ECONOMICS
versus
REALITY

How to Be
Effective
in the
Real World
in Spite of
Economic
Theory

ECONOMICS
versus
REALITY

John M. Legge

Transaction Publishers
New Brunswick (U.S.A.) and London (U.K.)

Library of Congress Catalog Number: 2015007956
ISBN: 978-1-4128-5716-1 (cloth), 978-1-4128-6251-6 (paper)
eBook: 978-1-4128-6194-6
Printed in the United States of America

Library of Congress Cataloging-in-Publication Data

Legge, John M., 1942-
    Economics versus reality : how to be effective in the real world in spite of economic theory / John M Legge.
        pages cm
    Includes bibliographical references and index.
    ISBN 978-1-4128-5716-1 -- ISBN 978-1-4128-6194-6 1. Economics. 2. Economic history. I. Title.
    HB171.L6128 2016
    330--dc23

                                                        2015007956

Contents

Preface

This work is not an economics textbook or monograph. What I have attempted is to set out a series of empirical facts about the way a modern market economy works and contrast these with predictions from the economics literature. By doing this I hope to explain to entrepreneurs, managers, and social and political activists when to rely on the advice of economists and, more importantly, when to ignore it.

The depth of the attachment of many academic economists to their discipline, and the fury with which they repel criticism from outsiders, surprises many of those trained in the physical sciences, as it surprised me when I first encountered it.

My undergraduate degree is in mathematics, and along the way I learned a certain amount about engineering; and I have never experienced, among engineers or mathematicians, anything resembling the aggressive defensiveness of economists when their assumptions or conclusions are challenged. My second career was in the computer industry, and there I certainly encountered the self-righteous aggression that any outsider who enters the economic debate experiences. I may have even exhibited some of these symptoms myself in my role as the public face of a number of computer systems development teams.

Engineers can afford to be casual about defending their discipline, because reality is the constant companion of every engineering hypothesis: if a bridge collapses or an airplane crashes, it does their designers no good to denigrate their critics as outsiders, unqualified to comment on the engineering art; but if the bridge stands and the airplane flies, even engineers who had nothing to do with either can see their discipline vindicated.

Mathematicians, at the cost of deliberately putting a gap between their discipline and reality, can be even less equivocal if that is possible: if a mathematical theorem can be shown to predict that $2 + 2 = 5$, it is the theorem that gets rejected, not those who performed the demonstration.

Economists lack this comforting certainty.

Economists believe that they know the "best" way to organize society; computer scientists often believe that they know the "best" way to implement a computer system. Proof is unobtainable for the economist. History cannot be rewound and restarted to find out if an alternative recommendation would have led to a better outcome. If an economy is managed according to the advice provided by an economist and the result is an unmitigated disaster, the economist can argue that any available alternative would have created an even worse mess. If this argument fails to carry sufficient conviction, the economists can claim that their prescriptions were not followed with sufficient precision: the problem was not in the advice but in the incompetence of those who attempted to implement it.

By contrast, if an economist's recommendations lead to a successful social outcome, there is no guarantee that the same economist's prescriptions will be effective in a different situation.

Computer systems developers enjoy one major advantage over economists: practically all of the time, a computer will do exactly what its program tells it to. If I code "GoTo Label_B," then I know with a confidence approaching certainty that when this instruction is executed, control will pass to the instruction sequence starting at "Label_B." There is no guarantee that this coding will actually produce the result that I had intended; but when a computer system does not perform as expected, the reason is practically always that the programming did not accurately reflect the requirements of the user who commissioned it. Economists, on the other hand, attempt to predict and modify human behavior; but even if their expectation about how the average person will respond to a proposed incentive is correct (in fact, it often isn't)[1] many people will not respond as expected, and the outcome can still be entirely different from that which the economist predicted.

The Harvard Law of Animal Behavior states that "under carefully controlled experimental circumstances, an animal will behave as it damned well pleases." People are a lot less predictable than laboratory rats; and while most people practice enlightened self-interest, their evaluation of their circumstances often differs from the way in which an economist may assume they are going to evaluate their circumstances. Economists have developed various terms to describe behavior that does not meet their expectations, starting with "irrational"; but ignoring such deviations, as many academic economists appear to do, does not improve the quality of their predictions or their policy advice.

Computer systems development experience teaches the practitioner a lot about sensitivity to initial conditions; it is no accident that modern interest in chaos theory coincided with the widespread availability of cheap but powerful computers. In a high-level language program of ten thousand lines, a single missing full stop can lead to plausible but wrong results; in an executable program (such as a file with an extension of .exe or .dll in Windows) a single bit set the wrong way, or not properly reset, can lead to serious errors or to program failure. ("Bit" is an abbreviation of "binary digit," the smallest possible unit of information; it can only take the values 0 or 1, sometimes called "true" or "false." Programmers generally treat 0 as true and 1 as false; digital design engineers treat 1 as true and 0 as false. This can be a source of endless amusement for spectators.)

By proper analogy an economist's predictions, no matter how soundly based in extensive studies of human behavior, can fail because a relatively small number of mavericks insist on acting "outside the square."

I began to take a serious interest in economics relatively late in life, when after some thirty years earning my living in the private sector, I accepted a temporary teaching position at the then Swinburne Institute of Technology (now Swinburne University of Technology). The then dean of engineering, Professor Murray Gillin AM, was pioneering an Australian postgraduate program focusing on innovation and entrepreneurship. Professor Gillin's interest was aroused when he visited Babson College in Boston, and in the early years of the program, Babson professors were frequent guests at Swinburne. I was appointed to teach marketing and business planning on the basis of my extensive practical experience, but I felt it necessary to add some academic reading to the mix; and I was appalled at the gap between the world as I had experienced it and the world as described in Samuelson's hugely successful economics textbook.[2]

It is now over twenty-five years since I first stood in front of a class at Swinburne, and during that time, I have read the academic economics literature reasonably extensively and corresponded with a number of economists, some of them leaders in their field. At the same time, I have deepened my understanding of the academic marketing literature and made a modest contribution to it, mainly on the topic of the diffusion of innovation.

Economics as a discipline and a profession has become subjected to a deep schism, but one that the leading figures of the profession are reluctant to acknowledge. There is the economics taught in the first year or two of an undergraduate course, which provides the slogans used by a thousand conservative polemicists; and there is the more complex and somewhat more realistic economics of the postgraduate student and of most faculty members. The first response of many of these more educated and humane economists to a criticism of "economics" based on the inconsistencies and unworldliness of the undergraduate syllabus is to point to the many respected economists who have made similar criticisms.

This book is not principally a critique of orthodox economic theories; there have been plenty of these, and there will no doubt be more. Many respected economists have made powerful logical criticisms of the orthodox theory, particularly the simplified (and, I believe, fundamentally misleading) economics of the undergraduate syllabus. As far as I am aware, none of the authors of these books and papers have had a breadth of industrial experience comparable to mine, so they have largely limited themselves to a debate "inside the tent."

Conventional economic theories may pose interesting logical conundrums and offer entertainment and intellectual stimulation to those familiar with them; but to use them to make recommendations for action at any level in the modern world is reckless at best and destructive most of the time.

Notes

1. Kahneman (2011: pp. 269 ff).
2. Samuelson and Nordhaus (1995).

Note on Measurements

I have used International units (liters, meters, kilograms) wherever measurements are relevant. A liter is about a quarter of a US gallon; a meter is a little more than three feet, a kilometer is about five eighths of a mile; and a kilogram is a little less than two and a quarter pounds. All measurements mentioned in the text are illustrative and rough conversions should be quite sufficient to convey my intended meaning.

Acknowledgments

This book could not have been written without access to Steve Keen's *Debunking Economics*. Keen offers a point-by-point deconstruction of the orthodox economic model, highlighting its many logical inconsistencies and absurd assumptions. His book is necessarily technical, since it has to stand up to criticism from other economists; so if any economist wishes to pick a fight over any of the technical assumptions I make, he or she should start by attempting to rebut Professor Keen.

A reviewer who prefers to remain anonymous kindly read and commented on my Chapter 3 several times and has made an invaluable contribution to that part of my book. I have reproduced his comments in some places and revised the text in several more after considering his advice; but the text as it stands reflects my views and opinions, and any remaining errors are strictly mine.

Shelby D. Hunt read and commented on Chapter 9. Avinash Dixit read and commented on Chapter 10 and made several valuable suggestions. David Legge, Richard Schmale, Anthony Dunn, Leonie Kelleher, and Max Kraynov all read a complete draft of the book and also made valuable suggestions. Lesley Vick performed a line-by-line edit of an advanced draft, adding immeasurably to its clarity and impact. I could have produced nothing without the support and encouragement of my wife, Robyn.

I owe a special debt of gratitude to Mary E Curtis and her readers at Transaction, for choosing to publish my book, and to Allyson Fields and her editorial team at Transaction for their careful preparation of the text for publication.

1

Uses and Abuses of Economics

If you can believe that you can believe anything.
—Arthur Wellesley, 1ˢᵗ Duke of Wellington

Terms from economics have entered political discourse in most developed countries. Governments are expected to promote productivity, or competitiveness, or welfare, and each of these is defined in economic terms. Economic theory has come to play a major role both in the regulation of business and in the expectations that the public and shareholders place on managers. A major political movement has been built on the assertion by the economist Ludwig von Mises (1881–1973) that participation in a market as a consumer is more important, and more rewarding, than participating in society as a citizen.

Economics is about economies, and in an economy, goods and services are produced and consumed. The conditions and arrangements under which goods and services are produced is a social construct: in a tribal society, production (mainly hunting and gathering) is a social obligation; in a slave-owning society, production takes place under the threat of punishment; in a feudal economy, peasants and artisans produce under the threat of the loss of their few privileges and sources of income; while in a more modern society, workers undertake production for wages.

History tells us that societal structures are transient: the few remaining hunter-gatherer societies are ethnographic curiosities; no contemporary society admits to sanctioning slavery, although in some cases the distinction is blurred; and most goods and services in the modern world are produced by workers in return for wages, aided by machinery and other capital items owned by capitalists or, more commonly, incorporated enterprises. Similarly, most produced goods and

1

services are bought and sold rather than being used by the producing organization or household.

Political economists look at societies to determine how production is organized and how the total value of production grows or declines. The modern study of political economy can be traced back to Bernard Mandeville in the early eighteenth century. Mandeville was writing about early capitalism, and in his poem and book *The Fable of the Bees*, he suggested that social progress was driven by envy, pride, and greed even while the official morality abhorred all three. Political economy is descriptive and explanatory; but in the mid-nineteenth century, Jevons sought to replace political economy with "economics," which he believed was, or could be made into, a science comparable to and as precise as astronomy.[1]

Political economy deals with relationships, some of which may be purely contractual but some of which involve mutual respect, affection, obligation, or all three. Economic theory deals with the interaction of maximizing agents that are rational, selfish, and with fixed tastes. Economic agents may be divided into classes such as "entrepreneurs" or "consumers," but all the agents within a given class are identical and interchangeable. The only motivation for economic agents is personal gain.

Managers of modern enterprises cannot avoid making economic decisions: if the wages that they offer are too low, they will not be able to hire or retain adequately skilled and motivated staff; and if the prices that they demand are too high, their sales and revenue will fall short of their targets and may not be sufficient to keep their enterprise viable. Their workers and customers do not, however, act entirely like the agents of economic theory are assumed to act. There is no magic wage at which a firm can recruit and retain all the workers that it needs, but which, if reduced by an infinitesimal amount, would leave the firm with no workers at all. Similarly, there is no magic price at which a firm can sell everything that it can produce, but which, if increased by an infinitesimal amount, would leave the firm with no sales at all.

While making economic decisions, managers cannot afford to ignore social relationships and individual differences. Most successful firms do not sell their products or deliver their services into a market; they sell to customers—the word itself signifying repeated transactions. Customers seek value for money, not the lowest price, and while courtesy and the recognition of individual needs won't overcome large price disparities, they can certainly overcome modest ones.

In a well-run firm, workers are treated with tolerance and respect and respond with diligent attention to their duties and care for the firm's interest: "For the scripture saith, Thou shalt not muzzle the ox that treadeth out the corn. And, The laborer is worthy of his reward."[2]

The American psychologist Frederick Herzberg (1923–2000) performed an extensive study of employee motivation and observed a clear split between those factors that encouraged diligence and those that discouraged it. Critically, while poor wages clearly caused dissatisfaction and were grouped by Herzberg under "hygiene factors," above-average wages could not compensate for poor administration or tactless, intrusive, or unfair supervision. Herzberg's list of "motivators" was topped by the opportunity to enjoy a sense of achievement and the recognition of effort and contribution.[3]

Political and social activists cannot ignore economic considerations any more than managers can. Any proposal that involves expenditure must be matched by a way to meet that expense, but it won't simply be the money. Expenditure implies effort, which in turn implies the deployment of human resources, which may need to be trained and which will certainly need to be redeployed from whatever they are currently doing.

When the money is to be raised from taxation, there must be broad community sympathy with the underlying proposals. When it involves redeployment from anything but the unemployment queues, those from whom labor services are being withdrawn or reduced must be conciliated. Since the mid-1970s, politicians, guided by economists, have tended to treat economic considerations as primary and social factors as tedious irrelevancies: this has led to widespread disengagement with the political process.

Success in business, politics, or social activity is impossible without some understanding of economics; but if all someone understands is economics, they will find success elusive and if achieved at all, transient.

Textbook Economics

Introductory economics textbooks take various approaches in their description of the purpose of economics, but most of them assert that economics is about allocation: how scarce resources may be divided among competing claimants to produce the best outcome. The "best" outcome will be that which delivers the "greatest good for the greatest number," following the advice of the philosopher Jeremy Bentham (1748–1832).

Efficient allocation of resources is supposed to achieve optimal welfare by eliminating profit through "perfect" competition, although the supposed proof of the welfare-enhancing effects of perfect competition rests on patently absurd assumptions, as does the assumed stability of perfect competition itself (see Chapter 3). In the textbook authors' devotion to certain slogans—in spite of the lack of a strong (or any) grounded foundation for them—economics as presented by think-tank polemicists often resembles a religious rather than a scientific movement.

An alternative view of the economic problem was initially proposed by the "Austrian" economist Ludwig von Mises, popularized by Milton Friedman (1912–2006) and actively promoted by Tony Blair (b. 1953, prime minister 1997–2007) when prime minister of the United Kingdom. In this view government, advised by economists, should adopt policies that maximize choice: freedom is identified with policies that place minimal limitations on what people are permitted to do by maximizing the scope of the market and minimizing both government provision and regulation.

Choices will, of course, be constrained by income and wealth, but by assuming that a market system is perfectly competitive (see Chapter 3 below) adherents of this view can assure themselves that everyone has the wealth and income appropriate to their natural talent and personal efforts; so any person whose choice is limited to various disagreeable alternatives by his or her limited income or wealth has only him or herself (or possibly his or her ancestors) to blame.

It would be a mistake to consider the economics profession as wholly or even mainly immune to change or dedicated to systematically ignoring the differences between reality as predicted by orthodox theory and reality as observed. David Colander and his colleagues suggest that the dominance of the "tight prior" assumptions—where any work that was not grounded in the assumption of selfish, rational behavior by fully informed individuals was denounced as "not economics"—has ended.

Some, but by no means all, textbook authors and lecturers in undergraduate economics programs now proceed from a description of reality to an exposition of theory, rather than an exposition of theory followed by an assertion that this is a sufficient basis upon which to describe reality.

Colander and his colleagues wrote:

> We argue that economics is moving away from a strict adherence to the holy trinity—rationality, selfishness, and equilibrium—to a more eclectic position of purposeful behavior, enlightened self-interest and sustainability.[4]

Colander and his colleagues go on to argue that the term "orthodox" is necessarily retrospective: it reflects what has been the consensus opinion rather than the opinions and arguments of the leading voices in the economics (or any other) profession that will be setting out the view that will become "orthodox" in the future.

Politicians, bureaucrats, and pundits often seem to be too involved in current affairs to absorb new ideas once they pass the age of thirty, and assuming that most of them are in their fifties or older, the economics that they recall and that influences their decisions was orthodox twenty or more years ago.[5] It is these current policies and practices, based as they are on largely superseded economic theory, which are the principal targets of this book.

Economics and the Environment

At a time when anthropogenic climate change threatens to devastate the global environment and cause vast economic as well as social damage, arguments about allocative efficiency within a model having almost no resemblance to anything found in the real world can seem somewhat irrelevant.

The subject of anthropogenic climate change has revealed significant differences between dogmatic and thoughtful economists. Leading voices from the think-tank universe have taken one of two basic positions: one is to assert that global climate change is a myth fabricated by an anticapitalist conspiracy of scientists; and the other is to assert that market forces will, if not interfered with, eventually resolve all the problems of climate change. It has been left to more thoughtful economists such as Lord Nicholas Stern[6] and Professor John Quiggin[7] to demonstrate the logical inconsistency of the dogmatists' approach.

An intriguing intervention into the global climate-change debate came from a group of exceptionally distinguished American economists.[8] To support their argument to the effect that the correct discount rate to be used in evaluating climate change amelioration should be 5 percent per year (rather than the 1 percent suggested by Stern and endorsed by Quiggin), they asserted that Stern had allowed ethical issues (like the rights of the yet-to-be-born and those too young to vote) to affect his judgment. The clear implication of their argument is that they consider that economic and political decisions should not be affected by ethical considerations.

This book should not be taken as a criticism of the work of Stern and Quiggin and many other thoughtful and insightful economists.

Rather, I hope to assist my readers to see economics as a tool—one of many—to be used in pursuing their business, political, or social aims and not as the source of irrefutable laws of behavior or the determinants of optimal policies. I intend to demonstrate that there can be a genuine alternative to neoliberal, "Washington Consensus" policies without violating any natural laws or reducing the welfare of any but the richest few tenths of a percent of the population. Even they may be better off in the medium term, given that persisting with neoliberal policies must ultimately lead to a fascist revolution, as similar policies did in Germany in 1929–32.

It would also be improper to suggest that only Stern and Quiggin among economists take ethics seriously. Irene van Staveren, among others, has explored the matter of ethics in economics and concluded that any attempt to split ethics and economics into separate fields of enquiry results in a set of economic theories devoid of relevance.[9] Deirdre McCloskey provides an accessible and very persuasive explanation of economics as an aspect of human behavior that only makes sense when the social and ethical environments are considered alongside the economic one. She observed that humans interact economically in market and quasimarket exchanges; socially with friends and relatives; and ethically (or morally) with strangers; and that few if any aspects of human behavior can be explained without reference to all three spheres of activity.[10]

Economics and Society

One of the seminal events in the selection of economic theories to be used in guiding government decisions came in 1973 when the American CIA promoted a coup in Chile to overthrow the democratically elected Allende government and install a dictatorship under Augusto Pinochet. Allende's government had been mildly socialist in the Western European tradition and attempted to pursue moderate redistributive policies; Pinochet claimed, at least initially, to be inspired by the work of Milton Friedman.

Pinochet's dictatorship intended to rule the state in accordance with economic theory as set out by the "Chicago School" and popularized by Friedman. Pinochet's government and its Chicago-educated advisors were not content with just reversing Allende's policies. They devastated the public-health and education systems that Chilean governments of all political persuasions had built up over the preceding century, privatized public enterprises and the pension system, and promoted market-based approaches to education and health. Their policies failed to produce the predicted results, and after persisting with them for some eight years, the "Chicago boys" were replaced by a slightly less ideological team of advisers, and Chile began to show signs of economic life.

Those who praise the economic transformation of Chile after Pinochet's coup are presumably treating the facts that the coup was accompanied by three thousand murders and thirty thousand incarcerations with torture, and that more than half the population was worse off thirty years after the coup than they had been before it, as irrelevant ethical issues trumped by the fact of increased GDP growth and higher average incomes.

Politics

Much public comment on economic issues does not come from academic economists of any persuasion, but from advocates of a particular point of view. Practitioners of this art trawl the economic literature to find arguments in favor of the interests of their patrons, often asserting a generality beyond any of the original researchers' claims. The qualifications and limitations from the original academic journal articles are typically ignored, and so a very specific result may be treated as a universal truth.

Hillary Clinton, US secretary of state in the first Obama administration, once referred to the vast right-wing conspiracy, a network of conservatively inclined individuals and foundations capable of gaining wide publicity and a certain degree of credibility for false and misleading information by creating the illusion of many independent sources for it. Many economist-advocates are employed or contracted by the think tanks that lie at the heart of the conservative network, and they have been remarkably successful in generating "hymn sheets" from which conservative and neoliberal politicians can sing.

The work of the economists Friedrich August Hayek (1899–1992) and Friedman provides the logical justification for neoliberal practice. When Mrs. (later Baroness) Margaret Thatcher (1920–2013, prime minister 1979–90) said that "there is no such thing as society," she was paraphrasing Hayek. Hayek asserted that the only interests that anyone should consider were their own and those of their immediate family. Hayek recognized that many people felt concern for the pain and privation of others, but argued that this was a relic of life in hunter-gatherer societies with no place in the modern world.

In particular, Hayek and his followers held—and hold—that any form of redistribution of income through the taxation and social welfare systems was immoral, damaging to economic efficiency, and a step on the "road to serfdom."[11]

Toleration of the price-driven allocation of necessities implies living in a moral vacuum: the rich man who accepts Hayek's argument may, without qualms of conscience, feed his pets steak while beggars starve at his gate. Hayek's (and Thatcher's) dismissal of the concept or at least the relevance of society is an attempt to avoid the charge of amorality: if there is no society, there can be no common interests and therefore no general obligations. The extreme advocate of this view was the novelist Ayn Rand.[12] In spite of the turgidity of her prose and the extreme unrealism of her depiction of industry and society, her works are still read and admired by many on the extreme-right-wing end of the political debate.

Work by the evolutionary theorist W. D. (Bill) Hamilton[13] (1936–2000), the sociologist R. D. Putnam[14] (b. 1941), the economist R. H. Thaler (b. 1935), and the psychologist Daniel Kahneman[15] (b. 1934), among others, has demonstrated that it is the existence of a community of interests that stops life becoming "solitary, poor, nasty, brutish, and short," as the English philosopher Thomas Hobbes[16] (1588–1669) imagined a state of nature to be. Only in communities where at least 70 percent of the population are prepared to forgo a short-term advantage in order to enjoy the longer-term benefits of cooperation are economic and social progress assured. In such societies the 30 percent or less who would prefer to seize a short-term advantage—even if this required them to defect from agreements for longer-term cooperation—are effectively ostracized if they give in to their preferences, so sabotage of the common purpose is restricted to a small class of criminals and psychopaths.

Game theory results, backed up by Putnam's research, suggest that if the number of potential cooperators should fall to less than half the population, cooperation will largely cease, and economic and social progress will stall. The Hayek/Thatcher/Rand dream of a world of selfish individualists is the direct route to a state in which life is truly "nasty, brutish and short" with no prospect of improvement in the future.[17]

Even Hayek recognized that people should not be motivated by short-term self-interest when inside their family: no woman acting out of pure self-interest would go through the discomforts of pregnancy and the pain of labor; and no man acting out of pure self-interest would use part of his income to support his children and their mother. Hayek's dichotomy is ultimately an unsustainable one: who is part of a family? Grandparents? Aunts and uncles? Cousins, and if so, what degree marks the boundary? Relatives by marriage? Next-door neighbors? Across-the-street neighbors? If we see a toddler about to step into traffic, do we stop him if he is the child of a third cousin, but permit him to get killed if the relationship is weaker? The theory may be clear, but the practice is impossible.

Economics and Infallibility

Some writers and commentators argue that the failure of the centrally planned economies of the USSR and Eastern Europe is conclusive evidence in favor of either Hayekian or simplistic neoclassical economics. Hayek argued that a centrally planned economy would necessarily misallocate investment because central planners could only have access to a fraction of the total economic wisdom diffused through a population and expressed through the price system.

The neoclassical arguments against central planning are rather weaker, given the reliance on a hypothetical "social planner" in much of the economics literature. To the extent that they have any coherence, they assert that a real planner (as distinct from a hypothetical one) would institutionalize inefficiency.

In the "socialist calculation" debates of the 1920s and 1930s, Ludwig von Mises argued that centrally planned socialism was impossible because the planner (or planning department) could not set prices across an economy. The socialist economist Oskar Lange (1904–1965) was deemed by most to have won the debate by drawing on the work of Léon Walras (1834–1910) whose models lay at the heart of neoclassical economics.[18] Von Mises's argument fails the reality test: as explained in Chapter 3 below, most prices in a real capitalist system are determined by marking up variable costs, an exercise well within the capacity of all but the most arithmetically challenged central planner.

Hayek offered a far more cogent argument against the sustainability of a centrally planned economy based on the dynamism of capitalism. Following Marx (with or more often without acknowledgement) Hayek claimed that the defining characteristic of capitalism was the search for improved—i.e., lower cost—means of production.[19] Central planners, like orthodox neoclassical economists, tended to take existing production processes as given. Under their various assumptions, every possible way of reducing costs will have been implemented already.

(This last point is best illustrated by a joke well known to economists: A professor and a graduate student are walking together when they see a $100 note on the ground. The student moves to pick it up; the professor calls him back: "If it was a real $100 note, someone would have picked it up already.")

Tyler Cowen approached the Socialist Calculation debate from a different perspective. He posed the following questions:

- How does rational calculation take place within the firm? Keep in mind that some corporate giants are larger in economic terms than the smaller socialist economies were.
- If one person owned (privately) all the firms in the economy, would rational calculation be possible?
- If one dictator controlled all the firms in the economy, would rational calculation be possible?
- If institutional investors or a diversified citizenry all owned the so-called "market portfolio" in equal proportions, like the Capital Asset Pricing Model suggests, would rational calculation be possible? [TC: Or is this scenario of "perfect capitalism" not much different from pure communism?][20]

Very large firms exist: many small countries have a lower total income than firms like GE or Toyota. While large firms employ a variety of means to provide appropriate incentives, they permit nothing resembling economic competition between individuals or business units; and resources, both current operating expenses (OPEX) and capital expenditure (CAPEX), are allocated from the center. The fact that they are successful in achieving growth and profit over extended periods indicates that a centrally planned economy, if organized on appropriate principles, could be equally successful.

Orthodox neoclassical economists, von Mises and his followers, and the unreconstructed advocates of socialist central planning make a common error. They assume that a competitive market will arrive at an equilibrium state that provides an optimal use of resources. Somehow economics became influenced by an engineering oddity known as the power transfer theorem, and from this it moved to a view that a competitive equilibrium is welfare maximizing. The error will be explained in some detail in Chapter 3 below.

The Austrian-American economist Joseph Alois Schumpeter (1883–1950) highlighted the one really critical flaw in socialist planning (and in simplistic neoclassical economic models at the same time). He pointed out that central planners could allocate investment successfully; their critical deficiency, when contrasted with market mechanisms, was their parsimony. Capitalism grows through a process of creative destruction; but the centrally planned economies had no destruction system.[21] The central planners were reluctant to spend "scarce" capital on, say, replacing a functioning plant simply because more productive methods had become available since it was built. They were equally reluctant to set prices high enough to pay for modernization and innovation.

Successful capitalist enterprises reduce prices, when they do so, in order to promote growth in their markets and to increase their profits either promptly or in the near term. Enterprises that reduce their prices because of competitive pressure or oppressive regulation or central planners' *diktat* are on the road to failure, since their squeezed cash flows will soon become, if they are not already, inadequate to support the level of investment necessary to survive.

The history of the Soviet and Eastern European steel industries in the years following World War II support Schumpeter's argument. That part of the Soviet steel industry that had not been destroyed by the Nazi invasion had been relocated to the Urals and destroyed just as effectively, if a little more slowly, by lack of maintenance and overuse. Few Eastern European countries had had a significant prewar steel industry, and those plants that existed had not been treated kindly by the war or the US Air Force.

In rebuilding and developing their steel industries after the end of World War II, the Soviet Union and the Eastern European countries paid careful attention to world's best practices, then represented by the Siemens-Martin open-hearth steelmaking system. The steel produced by these new and rebuilt plants was fully competitive in cost and quality with the best Western plants. While the open hearth was effective in producing quality steel, it was slow and labor intensive, and in the 1950s a number of Austrian firms pioneered the LD process, also known as the basic oxygen process, which produced an equally good product about seven times faster with fewer workers.

Capitalist competition was sufficiently effective to see the LD process adopted and open hearth and Bessemer plants scrapped across Western Europe and Japan quite rapidly. The transition was slower in the United States, where the steel companies preferred to lobby for tariffs on imported steel than upgrade their plants. Until the very last years of communist rule in Eastern Europe and the USSR, open-hearth furnaces were operated until they fell apart, and only then were basic oxygen converters installed. Even after the fall of communism, a few of these museum pieces were still in operation through the 1990s.

Economic Miracles

The period after the Second World War saw a number of "economic miracles" as societies that had been reduced to bare subsistence by the war did not merely recover—they rapidly surpassed the highest living standards enjoyed before the war.

The first of the post–World War II economic miracles took place in the USSR as the industries and cities destroyed in the war were rebuilt without any access to Marshall Aid and in spite of the added cost of nuclear weapons and space programs. Up until as late as 1960, the USSR and Eastern Europe's economic growth rates kept pace with Western Europe and outperformed the United States.

On the creation side of the equation, the Soviet central planners achieved a level of economic performance comparable to that of unplanned capitalism. When the Soviet leader Khrushchev realized, possibly after his US tour in 1959, that some destruction was needed if creation was to continue, the more conservative elements of the Soviet Communist Party organized a political coup and installed Brezhnev, who oversaw twenty years of stagnation.

By 1985, when Gorbachev tried to return to Khrushchev's program of renewal, the bulk of the Soviet population had long forgotten or been born too late to remember the hard-won victory in the Second World War and the triumph of postwar reconstruction; their memories and their everyday experience were of the failures of an economy twenty-five years past its use-by date.

The noncommunist economic miracles—first West Germany, then Japan—were not organized according to the principles of Hayek and Friedman, but rather those of Bismarck and Keynes. Britain's postwar recovery was slightly less miraculous, but impressive all the same: by 1957 Harold Macmillan (1894–1986, prime minister 1957–63) could tell the British public that "You've never had it so good" and go on to win the election of that year. The British welfare state owed more to Beveridge than Bismarck, but its economic management owed everything to Keynes.

Class War

Evolutionary competition is between individual agents as is most economic competition; but many animal species show evidence of group cooperation against common enemies, including those of their own species. Humans are no different. Businesses that compete vigorously with each other in their shared markets will cooperate to oppose policies that threaten their common interests and to promote policies that would advance them.

"War" may seem an extreme metaphor for people who have to delve deep into their history books to find accounts of deadly force being used in essentially political disputes; but the suppression of the Paris Commune in 1871 still resonates in France, as does the American Civil War in the Southern states of the United States. The behavior of the brutal and repressive oligarchies installed by American power in many South and Central American countries in the second half of the twentieth century certainly qualifies as warfare, with huge death tolls among combatants and bystanders alike.

In practically every war, there comes a time when the shooting stops, occasionally reflecting an outbreak of common sense but more often the total exhaustion of one of the parties and the depletion of its combatant capability. The victors always claim that their victory has put an end to the conflict and the users should adjust to the new circumstances; but as long as the causes of conflict remain, the potential for active conflict—possibly political but possibly violent—remains.

The clash between Right and Left has historic roots going back well over two thousand years. It can be seen in the tyranny of the Peisistratids in ancient Athens and the revolt against it in 510 BCE, and in the history of the Roman tribunate under the Gracchi in the second century BCE and the murder of Tiberius and Caius Gracchus.

In every property-owning society, the distribution of wealth tends to become progressively more uneven over time,[22] and parties arise to assert the interests of those whose wealth has increased against those whose wealth has not. The struggle is usually cast as a battle of rights against obligations: those with property assert their right to do with it what they will, while those without seek to enforce obligations on the property owners to devote part of their wealth to the support of the rest of the community.

There are often religious overtones: in nineteenth-century England, the wealthy enjoyed the moral comfort provided by the Church of England, whose comfortable vicars preached the glories of a divinely ordered society; while the Methodists, preaching to their lower middle-class and working-class congregations, were more likely to refer to the Sermon on the Mount and discuss camels struggling through the eye of a needle.

The work of Newton and later astronomers and scientists triggered an attempt to devise a rational as distinct from a divine explanation for the ordering of society, and the book by Adam Smith (1723–1790) *An Inquiry into the Wealth of Nations*, first published in 1776, was held by many to stand alongside Newton's *Principia* as a definitive explanation of Life, the Universe, and Everything. While actually reading Smith's work does not reveal an unqualified argument for a deregulated, market-oriented society, he is often cited as the founder of modern liberalism, and Hayek is treated as his direct heir.

Hayek most certainly did argue for extreme liberalism and turned the classic Methodist argument on its head: far from accepting the historical evidence and Marxist argument that an unregulated market economy divided society into a few masters and many servants, Hayek opposed any interference with the rights of the wealthy.

For over seventy years from the publication of *The Wealth of Nations* in 1776, there was no theoretical argument developed to support the Left beyond simple Methodism. The Chartists and the Corn Law Leaguers, while seen as dangerous revolutionaries by English Conservatives, actually adopted a relatively liberal position; they certainly did not want to be associated in the public or their own mind with the excesses of the French Revolution. Their argument was for equal treatment, not redistribution. (Of course, for believers in a hierarchical society, calls for equal treatment sound revolutionary.)

The only direct theoretical attack on the foundations of capitalist society came from Marx and his associates and followers; and the basis of their attack was the assertion, based on an apparently sound argument, that market capitalism was bound to descend into a series of ever-deepening economic crises with a rising concentration of wealth and the progressive immiseration of the working classes. As the nineteenth century turned into the twentieth, Marx's followers could cite the economic crisis of the 1890s, the First World War and the ensuing depression in the early twenties, the Great Depression of the early thirties, and the recession of 1937 as evidence of the accuracy of Marx's prophecies.

While the mainstream Left in Britain and Continental Europe never formally adopted Marxism, it certainly slipstreamed it, adopting interventionist and redistributive policies with gusto. The economic success of the Soviet Union from the end of the civil wars in the early 1920s to the early 1960s provided the orthodox Left with additional arguments: their policies could produce welfare and economic growth without the repression and hypocrisy so evident in the USSR. The Russian invasion of Hungary in 1956 demonstrated beyond doubt that the Soviet system was based on coercion; the economic stagnation from the early 1960s onward stripped the Soviet model of even the attraction of apparently superior economic performance.

The nearest the orthodox Left had ever come to a theoretical base was the "bastard Keynesianism"[23] that emerged following Keynes's relatively early death; and few on the Left noted that Keynes had seen his mission as preserving capitalism, not burying it. Keynes had no problem with the class system; he just wished to warn his own class that they should not grind down the proletariat to the point that made revolution an attractive alternative to submission.

Models and Reality

The world that we live in is an incredibly complex place. From minute to minute, we are affected by the natural environment, the built environment, and the actions of our fellow humans. Activities as simple as walking or talking involve hundreds of muscles and thousands of nerves, none of which we consciously control or are aware of until they are damaged or act erratically.

As Kahneman explains, we have two systems for interacting with our environment: the "fast," intuitive, multitasking system where our reactions are almost reflexes; and the "slow," deliberative system where we take account of the circumstances and our prior experience and make a reasoned judgment before taking any action. Using the slow system is stressful and time-consuming, and most of us are content to leave most of our decisions in the hands of our fast processes—to make "snap judgments."[24]

The fast system works off mental models that are "good enough" for most purposes, and our brains are built to select the "best fit" model rapidly and automatically when we need to make a decision. A great deal of education and training is about developing mental models to support our fast-thinking capability. An infielder in baseball, or a close-in fielder in cricket, catches flying balls before his conscious mind even realizes that the ball has been struck in his direction: if he stopped to think about what he should do, the ball would be halfway to the fence before he could react. (Only one fielder in cricket occupies a fixed position; the rest are placed at the fielding captain's discretion.

One position about three meters from the batter became known as "silly (or suicide) point.")

As Kahneman points out, in situations unlike any previous ones that we have experienced, the decisions that our fast system makes are often objectively wrong. Our fast-thinking mind works by finding the best fit model for a given situation, and there are no alarm bells rung if the learned model is a poor fit to present reality. The curve ball in baseball and the googly or wrong'un in cricket are effective because the batter's fast-thinking mind is tricked into selecting the wrong model for his or her response.

Using mental models to limit the need for intellectual effort, and the consequent delays in responding to a situation, goes a long way beyond sport. Top performers in the professions, including academics, form models and use them to make decisions all the time: "If this, this, and this, then do that." Professional judgment only comes into play when the situation doesn't fit any model or when the action prompted by the model doesn't have the expected result.

The construction of models is an important part of the ordinary activity of academics in all disciplines, and under the rule of "publish or perish," academics describe their new models, or their suggested changes to existing models, in papers that are then subject to peer review before publication. The models may be called theories, or theorems, or rules, or even laws, but they remain abstractions that might or might not have some resonance with the real world. When the authors of models claim that their results have real-world relevance, they may be expected to demonstrate this. In the physical sciences, it is often possible to arrange an experiment, and if the experimental outcome is the one predicted by the model, the model survives, at least until a result incompatible with the model is demonstrated.

There are practical and ethical issues involved in experiments in the life sciences, and while these can be managed in some cases, in others hypotheses can only be tested by statistical observation. Such tests can almost never be more than indicative because there will always be cases that don't fit the pattern.

Epidemiologists demonstrated that regular cigarette smokers were twenty times more likely to die of lung cancer than nonsmokers; but some nonsmokers develop lung cancer and some smokers die at a ripe old age without any indication of it. For years these anomalies were cited by lobbyists for the tobacco companies as they tried to dissuade governments from taking action to discourage smoking.

People who have developed models or those who have been taught to use a particular model and have done so extensively may have much invested in their model and react strongly to any criticism of it. We may look back on the dispute between Galileo and the Catholic Church over Copernican theory as a quaint historical anomaly; but scientists with far stronger evidence than anything Galileo relied on report that human activity is warming the planet and get denounced as conspirators, dupes, or frauds by people for whom global warming conflicts with their mental models.

Models can take on a different role: that of ideals. Plato, the ancient Greek philosopher, was keenly aware of how erratic, messy, and unjust the real world could be. As a believer he could not accept that the god or gods who had created the Earth and the people on it could have made such a mess deliberately. He concluded that the *real* world was in fact perfect and predictable, but the gods had deliberately clouded human perception so that we could not see reality clearly. We could, Plato argued, get some idea of what reality was really like by studying mathematics, particularly geometry. He had "No entry without geometry" engraved above the entrance to his academy in Athens.

The astronomer Johannes Kepler (1571–1630) straddles the Platonic and the modern scientific eras. He had access to a huge series of astronomical observations, a series sufficient to reveal errors in both the old Ptolemaic models and Galileo's version of the Copernican one. Both Ptolemy and Galileo had assumed that the planets moved on the surface of perfect spheres, and initially Kepler retained that assumption. Kepler went further and assumed that the diameters of the spheres bore some relationship to the five regular polyhedrons described by the ancient Greek philosopher and mathematician Euclid.

After putting himself though unspeakable mental torture, Kepler abandoned the idea of spheres and polyhedrons and demonstrated that the planets (or at least Mars) orbited the sun in ellipses. He set out three laws of planetary motion, which became the foundation on which Sir Isaac Newton (1642–1727) developed the Law of Universal Gravitation. Kepler, and even more decisively, Newton, ejected Platonic ideals from physics: physicists find facts and fit theories to them, rather than the other way around.

Antoine Lavoisier (1743–94) did the same for inorganic chemistry at the end of the eighteenth century, and Friedrich Wöhler (1800–82) started the process of eliminating vitalism and ideals from organic chemistry in 1828. Louis Pasteur (1822–95) put biology on a scientific basis, and biochemistry emerged at the start of the twentieth century as the science of living cells. In the late twentieth century, the convergence of neurophysiology and psychology saw many psychologists adopting a scientific approach.

The one discipline that calls itself a science but largely refuses to adopt the scientific method is economics. An economist who simply collects facts may be denounced as pursuing "measurement without theory": papers that appear in the most prestigious economics journals set out a theory, often in the form of an elaborate set of mathematical equations, and such papers then offer a set of facts, or a statistical analysis of some data sets, that appear to support the theory.

When the MIT economist Robert Solow (further discussed in Chapter 9) tried to fit the economic history of the United States in the first half of the twentieth century to the standard model of economic growth, he found that 80 percent of observed growth could not be explained by the standard model. The discrepancy became known as the "Solow residual" and is ignored by orthodox economists.

Finance economics developed around the "efficient market hypothesis" or EMH, although most interesting work in finance economics now is devoted to examining deviations from it. The language used remains that of the Platonic ideal: the model, or hypothesis, says how financial markets *should* behave, and the departures from this ideal are described as "noise" or the consequence of "irrational" behavior by market participants.

Notes

1. See p. 25 ff.
2. 1 Timothy 5:18.
3. Herzberg (2003).
4. Colander, Holt & Rosser Jr. (2004: p. 485).
5. Keynes (1936 [1961]: pp. 383–84).
6. Stern (2007).
7. Quiggin and Horowitz (2003).
8. Arrow (2007).
9. Van Staveren (2007).
10. Mccloskey (2008).
11. Hayek (1944).
12. Rand (1957).
13. Axelrod & Hamilton (1981); see also Guttman (2003).
14. Putnam (1993, 1994).
15. Kahneman, Knetch & Thaler (1986), Kahneman (2011).
16. Hobbes (1651 [2010]).
17. Dawkins (1989: Ch 12).

18. Cottrell & Cockshott (1993).
19. Hodgson (1998: pp. 107–133).
20. Cowen (1995: pp. 243–249).
21. Schumpeter (1942).
22. Piketty (2014).
23. Term attributed to Joan Robinson. Davidson (2009: pp. 18–20) describes and critiques the distortion of Keynes's views in the years immediately following his death.
24. Kahneman (2011).

2

Names to Reckon With

A man who has never been engaged in trade himself might undoubtedly write well upon trade, and there is nothing which requires more to be illustrated by philosophy than trade does.
—Dr. Samuel Johnson

Economics is not, in spite of the hopes of some major nineteenth-century figures, an exact science, and many issues that a practical person would consider settled are the subject of continuing debates. Each of the figures discussed below has acquired passionate followers and, in many cases, even more passionate enemies.

I have not attempted an authoritative biography of any of these important names, but I have tried to avoid attaching ideas to them that they would have repudiated.

The Classical Economists

The eighteenth-century Enlightenment saw people looking for logical rather than divine explanations for the state of the world. While this started with astronomy, it rapidly moved into the other "hard" sciences and then into the study of human relations. The first or "classical" economists concerned themselves with two main issues: the explanation of how an economy functioned and the generation of proposals to improve it.

Adam Smith

Adam Smith (1723–1790) was a Scottish clergyman who was engaged by the Duke of Buccleuch to accompany the duke's son on a grand tour of France and Italy. Smith's duties were not onerous, and he spent some time becoming familiar with the French "philosophes," including the encyclopedist Diderot. His reward for bringing the young man back alive and in reasonable health was a pension of £100 per year at a time when no shame attached to accepting patronage from a wealthy sponsor. For his own merits, augmented by the influence of his wealthy patron, he became a professor at Glasgow University.

Smith's major contribution to economics came when, in 1776, he published *An Inquiry into the Nature and Causes of the Wealth of Nations*. This proved to be a profoundly influential work; it has been republished in numerous editions and is still in print. It has become almost obligatory for anyone writing on economic issues to quote Smith. I do here, several times. Because the work is long and the language colorful, *Wealth of Nations* has become something of a Bible: quotations may be found to suit almost any opinion.

Smith took the "Inquiry" part of his title very seriously: he assembled a vast amount of data and used it to support his arguments. He argued that the England of his day suffered from excessive regulation; in particular, the guild and apprenticeship systems served to raise prices and limit supply without any compensating benefits to society generally.

Smith coined the phrase "invisible hand" to describe how appropriate liberal policies would encourage industry development without any firm-specific or industry-specific measures. The phrase is most commonly quoted today to give historic authenticity to the "law" of supply and demand. Smith did observe that shortages drove up prices, the higher prices attracted merchants, and the new supplies brought prices down; but he saw nothing invisible in the process.

Smith is sometimes described as the father of modern economics, but it is obvious to anyone who has read his work—as distinct from trawling it for quotations—that he would regard the selfish, rational individual of modern economic theory with horror. Smith's lecture notes survive, as does his work *The Theory of Moral Sentiments*, and it is clear from both that he considered that an economy could only operate within and subject to a society, and that merchants and manufacturers were expected to observe moral boundaries.[1]

David Ricardo

David Ricardo (1772–1823) was a banker and politician. He is primarily remembered today as the author of the Comparative Advantage argument for free trade. He also developed the labor theory of value, a concept further developed by Karl Marx.

Ricardo was a prolific writer, and his collected works and correspondence occupy several volumes. He was also a skilled debater who sometimes appeared more eager to win an argument than to begin it from properly grounded assumptions. Schumpeter coined the term

"Ricardian vice" to describe economists who, like Ricardo, built their conclusions into their assumptions and then "proved" them with faultless logic.

Ricardo has also been cited by economists opposed to any use of taxation and spending policy by governments to speed recovery from recessions. The term "Ricardian equivalence" applies to the proposition that, if a government should borrow money in order to stimulate the economy, the citizens would decide that this would require increased taxation in the future to repay the accompanying debt. Fear of increased taxation would persuade the citizens to save just as much money as the government borrowed, negating any stimulus effect. There is little reason to believe that Ricardo saw this proposition as anything more than a debating tactic, and history has proved it false in any case.

Thomas Malthus

Thomas Malthus (1766–1834) was a scholar and clergyman most famous for his *Essay on the Principle of Population*, in which he argued that the potential for population increase would always outrun food production, meaning that the population would ultimately be limited by starvation. He regarded it as unfortunate when unemployed laborers and their families starved to death but considered such deaths as a necessary part of the operation of an economy.

Malthus also set out a "law of proportion" arguing that the extreme application of any policy was necessarily worse than seeking a balance between opposing tendencies, and he acquired a reputation for vacillation in consequence. His work influenced both Marx and Keynes.

Karl Marx

Few people can have been as unfortunate in their followers as Karl Marx (1818–1883). Fiends incarnate would shudder if told that they were the inspiration for the acts and ostensible beliefs of Joseph Stalin or Pol Pot.

Marx was born into a middle-class German family and received an education appropriate to his time and class. He became a journalist, and his reporting irritated the authorities in several of the independent principalities that made up Germany at the time, so he found it convenient to move to London, where he formed a lifelong friendship with Frederick Engels (1820–1895). Engels was the son and heir of a major Manchester cotton master, operating one of the largest factories there. He was deeply concerned about the fate of the working classes but showed no wish to join them, working in the family business to the extent needed to maintain its prosperity and his income. He periodically bailed Marx out of debt.

Marx was deeply moved by the plight of the working man. Not that he learned of it directly: his information came from Engels and from his study of parliamentary reports in the great reading room of the British Museum.

Marx may have been the first significant economist to interpret capitalism as a dynamic system, and he offered a persuasive but ultimately flawed explanation of the economic crises that marked the nineteenth century. He adopted and expanded Ricardo's labor theory of value and argued that under capitalism workers generated "surplus value"—the value they added in each working day exceeded their wages—and this value was "expropriated" by their employers.

Marx can be read as advocating revolution, but equally as describing capitalism as simply one stage in human development to be succeeded in due course by socialism. Charles Darwin (1809–1882) was a contemporary of Marx, and Marx was quick to explain human societal development as an evolutionary process: he believed that socialism would replace capitalism like mammals replaced dinosaurs.

Neoclassical Economists

Background

The late seventeenth and the eighteenth centuries saw the birth of the Enlightenment, a period of extraordinary intellectual ferment in Northern Europe. Mathematicians and astronomers achieved extraordinary numerical precision, establishing the movements of the moon and the planets with an accuracy of seconds per year. In 1781 Herschel predicted the size and orbit of the planet Uranus from observing tiny discrepancies between the calculated and observed orbits of Saturn and Jupiter: his prediction was triumphantly confirmed by observation.

The early engineers—James Watt (1736–1819), George (1781–1848) and Robert (1803–1859) Stephenson, and Isambard Kingdom Brunel (1806–1859)—were pragmatic men who succeeded without much reliance on theory, or in Brunel's case, in spite of an ostentatious disregard of it. As the nineteenth century proceeded, scientists sought to explain the operation of a steam engine, and in due course to advise mechanical engineers of the directions in which to look for improvements. Sadi Carnot and Thompson, Lord Kelvin, created the science of thermodynamics, which pointed the way to the building of far larger and more efficient engines.

International trade grew on the back of the triple-expansion compound steam engine, built with thermodynamic principles very much in mind. The first steamboat (as distinct from a sailing vessel with an auxiliary steam engine) to cross the Atlantic could barely complete the journey with coal in every hold and in heaps on the decks. By the end of the nineteenth century, a cargo ship could travel from Liverpool to New York with no more than five percent of its total mass at sailing consisting of fuel.

Jevons and Walras

Léon Walras (1834–1910) and William Stanley Jevons (1835–1882) attempted to apply the mathematics that underlie mechanical engineering to economics (Mechanical engineering is the practical use of machines that convert heat into mechanical energy. The term was invented by the English railway engineer Robert Stephenson to distinguish his profession from civil engineers (who built structures) and military engineers (who blew them up)). To do so Walras and Jevons had to make certain assumptions, notably that equations involving continuous, differentiable variables could adequately describe real human populations.

Scientists and engineers already knew that real gases were not truly continuous, but rather were made up of molecules with empty space between them; but when dealing with the sort of volumes and velocities occurring in a nineteenth-century steam engine, at least before Parsons invented the steam turbine, the errors implicit in assuming that gases were actually uniform are completely insignificant. They are undetectable with any instrument available before the late nineteenth century.

Mechanical engineers simplified their calculations further by substituting the parameters appropriate to an ideal, or perfect, gas in their equations and then making a small adjustment to their final answers to allow for these imperfections. Even then engineers and their clients did not rely completely on the calculated performance of their engines but rather insisted on careful tests and trials before taking delivery and making final payments.

Using the mathematics of ideal gases, which were known to be only an approximation to the behavior of real gases, and applying it to the behavior of people was a bold step; but it lay on a road on which Walras and Jevons boldly strode—and a road on which a very large number of modern economists travel without any sign that they are aware of their lack of rigorous mathematical support.

Walras and Jevons clearly had an agenda. Jevons wrote, in the introduction to his textbook on political economy:

> In this work I have attempted to treat economy as a calculus of pleasure and pain, and have sketched out, almost irrespective of previous opinions, the form which the science, as it seems to me, must ultimately take. I have long thought that as it deals throughout with quantities, it must be a mathematical science in matter if not in language . . . . The nature of wealth and value is explained by the consideration of indefinitely small amounts of pleasure and pain, just as the theory of statics is made to rest upon the equality of indefinitely small amounts of energy.[2]

Physics envy has never been clearer than in this quotation from Walras:

> The establishment of economics as an exact science . . . need no longer concern us. It is already perfectly clear that economics, like astronomy and mechanics, is both an empirical science and rational science . . . . [In time] mathematical economics will rank with the mathematical sciences of astronomy and mechanics; and on that day justice will be done to our work.[3]

The majority of academic economists today continue in the tradition established by Walras and Jevons, and they credit Walras and Jevons with creating a "marginalist revolution" leading to the dominance of "neoclassical" economics. Many contemporary economists appear to believe that economics does permit precise and accurate predictions of future outcomes, comparable to the work of Herschel.

Alfred Marshall

Alfred Marshall (1842–1924) built on and expanded the work of Jevons and Walras. He was born into a middle-class family and matriculated to Cambridge, where he studied mathematics and physics; but after graduating he turned to philosophy and was awarded a college fellowship and a lectureship on that basis.

The study of philosophy aroused his interest in economics, and he published a number of papers that became a series of books published from 1879 on. In 1884 he was invited to become professor of political economy at Cambridge, a position that he held for the rest of his life. In 1890 he published the first of many editions of his *Principles of Economics*, a work that became profoundly influential.

Marshall is credited with developing the law of supply and demand (see Chapter 3 below) and the concept of present value (see Chapter 10 below). He researched industrial structures and observed the formation of industrial clusters, anticipating the later work of Paul Krugman[4] and Michael Porter.[5]

When Keynes matriculated to Cambridge, Marshall was his tutor; when Marshall died Keynes wrote his obituary.

Paul Samuelson

Paul Samuelson (1915–2009) was an American economist who enjoyed a long and successful career. In 1947 he published *The Foundations of Economic Analysis*, a scholarly work that codified the key principles and methods of neoclassical economics. The principles included maximizing agents and an equilibrium state; the methods drew on previous work on thermodynamics.

In 1948 he published *Economics: An Introductory Analysis*, an introductory textbook now in its nineteenth edition. This became by far the most widely used economics textbook and possibly the most widely used higher-education textbook in any discipline. He is important to historians of economic thought as an economic theorist, but in the context of this book, his impact came from the widespread use of his textbook. Samuelson considered it proper to analyze an economy as if it were in a state of perfect competition and declared that all departures from perfect competition reduced welfare, making society as a whole worse off.

The Heroes

Peter Drucker dominated management education from the publication of his book, *The Practice of Management,* in 1954 until neoclassically trained economists successfully colonized management education in the 1990s. He described John Maynard Keynes and Joseph Alois Schumpeter as the two greatest economists of the twentieth century,[6] using the perspective of a practical management consultant and educator.

Drucker based his opinion on the profound influence both men had had on him and the study of economics and business. At least at the time Drucker was writing, the great majority of economists worked in mathematical abstractions with little or no apparent connection to reality. Keynes and Schumpeter based their economics firmly in the real world, recognizable to anyone with management or marketing responsibility.

Unfortunately, relatively few modern economists are familiar with their work except at a somewhat distorted second hand. The persistent use of reality by both men makes it impossible to fit their work into neat mathematical models; their implicit rejection of neat mathematical models is profoundly disturbing to those whose entire careers have been built on their ability to construct and interpret such models.

Schumpeter

Joseph A. Schumpeter was born in Austria-Hungary in a town that is now part of the Czech Republic and received his doctorate in 1906. He held university appointments before World War I and at the end of the war served briefly as Austria's Finance Minister and then as the chairman of a bank. From 1925 to 1932, he was professor of economics at Bonn University, and from 1932 until his death, he held the senior economics chair at Harvard.

Schumpeter explained the process of economic growth. He assumed that entrepreneurs were more or less rational profit seekers who intended to introduce an innovation into existing markets. How this leads to economic growth is explained at some length in Chapter 9.

Schumpeter rejected both the prevalence and the desirability of perfect competition. He observed that the conventional economic theories of his time (and ours) assumed that price competition dominated other forms of competition and pointed out that innovation, and therefore most economic growth, would be impossible if all competition was perfect. At the very least, he wrote, the rules of perfect competition would have to be suspended until the innovator had become established. He also noted that the rise of the great corporation and the ascendancy of oligopolistic[7] competition accompanied an acceleration of economic growth, and suggested that the conventional assertion that more competition would lead to more growth could not be supported on the evidence.

Schumpeter rejected a key foundation stone of neoclassical economics: the idea that an economy was at or near an equilibrium state. "Capitalism, then, is by nature a form or method of economic change and not only never is but never can be stationary."

Schumpeter concluded that the real economy was not in a state of perfect competition; it could not be realistically analyzed as if it were in such a state; and if it ever got into such a state, the consequences would not be desirable. He wrote:

> The first thing to go is the traditional conception of the modus operandi of competition. Economists are at long last emerging from the stage in which price competition was all they saw. As soon as quality competition and sales effort are admitted into the sacred precincts of theory, the price variable is ousted from its dominant position. However, it is still competition within a rigid pattern of invariant conditions, methods of production and forms of industrial organization in particular, that practically monopolizes attention. But in capitalist reality as distinct from the textbook picture, it is not that kind of competition which counts but the competition from the new commodity, the new source of supply, the new type of organization (the largest-scale unit of control for instance)—competition which commands a decisive cost or quality advantage and which strikes not at the margins of the profits and the outputs of the existing firms but at their foundations and their very lives. This kind of competition is as much more effective than the other as a bombardment is in comparison with forcing a door, and so much more important that it becomes a matter of comparative indifference whether competition in the ordinary sense functions more or less promptly; the powerful lever that in the long run expands output and brings down prices is in any case made of other stuff.[8]

In describing how competition through innovation affects large companies, Schumpeter referred to "the gales of creative destruction" as new products and processes, new levels of product quality, and new forms of organization rendered established ones obsolete and forced their owners and operators to take drastic efforts in order to stay solvent. The phrase is often used today by people who reject or ignore the rest of Schumpeter's work.

Keynes

John Maynard Keynes (1883–1946) was born into an upper-middle-class English household and educated at Eton and Kings College, Cambridge. He was tutored in economics by Alfred Marshall and A. C. Pigou, and graduated in 1905. After qualifying for his MA in 1908, he took up a lectureship in economics at Cambridge. While he maintained his connection with the university for the rest of his life, he was frequently summoned to Whitehall to advise the British government on economic and financial issues.[9]

Keynes's most influential work was *The General Theory of Employment, Interest and Money*, in which he demonstrated that even under all the assumptions of perfect competition, there could be an unemployment equilibrium with people ready and willing to work and no jobs available to them.[10] More controversially, Keynes suggested that governments should step in under such circumstances with public works and other programs.

Keynes predicted that the additional demand created by government investment would stimulate private investment, creating a multiplier effect: only a fraction of the formerly unemployed needed to be engaged by public investment projects in order to lead to the complete absorption of the unemployed into the resulting growing economy.

Keynes also completed important work on the subject of money and interest. His major contribution in the context of this book was his insight that an economy could not be analyzed successfully as the sum of the efforts of isolated individuals, but had to be analyzed as a system. The analysis of economies as systems is now described as macroeconomics, and Keynes set out the basic principles of macroeconomic analysis.

Among the crucial differences between Keynesian and standard neoclassical economics are:

- Keynes wrote that firms stop producing when they can no longer sell their output: total economic activity is limited by total economic demand. In the neoclassical model, firms stop producing when diseconomies of scale are about to force their costs above a market-determined price while demand is infinite, limited only by consumers' income.
- Keynes wrote that the quantity of available money affected the real economy because contracts for wages and for exchange are expressed in money terms. In the neoclassical model, money is a mere lubricant, and all transactions take place in real—i.e., inflation-adjusted—terms.

The Chicago School

The economics faculty of the University of Chicago is generally associated with continuing attempts to "disprove" Keynes by well-formed logical arguments based on the neoclassical paradigm of equilibrium and rationality. Sympathetic economists from other universities may consider themselves part of the "New Classical" movement, and the term may be used to embrace the Chicago School as well. The New Classical movement appears to be an attempt to capture the authority of Smith, Ricardo, and Malthus without actually reading their work or taking any account of their conclusions.

The Chicago School is known for its "tight prior" approach, rejecting any conclusion that cannot be built upon the assumption of rational, selfish behavior by individual agents in an equilibrium state. They are then free with conclusions drawn on this basis that are stated as irrefutable facts with no reference to the highly dubious underlying assumptions.

Leading Chicago School figures include Roger Lucas (b. 1937), who developed a theory of rational expectations that led to the conclusion that the average expectation of a population for the outcome of an economic policy was an accurate prediction of the outcome. From this he concluded that fiscal stimulus policy would be ineffective because the prospect of future tax increases to pay down the debts would suppress demand and offset all the effects of the stimulus. Lucas summoned the ghost of Ricardo to his aid—hence "Ricardian equivalence."

Gary Becker (b. 1930) is another ornament of the Chicago School famous for extending the use of economic analysis into matters such as marriage and divorce.

Eugene Fama (b. 1939) developed the Efficient Market Hypothesis, which became the basis for the conventional (but flawed—see Chapter 10) theory of investment evaluation. The Efficient Market Hypothesis asserts that the market price of a commodity or security is the best possible estimate of its value. In consequence, a public company with shares traded on a stock exchange should only make investments and other decisions that lead to an increase in its stock price.

The efficient market hypothesis implies that it is impossible for corporate executives to affect the stock price by concealing information or publishing false information. This conclusion has given great comfort to many corporate fraudsters and may partly explain the reluctance of authorities in the United States and elsewhere to pursue criminal prosecutions for corporate misbehavior and their willingness to accept a cash settlement with no conviction recorded or confession required.

Neoliberalism[11]

Origins

Stedman Jones, in his profound work *Masters of the Universe*, identifies two seminal thinkers in the development of neoliberalism. The first was the Austrian economist Ludwig von Mises, who argued that socialism was economically impossible because prices could only be set in markets. Von Mises at the same time redefined democracy as the freedom of consumers to choose between competing suppliers in a market: their cumulative individual choices would direct producers to address all their needs.

The more important contribution came from Friedrich Hayek. Hayek was appalled by the actions of Nazi Germany and the practices of the USSR and was concerned that the successful use of central planning by the Allies during World War II would reconcile the population to the widespread adoption of socialist planning. He implicitly adopted von Mises's definition of democracy and argued that the only guarantee of freedom from Nazi or Communist tyranny was free markets.

Keynes wrote to Hayek after reading what was to become Hayek's most popular work, *The Road to Serfdom*, and commented that the idea of a society with no laws or regulations beyond the preservation of markets and the protection of property was not entirely practical:

> You admit here and there that it is a question of where to draw the line. You agree that the line has to be drawn somewhere, and that the logical extreme is not possible. But you give no guidance whatever as to where to draw it. In a sense this is shirking the practical issue. It is true that you and I would probably draw it in different places. I should guess that according to my ideas you greatly underestimate the practicability of the middle course. But as soon as you admit that the extreme is not possible, and that a line has to be drawn, you are, on your own argument, done for, since you are trying to persuade us that so soon as one moves in the planned direction you are necessarily launched on the slippery path which will lead you in due course over the precipice.[12]

In this Keynes was following Adam Smith, who wrote that many essential public goods (see Chapter 11) had to be delivered by governments if they were to be delivered at all:

> The third and last duty of the sovereign or commonwealth is that of erecting and maintaining those public institutions and those public works, which, though they may be in the highest degree advantageous to a great society, are, however, of such a nature that the profit could never repay the expense to any individual or small number of individuals, and which it therefore cannot be expected that any individual or small number of individuals should erect or maintain. The performance of this duty requires, too, very different degrees of expense in the different periods of society.
>
> After the public institutions and public works necessary for the defense of the society, and for the administration of justice . . . the other works and institutions of this kind are chiefly those for facilitating the commerce of the society, and those for promoting the instruction of the people. The institutions for instruction are of two kinds: those for the education of youth, and those for the instruction of people of all ages.[13]

Neither Smith nor Keynes believed that a pure market society was possible, much less desirable, and even Hayek considered that government action might be necessary to prevent the emergence of monopolies and to ensure that public goods were provided by "the market."[14] Hayek had no practical experience of commercial or manufacturing activity, and his view of markets and production was naïve in the extreme; but he pursued his vision of a pure market society with extraordinary persistence and dedication.

Public Choice and Regulatory Capture

The utility-maximizing consumer used in economic theorizing is a caricature of a real human being, a concept invented to enable the calculus to be applied to economic problems. The concept is not essential in fundamental neoliberalism: von Mises developed the key distinction in "Austrian" economics when he pointed out that real people differ from each other and cannot logically be replaced by an average or representative person when developing economic arguments. The utility-maximizing consumer is, however, a critical concept in neoclassical economics and has been absorbed into contemporary neoliberalism.

The psycholgist and author Daniel Kahneman (b. 1934) recalls his first contact with the neoclassical economists' substitute for humans when he read an article by the economist Bruno Frey, who wrote, "The agent of economic theory is rational, selfish and his tastes do not change."

As a practicing and academic psychologist, Kahneman knew that people weren't like that:

> I was astonished. My economist colleagues worked in the building next door, but I had not appreciated the profound difference between our intellectual worlds. To a psychologist, it is self-evident that people are neither fully rational nor completely selfish, and that their tastes are anything but stable. Our two disciplines seemed to be studying different species, which the behavioral economist Richard Thaler later dubbed Econs and Humans.[15]

Rational behavior, in the sense that neoclassical economists use the term, is a practical impossibility. Kahneman confirms that a great deal of human behavior is far from perfectly rational even in experimental situations where the complexity of the real world is hidden, and he provides a convincing explanation based on our evolutionary history.

Treating the assumption of selfish, rational behavior as a fact led neoliberal economists toward the theory of public choice. If real people were truly rational and selfish, then putting them in charge of a public enterprise would automatically see its operations distorted in order to deliver private benefits. Treating this ungrounded assumption as a fact led to arguments for the privatization of public authorities and public enterprises, even when the enterprises operated a natural monopoly such as water supply.

It is not hard to find examples of people who have abused positions of trust for their own gain; and as Jon Ronson pointed out, psychopathological selfishness is no handicap when seeking promotions through an organization where promotions are made on mainly subjective grounds.[16]

The fact that some chief executives are psychopaths who, if born into a lower social class, might well have turned into violent criminals does not mean that all chief executives are psychopaths or that a majority of real people are psychopathically selfish. Military and social history has many examples of people putting their lives at risk and often losing them to save a stranger or to support a cause from which they could expect little personal gain. The use of public choice theory to justify privatization involves at least two false assumptions:

- That every possible candidate for a management position in a public enterprise is psychopathologically selfish.
- That senior managers of privatized monopolies will have their psychopathological tendencies suppressed by the vigilance of their shareholders.

Recent history has demonstrated that shareholders in public companies are almost totally ineffective in preventing senior management practicing greed and opportunism if they choose to do so. Even when the incompetence of chief executives becomes impossible to ignore, they are sent on their way with massive "golden parachutes." Even shareholders in smaller companies are reluctant to vote against the reelection of directors. The current directors will have befriended them and organized entertainment and refreshments at the various general meetings and offered exculpatory explanations for disappointing results. Not only would it be bad manners to vote against the reappointment of such nice people, but the typical shareholder would not know who to propose as a replacement.

Hayek's argument for what became known as privatization is more subtle: he followed von Mises in arguing that public servants—bureaucrats—were judged by their ability to administer regulations, not to respond to circumstances. He did not challenge their honesty or diligence, but rather argued that private, profit-seeking firms would respond more rapidly and effectively to their customers' requirements. As Hayek's ideas developed, the range of activities that he permitted people to participate in as citizens steadily shrank. In a perfect Hayekian world, there would be no citizens, only consumers/customers.

The assumption that everyone is rational and selfish leads inexorably to the theory of public choice. Someone whose sole concern is their own advantage will not consider issues of right and wrong, but only what he or she can get away with.

The doctrine of regulatory capture makes somewhat weaker assumptions than does public choice theory. Its adherents argue that even if some regulators intend to serve the public interest they will fail to do so because, by assumption, the public interest will always be served best by unrestricted competition. Regulators must be in frequent contact with the managers of the firms that they regulate, and will be presented with many highly specific opportunities to assist these firms, backed up by persuasive arguments. Their interactions with the public will be of a more general nature and no one will present the public's case to these regulators.

There are fundamental problems with the assertion that regulatory capture is both inevitable and contrary to the public good. One is the implicit assumption that any action that assists firms in an industry must be to the detriment of the customers of that industry. A second is the deeper assumption that an unregulated market will necessarily offer better customer outcomes than a regulated one. In Chapter 3 I will show that a monopoly will set lower prices than would rule in a market with many participants; and price is only a proxy for the costs and benefits of user participation in a market.

To deny that regulatory capture is inevitable is not to deny that it can occur. According to a report in the *Washington Post*, one of two administrative law judges in the Commodity Futures Trading Commission told his colleague that he had promised the commission chairperson who appointed him "that we would never rule in a complainant's favor," and the report notes that "a review of his rulings will confirm that he fulfilled his vow." The judge did not need to be captured; he accepted an appointment on the basis that he was a servant of the industry he was charged with regulating.[17]

While some regulations and regulatory agencies may restrict or have restricted competition, many specifically address conduct. For example, in America the operators of restaurants and food processing establishments are required, among other hygiene related procedures, to erect signs in washrooms instructing employees to wash their hands before returning to their duties. It has been argued, apparently seriously, that these regulations impose a needless cost on restaurants because if a restaurant's customers started to die of food borne diseases this would adversely affect its business. Since, by assumption, all managers are rational they would enforce hygiene standards even if no regulations ordered them to.

The regulation of finance under the New Deal following the Great Depression has been a particular target of the neoliberal movement. The advocates of financial deregulation claim that regulating their industry discourages innovation and adds unnecessary cost. A similar logic applied to zoos would see the locks on the gates of the tiger enclosures removed, saving the expense of employing a locksmith. Rational parents would prevent their children opening the gates, so no one would get hurt.

Milton Friedman

Neoliberalism could not have progressed beyond an association of naïve eccentrics and unworldly professors without the tireless efforts of Milton Friedman. Friedman's undergraduate degree was in mathematics, and his first postgraduate degree was in statistics. During the 1930s he was a supporter of Roosevelt's New Deal and worked in New Deal institutions. After the end of World War II, he became convinced by Hayek's (and von Mises's) arguments linking freedom to markets, and he was one of the earliest US authors to use the term "neoliberalism."[18]

In his 1951 paper, Friedman argued that nineteenth-century laissez-faire, the philosophy of classical liberalism, had failed to maintain popular support, leading to the rise of collectivism and socialism in the first half of the twentieth century. His definition of socialism displayed the talent for bold generalization that made him such a formidable debater and propagandist: he included everything from the New Deal regulation of finance to Soviet central planning in his definition, and he boldly claimed that these were proven failures *in toto*. Neoliberalism was to be a modern form of liberalism where the state played a restricted but positive role in maintaining competitive markets.

Hayek believed that the rise of the welfare state during the first half of the twentieth century and the displacement of traditional laissez-faire liberalism, were the result of the activities of the Fabian Society, which had made collectivist ideas acceptable and identified classical liberalism with troglodyte conservatism and brutal exploitation. Hayek did not appear to consider that objective factors, such as ruthless exploitation and grotesque inequality, had played any part in these changes. He founded the Mont Pèlerin Society in 1947 in order to restore academic credibility to his free-market ideas.

Friedman, at least in his 1951 paper, did recognize that there had been objective factors in the rise of "collectivism" and blamed these on the tolerance of anticompetitive behavior by various individuals and firms. Neoliberalism would solve these problems by the adoption and enforcement of effective procompetition policies. Such minor differences of opinion about the basis of the acceptability of "collectivism" did not prevent Friedman becoming Hayek's close ally in their mission to conquer academia and, from there, the world for neoliberalism.[19]

While Friedman never abandoned academic publication, he devoted considerable effort to polemical works, partly intended to influence public opinion directly but more significantly to gain wealthy sponsors for think tanks and endowed chairs where his and Hayek's ideas would be propagated. He was aware of both Hayek's unworldliness and the prevalence of imperfect competition in the economy, and his invention of the F-twist (page 63) was intended to render his and Hayek's arguments immune from reality-based refutation.

Friedman's effort led to hundreds of millions of dollars being directed to projecting free-market ideas; association with all these wealthy donors led to a shift in Friedman's own opinions, and he came to assert that there was no such thing as anticompetitive behavior by firms and that procompetition laws and authorities were a waste of money: the only form of anticompetitive behavior that should be prohibited was the operation of trade unions.

Hayek's and Friedman's agenda bore fruit when, during the later 1970s, the Democratic administration of Jimmy Carter (b. 1924, president 1977–81) in the United States and the Labour government under James Callaghan (1912–2005, prime minister 1977–1979) in the United Kingdom turned to neoliberal ideas in an attempt to break out from the stagflation of the time. The conservative administrations that followed pursued neoliberal ideas more enthusiastically and in much greater depth, but the extended success of the neoliberal project owes a great deal to its initial adoption by left-liberal governments in the 1970s and the failure of the left-liberal governments of Clinton (b. 1946, president 1993–2001) and Blair to repudiate it.[20]

The fact that distinguished academics and Nobel Prize winners such as Paul Krugman and Daniel Kahneman ridiculed the foundations and the logic of neoliberalism did not break its dominance of the conventional wisdom. Even the economic disaster of the Global Financial Crisis (GFC) leading to the Great Recession (2007–10) in the United States and the Eurozone Crisis (2010–) in Ireland and the countries of "Southern" Europe has not entirely discredited it.

Ordo-liberalism

A number of German economists associated with the journal *Ordo* hold strong beliefs in the advantages of competitive markets. *Ordo* accepted papers by Hayek and his associates and, in Stedman Jones's view, is an advocate for "stage 2" neoliberalism. The group has great influence in Germany and substantial influence in the EU, where the Competition Directorate generally follows its precepts.

What distinguishes the Ordo-liberals from contemporary neoliberals ("stage 3" neoliberals in Stedman Jones's term) is their strong adherence to the Bismarckian settlement: they draw a clear line between the state and the market. In Germany the state retains responsibility for health and education, and does so administratively: there is no pretense of a "health" or "education" market. Manufacturing industry in Germany is wholly in private hands and the competition laws are strictly enforced.

In this the Ordo-liberals are the true heirs of Adam Smith while the neoliberalism of the later Friedman and institutions such as the Adam Smith Society are mere pretenders.

Neoliberalism Stage 3 in Practice

The "stagflation" in some (not all) of the developed economies following the "oil shocks" of the 1970s clearly demonstrated a fundamental flaw in Keynesian economic management as practiced by the US and British governments. The fivefold increase in the cost of crude oil led to higher energy prices, which flowed through to consumer prices generally; these triggered wage demands that, when acceded to, put further pressure on consumer prices. At the same time, firms attempted to cut their costs, leading to increased unemployment and reduced economic growth; hence "stagflation" = stagnation + inflation.

The Carter administration in the United States and the Callaghan government in the United Kingdom turned to the neoliberal playbook in an attempt to limit inflation and in doing so implicitly abandoned the full employment policies that all administrations and governments had followed since the end of World War II. The Callaghan government set cash limits for public authority pay; these were bitterly resented by the low-paid workers most directly affected, leading to a prolonged "dirty jobs" strike, with garbage piled high in London's streets. Although the strike was settled before the 1979 election, the memory lingered and was a factor in the Labour Party's loss.

Carter was defeated by Ronald Reagan (1911–2004, president 1981–1989) in the 1980 election. Carter was one of the most thoughtful American presidents, but his natural caution and determination to understand issues before acting was portrayed by his opponents as indecisiveness. Reagan had been an actor and then the narrator for a series of programs sponsored by General Electric promoting the benefits of private enterprise. If Reagan ever suffered from doubt, it was not apparent to the public, and he was aided by some outstanding speechwriters. His personal confidence and his excellent delivery secured widespread agreement with his policies and ideas and made his opponents appear hesitant and confused.

The Reagan administration in the United States also attempted to put Freidman's ideas into practice and control inflation by controlling the money supply. The result was soaring interest rates and a huge appreciation of the US dollar, bankrupting some manufacturing businesses and forcing others to relocate or become importers. The rising dollar had a catastrophic effect on several Latin American countries, which had raised loans on the New York market and found the cost of servicing them more than double due to the combination of higher interest rates and the dollar appreciation.

The Reagan administration also cut taxes, particularly on higher-income earners. The cuts were partially offset by cuts to domestic programs, but any domestic savings were swamped by large increases in defense expenditure. The United States entered a period of both trade and fiscal deficits that, with some brief pauses, continues to the present day.

Margaret Thatcher came to office as the Conservative prime minister in Britain in 1979. The Thatcher government in Britain abandoned "Keynesian" demand management policies, reduced the progressiveness of the taxation system, abolished foreign currency restrictions, and raised interest rates to previously unheard-of levels. The huge rise in the exchange rate resulting from the interest-rate increases bankrupted approximately 30 percent of British manufacturing industry and so created a reserve army of the unemployed sufficient to suppress wage demands. Interest rates were then slowly reduced, but the damage had been done. Thatcher's government also privatized most of the profitable state trading enterprises, including British Telecom and British Gas.

The combination of higher unemployment, the loss of manufacturing jobs, administration hostility to trade unions, and a failure to maintain the real value of the minimum wage saw median US incomes stagnate, and the American median income, adjusted for inflation, has barely moved from its 1979 level in the following decades.

In 1989 Reagan was succeeded by his vice president, George H. W. Bush (b. 1924, president 1989–92). Bush senior was far from blasé about the US fiscal deficit and legislated some modest tax increases in order to restrain it. His administration was successful in controlling the deficit but was bitterly criticized by much of the media, and he was defeated in the 1992 election by Bill Clinton.

Clinton made further modest tax increases, and during his administration (1993–2000) the US government ran modest fiscal surpluses; but Clinton did little to reverse the broader policies introduced under Reagan.

The Washington Consensus

The policy combination of flatter tax scales, a move from income to consumption taxes, privatization of state-owned enterprises, and contracting out of government services became known as the Washington Consensus, and the World Bank and International Monetary Fund (IMF) forced client governments in the developing countries to adopt these policies. The theory, such as it was, underlying the Washington Consensus became known in the United States as Reaganism and in Australia as "economic rationalism" but is more broadly referred to as "neoliberalism."

Neoliberal policies were adopted by many developing countries under pressure from the World Bank and the IMF; they were more or less voluntarily adopted in the transition economies of Eastern Europe as the opposite of state socialism; and they were adopted out of conviction by a number of English-speaking countries, including the United States and Britain. They were emphatically not adopted in France, Germany, or Italy and only adopted after heavy modification if at all in the Benelux and Scandinavian countries.

Reagan and Thatcher were able to justify their position as logically consistent with the use of mainstream economics. In a theoretical economy where competition is perfect or nearly perfect, government intervention must necessarily involve welfare losses. If, for example, governments levy progressive taxation in such a perfect economy (see Chapter 3) the highest-paid people must be the most productive, and by reducing their incentive to produce, one must reduce the total output of the economy and with it the average income of all people within it.

If, of course, one starts from a sufficiently ridiculous assumption, one can arrive at an even more ridiculous conclusion, and this is a good example: actual studies have shown that there is in fact very little correlation between value created and income at the top of the income scale, and that increasing incomes over a certain level does not bring on an increased effort.

Many on the Left were seduced by orthodox economists who argued, on the basis of their deeply flawed models rather than any observable facts, that the more perfect and less regulated the economy became, the fewer chances the capitalist class would have for rent seeking and skimming excess profits, and the greater the share of economic output that would accrue to workers.

Many politicians on the Left found these arguments persuasive and persuaded their parties to abandon socialist policies, or anything that could be associated with them, in favor of microeconomic reform. The Left parties ceased to oppose uncontrolled capitalism; rather, they based their appeal on a claim, backed up by the mainstream economics profession, to be better managers of capitalism—or better at letting capitalism manage itself—than the parties of the Right.

In a strange inversion, the Left parties have become more devoted to neoliberal purity than the Right. While this book was being written, the Socialist president Hollande of France was squandering the popularity that led to his election by enforcing austerity and other neoliberal-inspired policies while his country was suffering from high unemployment and sluggish growth.

If neoliberalism truly pointed the way to an ideal society, none of this would matter, but if it doesn't, then having both sides of the political system committed to neoliberalism and neither open to any alternatives will stifle economic and social progress. Voices on the Left are strengthened by making suggestions that reflect economic reality rather than economic theory and ordinary people's aspirations rather than the policies espoused by the narrowly owned business press. When left-wing politicians do offer reality-based policies, they are routinely denounced as "populists" and their suggestions as "populism."

There remains the risk that policies selected for their popularity may be genuinely damaging to the economy, and in the absence of a coherent theoretical framework, the advocates of such policies may be portrayed as being divorced from reality and selling illusions. A realist economic theory, once developed, could be used to test popular policies for practicality and logical consistency.

The term "populism" carries the clear implication that setting out policies that appeal to the electorate is somehow improper. Such policies do, of course, have the advantage of popularity: those who advise the Left to avoid popular policies may not be the Left's best friends.

Notes

1. Kennedy (2010) provides an approachable but thorough account of Smith's work, including an account of the hijacking of his name in the support of propositions not supported by his actual work.
2. Jevons (1871 [1970], Preface, p. 3) quoted in Grieve (2012).
3. Walras (1874 [1977], pp. 47–48) quoted in Grieve (2012).
4. Krugman (1996).
5. Porter (1990).
6. Drucker (1989).
7. See Chapter 3.
8. Schumpeter (1942).
9. Skidelsky (1983).
10. Keynes (1936 [1961]).
11. This section is based on Stedman Jones (2012); most individual page references have been omitted to avoid clutter.
12. Letter from Keynes to Hayek, June 28, 1944, reproduced from Stedman Jones (2012: p. 67).
13. Smith (1776: Bk V, Ch I, Part III).
14. Wapshott (2011).
15. Kahneman (2011: p. 279).
16. Ronson (2011).
17. Hilzenrath (2010).
18. Friedman (1951); the term did not "take" in the United States and was generally superseded by "Libertarianism."
19. Stedman Jones (2012: pp. 73–84).
20. Stedman Jones (2012: Ch. 6).

3

Competition: Real or Perfect?

Some people believe football is a matter of life and death;
I am very disappointed with that attitude. I can assure
you it is much, much more important than that.
—Bill Shankly, Legendary Manager of Liverpool Football Club

Real competition is about winning. In sport the winner gets the gold medal or the silver ewer and the endorsement contracts. In business the winner gains a customer or a new and profitable contract. Losers must try harder and hope to win next time, or look for an alternative competition with weaker opponents. Sport has rules, and some of the most important concern resources: a golfer is only allowed so many clubs and a football team can only have so many players on the field at one time. All the players in a competition have scoring opportunities, and the winner is the one with the highest, or in a few sports the lowest, score.

Business also has rules, and some of the most important concern resources: a business must either own the resources that it deploys or use them with the permission of their owner. Money is an essential resource for a business like a golfer's clubs or a football team's players: without it nothing happens. Money is also the basis of business rule number 1: at the end of each operating cycle, a business should have more money under its control than it started with; over a period of no more than a few years, "should" becomes "must," or the business leaves the game. The final role of money is the measure of the score: the business that makes the greatest amount of money, relative to the value of the resources that it controls, is the winner.

Business winners don't usually get gold medals, but they get to use the money they make in one operating cycle to be more aggressive in the next one. They can buy the best assets of failed competitors cheaply; they can replace old equipment with newer, better-performing equipment and old premises with newer, better-located ones; and they can spend more on sales and marketing. They can demonstrate their success to investors and obtain more money to enable them to be even more successful. Like a football team moving to a higher division, they may enter new markets, or like a team with a promising nursery club, they can create new and higher-quality products.

Real competition is a process: two or more parties strive for some goal, and the most successful is declared the winner. That is not, unfortunately, how most economists see competition or what they mean by the word.

Perfect Competition

Most economists see competition as a state, and they call the ideal state "perfect competition." Under perfect competition there are no winners, and if profit is the score, no scores either. Under perfect competition all firms are price takers, and their actions cannot affect the price that they receive. The limit on their output, and revenue, is the progressive increase in their costs as their output rises. The idea of perfect competition has roots in the nineteenth century.

Keen demonstrated conclusively[1] that the theorems emerging from standard neoclassical economics to describe the state of perfect competition assume that an entire economy consists of a single product created by a single worker or a number of identical workers and supplied to a single consumer or a number of identical consumers. When the first edition of Keen's book appeared, the reaction of many orthodox economists was, in effect, "So what? We already knew that."

To take a recent example of the sort of economics that Keen was criticizing, Denicolò and Zanchettin, in an article published by the prestigious *Economic Journal*,[2] claim to have shown among other things that "stronger patent protection may reduce innovation and growth." As a prelude to forty pages of mathematics, they state of their model, "The economy is populated by L identical, infinitely lived, individuals. . . . There is a unique final good in the economy that can be consumed, used to produce intermediate goods, or used in research. . . ." Not only are all the people in this model world identical and immortal, they only produce a single product. The product has properties that are entirely unreal—not so much science fiction as pure magic. The conclusion may be justified, or not; but the idea that a model so remote from reality can be used to make public policy recommendations is, to anyone but a fully certified neoclassical economist, staggering.

Nineteenth-century mechanical engineers designing steam engines knew that real steam would not pass instantaneously from the boiler to the cylinder as soon as the valves were opened; even an ideal gas would have some inertia and consequent "Newtonian" viscosity, which would limit the speed at which it could travel. At the piston speed typical of late-nineteenth-century engines, the discrepancy was minor, although neglecting or miscalculating these effects often led to designs for engines that failed to meet their specifications. Engineers soon learned the risks involved in assuming perfection while dealing with the real world. These lessons were slow to pass to economists.

Perfect competition is a theoretical state in which an economy, or part of an economy, may exist on the assumption that consumers and producers behave like a frictionless, weightless ideal gas: if producer A offers a lower price than producer B, every consumer will instantaneously transfer their business from A to B, no matter how small the price differential. This is known to economists as the Law of One Price, and as such is part of the dogmatic core of the theory of perfect competition. Industrial Organization (IO) economists, as discussed further below, do not consider that perfect competition exists in reality, although they tread fairly carefully around the Law of One Price.

Orwell, in his book *1984*, suggested that control of language could become control of thought. The economic concept of perfect competition is an example of this: if there is such a thing as perfection, why should anything else be tolerated? Some economists may believe that perfect competition is a practical possibility; others realize that the preconditions for perfect competition are so stringent as to render it impossible to actually exist as a practical matter of commerce.

The best that can be hoped for is "nearly perfect" competition, whatever that may be. J. M. Clark introduced the idea of "workable competition" in 1940.[3] "Workable" competition is defined as the closest practical approach to "perfect" competition, recognizing that there aren't an infinite number of firms or consumers and that all products are not fully interchangeable. Clark's proposal does not seem to have satisfied the generality of economists. S. H. Sosnick published a critique of workable competition in 1958,[4] but the critique itself is not entirely convincing.

Under the European Union's Competition Directive, regulations establishing workable competition are required when deregulating or privatizing utility systems such as the gas or electricity supply networks. If British or Californian experience with electricity privatization is any guide, such regulations have not delivered net consumer benefits. They have given comfort to those economists who believe that perfect competition makes perfect.

Teaching Perfection

The path by which young minds are seduced into believing in the desirability of perfect, or almost-perfect, competition is deceptively simple. They are asked to consider a simple farmers' market selling, let us say, potatoes. If there are many eager buyers and not many potatoes, the price will go up, while if there are few buyers and many potatoes, the price will drop. The price will not, the class is assured, fall to zero; because the farmers will not sell potatoes below the cost of their production. Equally, the price will not go stratospheric: high prices will deter buyers, and in the absence of willing buyers, the farmers will have to reduce their asking price.

If buyers are eager enough to push the price of potatoes over the cost of production, the students are assured that the farmers will produce more; but to increase production they will have to work lower-quality land, and this will push their cost of production up, so the price will settle at the point where the price exactly equals the cost of producing the last potato. In symbols the price (P) will equal the marginal cost (MC).

Well before this point is reached, any farmers' children in the class will have exploded, and the class may be exposed to some classical condescension as the lecturer explains that although their parents may have had to sell produce below cost (or had produce that they couldn't sell at all) this must have been due to irreproducible circumstances, and no other farmers have ever had to face this problem.

Economists generally use the term "welfare" to refer to overall consumption; most of them are not particularly worried about who does the consuming. If a change allows Mr. Dives to eat steak for breakfast as well as dinner, most economists would say that welfare has improved, even if Mr. Lazarus has to continue subsisting on thin gruel. Perfect competition is described as desirable because it appears to maximize "welfare."

Once the farmers' children have stormed out of the class, the lecturer will now assert that "welfare" is at its maximum when prices equal marginal cost, and because we live in the best of all possible worlds, this must be the case in ours. The lecturer will go on to argue that the perfect operation of supply and demand will set prices (and wages, the price of labor) to their welfare-maximizing level across the whole economy, and that anyone who interferes with the perfect operation of the market is both stealing "rents" or "excess profits" from the general public and inflicting on it deadweight losses (so called because the loss to consumers is not matched by a gain to producers).

Students who make it to later-year economics studies and those Econ 101 students lucky in their lecturer are taught that prices can rise above or fall below the marginal cost of production, and even that prices can fall to the point that farmers lose less by leaving a crop unharvested than by harvesting it and taking it to market. They are reassured that the desirable welfare properties of a perfectly competitive market hold in long-run equilibrium, when the number of firms has adjusted so price equals average cost as well as marginal cost.[5]

There are at least three critical problems even with this less dogmatic approach. Even in the long run, prices may never converge on a single, equilibrium price:

- If a complex system ever gets out of equilibrium, it may never return to it, but rather it may fluctuate cyclically or chaotically.
- The long run may never arrive, because every instance of innovation postpones it until the effects of the innovation have been absorbed into a new equilibrium.
- Real farmers would plant less than the quantities that they expected would lead to pricing at marginal cost.

As Mordecai Ezekiel demonstrated empirically in 1938 after studying the Chicago hog market, the price may never reach an equilibrium point, cycling in an indefinite cobweb.[6] Ezekiel anticipated work in chaos and complexity theory that demonstrated that real systems do not, in general, settle to an equilibrium point, and even the limit cycle described by Ezekiel is a highly specific result.[7]

On the second point, Schumpeter pointed out, "Capitalism, then, is by nature a form or method of economic change and not only never is but never can be stationary."[8] If the long run ever arrived, the economic system would no longer be capitalism in any form. Every innovation restarts the countdown to the long run.

Thirdly, from the farmer's point of view, planting to the point where the marginal cost equals the anticipated price is a poor strategy. If she plants somewhat fewer potatoes, the price will be higher, and although she will have fewer potatoes to sell, she wasn't going to make a profit on the last potato anyway had she followed the economists' rules.

Of course, if she plants far too few potatoes, the rising price will not compensate her for the lower volume, and so she should seek the happy medium where her gross profit is as large as possible.

There are at least two flaws in this justification for trying to make competition perfect. The first is the "welfare flaw": perfect competition, if it happened, wouldn't actually maximize welfare. The second is that no real market would actually deliver marginal cost pricing. Both are explained below.

Industrial Organization, or IO, economists take a more realistic view of markets and competition, and explicitly deal with markets with a finite number of suppliers. They represent a minority of academic economists.

The Welfare Flaw

Somehow economics became infected with an engineering oddity known as the power transfer theorem. The theorem states that the maximum possible amount of power between a source, such as a generator, and a sink, such as a motor, occurs when the internal resistance of both are equal.

This deceived some early engineers into using small generators to drive big loads: they soon discovered that this meant wasting a lot of power in the generator. A bigger generator might cost more up front, but it soon paid for itself by cutting the internal losses.

A competitive equilibrium in economics is a similar state, where the maximum possible value is transferred from "producers" to "consumers."

Welfare economics idealizes the situation where the cost of producing a consumer benefit equals the value of the benefit: price equals marginal cost. This is a close analogy to reducing the size of the generator until its internal resistance is equal to the resistance of the load. In the case of an electrical system, system efficiency rises even while power transfer efficiency falls.

A benevolent social planner would divert a proportion of productive effort into capital goods and delivering the benefit of lower variable costs; but the price must then be high enough to deliver a return on the capital investment as well as covering the variable costs. A price that simply covers capital costs and variable costs is still inadequate: there must be money available to cover depreciation and to invest in product and process innovation. (Economists may include depreciation as part of the cost of capital, so if they don't mention it they may not be neglecting it.) Discussing benevolent social planners is a little unrealistic, given that such creatures are rare if they exist at all.

More realistically, firms that do not collect enough revenue to cover their variable costs, generate a return on their capital, including depreciation, and provide funds for investment in marketing and innovation do not stay in business; they will be nearly as rare as benevolent social planners.

A competitive equilibrium does not maximize welfare; all it does is maximize transfers from producers to consumers at a given level of technology. Once we remember that a typical consumer is a producer who has gotten home from work (and not an economist enjoying an annuity paid by a landowning duke), we can stop being concerned about the injustice done to consumers when producers enjoy a surplus and start worrying about the net welfare enjoyed by producer-consumers. (Adam Smith enjoyed a pension of £100 per year to top up his stipend from Glasgow University (see pages 21ff). A Scottish laborer who was lucky enough to be employed for a full year would, at that time, have earned a total of eleven pounds and fourteen shillings.)

The Mathematical Error

First-year economics students are taught that the economy consists of "consumers" and "producers," and consumers maximize "utility" while producers maximize profit.[9] Some elementary calculus leads to the conclusion that a profit-maximizing monopolist will produce a quantity Q at a price P such that marginal cost equals marginal revenue.[10]

They are then introduced to the idea of a "competitive" market with many producers and are assured that the actions of a single producer cannot affect the price.[11] At the same time, they are assured that the aggregate supply of all producers *does* affect the price;[12] but the aggregate supply is only the sum of the individual producers' contributions. By glossing over this contradiction, they are taught that, while in a monopolized market the price will settle at a level where marginal cost equals marginal revenue, in a competitive market the price will settle at the lower level where the price equals marginal cost. The argument is reinforced by the use of elegantly drawn graphs.

Keen and Standish[13] have shown that "competitive" pricing is a fiction—at its kindest, an error arising from confusion between "many" and infinity. Even in the more elaborate models developed by IO economists, a near-competitive price is only possible in markets where prices must be set once and observed forever. When producers have frequent opportunities to adjust their prices, the result will again be a price approximating the price a single monopoly supplier would have charged.

Defenders of the theory of marginal cost pricing have run experiments in which students are required to play a business game involving price setting, and in such games the price may approach the marginal cost level. Since such games are designed by people attempting to refute criticisms of conventional price theory, the results must be taken with a grain of salt.

A game in which students were required to meet fixed costs from a limited cash base and were rewarded for maximizing profit, while those who exhausted their cash were eliminated from the game, would be more realistic. As discussed below, real firms use mark-up pricing that, assuming that the mark-up is calculated correctly or adjusted in line with experience, will converge on the monopoly price. The board game Monopoly has many of the necessary characteristics but lacks any price-setting functions or opportunities for willed choice in purchasing. It does capture the essential nature of capitalist competition, which may account for its lasting popularity.

Firms lack the information required to set a profit-maximizing mark-up *a priori*; but as long as they have a moderately effective accounting system, they will have no trouble in adjusting their price until the earned margins are satisfactory, possibly not perfectly converged on the monopoly price but not far from it.

The Attractions of Perfect Competition

The political conclusions from an assumption of perfect competition are extremely attractive to radical individualists, since under perfect competition all economic rewards will be precisely matched to economic contribution. Many indolent heirs to dubiously acquired fortunes have been persuaded to support economists such as Hayek and Friedman as an alternative to the command "Go and sell all that thou has, and give to the poor, and thou shalt have treasure in heaven."[14] These economists justify radical individualism in part on the basis of an assumption of perfect competition; a (relatively) small donation to suitable think tanks and universities enables such indolent heirs to combine affluent indolence with moral rectitude.

Samuelson, in his influential textbook,[15] declared that the defining characteristic of "almost-perfect" competition was that output was limited by the capacity of each individual producer; and if output was limited by the extent of demand, then the resulting competition was not even nearly perfect.

To discover whether an individual firm is subject to (nearly) perfect competition, one asks its manager or owner the following question: "If a prospective customer asked you for one additional unit of your firm's output at the average price that you are currently receiving, would you be able to supply that customer profitably?"

When that question is asked, 90 percent of nonagricultural businesses reply to the effect that they could supply an additional customer either immediately or after a short delay to cover purchasing or manufacturing lead times; the remaining 10 percent reply to the effect that it would take them some time and/or effort to supply an additional customer, but given that time they could do so profitably at their ruling price.

Toyota, and companies that follow its lead, deliberately builds factories that can meet their anticipated demand in two shifts. If there is an unexpected rise in demand, it can be satisfied by offering each shift overtime work: there is no question of Toyota turning away buyers because there were more of them than it had planned for, or for delaying delivery while expensive capital works are completed.

The critical factors that make perfect competition impossible for manufacturing and service businesses—even if they ignored their strategic interests—are that their variable costs do not rise significantly with output, and they have fixed costs that must be paid whatever the price they are receiving for the goods and services that they produce.[16] When the fixed and variable costs are combined, it becomes clear that marginal costs *fall* with increasing output as the fixed costs are allocated over an increased quantity. Even when overtime must be paid at higher rates than ordinary time, spreading fixed costs over a greater volume means that total unit costs continue to fall.

It is obvious with service businesses, now the largest part of a modern economy, that their output is limited by the number of customers, not the marginal cost of serving the last one: a hairdresser can't cut hair when there is no one in the salon, and no restaurant serves meals to empty tables.

The F-twist

Milton Friedman was the inventor of what Paul Samuelson called the "F-twist": the assertion that a theory that explained observed facts (and more importantly, justified a particular line of advocacy) could be described as proven in spite of a radical disconnect between the assumptions upon which the theory rested and the observed world.

Friedman's logic could only convince someone who already had faith in his conclusions; unfortunately, this includes a major proportion of those engaged to teach undergraduate economics courses.

When Friedman was confronted with evidence that typical businesses did not believe they were subject to perfect competition where they had no control over their prices but rather estimated their variable costs and set a price based on a suitable uplift, Friedman drew an analogy with a billiards player who did not understand Newton's laws of motion but rather ascribed his success to his lucky rabbit's foot.

In fact the successful billiards player plays each shot so as to impart a velocity and spin to the cue ball that will, according to Newton's laws of motion, achieve his game objective; while a manager who consciously or otherwise adopts the laws of perfect competition will rapidly send his business bankrupt. The mere fact of survival of a business proves that its managers, intuitively or otherwise, are making strategic decisions; they are not behaving as the managers of firms in a state of perfect competition are assumed by economic theory to behave.

One of the great attractions of the assumption of perfect competition is that it permits the production of unambiguous recommendations to resolve many important policy issues. Mencken noted that "for every complex problem there is an answer that is clear, simple, and wrong." Conventional economists use the assumption of perfect competition to produce a clear and simple answer to every problem; and whether such answers are wrong or not takes second place to the fear that recognizing the complexity of a modern economy would mean losing the ability to generate unambiguous answers to every question.

Conventionally trained economists without substantial practical experience often underestimate the uncertainty cascading throughout the economy. Farmers are affected by the weather and other caprices of nature, but every business is in a perpetual state of uncertainty about its customers and its rivals. This, as Dixit showed, leads to a fundamental state of hysteresis[17] in decision making: people, and businesses, are cautious about making irreversible decisions, and this includes decisions to abandon projects once started.[18]

To anticipate Chapter 10, rational entrepreneurs will not enter a market unless the prospect of supernormal profits overcomes their reluctance to make an irreversible investment in conditions of uncertainty. Dixit's demonstration of hysteresis in investment decisions shows that entry to a market will stop before prices are forced even as low as long-run marginal cost, and incumbents will continue to earn "supernormal" profits.

Realistic Competition

In 1926 Keynes's younger colleague, Piero Sraffa, published a paper in the *Economic Journal* that injected a remarkable level of realism into microeconomics.[19] He was neither the first not the last economist to point out that there were crucial elements in neoclassical theory that were directly contradicted by everyday experience. Sraffa pointed out that the decreasing returns—or rising marginal cost—that were essential to equilibrium in neoclassical models were based, quite reasonably, on English agriculture in the eighteenth and nineteenth centuries. During this period land was owned by great magnates and rented, complete with houses, barns, and stables, to farmers on an annual basis; each farmer's fixed costs were trivial, and obviously the best land would be rented and worked first. Poor land would only go under the plough when prices were very high.

Farmers working their own freehold land, manufacturers, and service enterprises had substantial capital costs and no particular reason for variable costs to rise before physical limits stopped production growing entirely. As production rose, fixed costs were allocated across a larger volume of output, and so total unit costs fell—real enterprises experienced increasing, not decreasing returns.

Sraffa then needed to explain why all firms did not increase production until they were stopped by physical limits. He pointed out that real firms incurred sales and marketing expenses when they tried to increase their sales. Even if, as some economists glibly assert, "human wants are infinite" the demand for every real firm's output is definitely finite, limited by the number and appetite of its customers; and gaining new customers is costly. I describe how marketing works and how to make a broad estimate of the likely cost of any marketing initiative in Chapter 9.

A further gap between realistic competition and the standard neoclassical model was opened up by the American engineer and aviation pioneer T. P. Wright (1895–1970) when he discovered the experience curve in the 1920s.[20] The experience curve stated that the variable costs of production declined by a constant fraction with each doubling of cumulative production: the two hundredth unit produced would cost about thirteen percent less than the hundredth unit, and the thousandth unit would cost over twenty-five percent less than the two hundredth unit.

Variable costs are, from the neoclassical viewpoint, worse than constant: the more a firm produces, the lower its variable costs, compounding the effect of allocating fixed costs over a greater volume.

While Wright based his work on aircraft manufacture, subsequent studies starting with the work of Bruce Henderson (1915–1992), founder of the Boston Consulting Group, have found that it applies to practically every business activity; for example, the cost of storing one byte of information has fallen in line with the experience curve's predictions over eight orders of magnitude.

Sraffa, and later Schumpeter, hoped that these demonstrations of the gap between reality and the neoclassical model would lead economists toward more realistic models, but unfortunately, they proved overoptimistic. Economists as a group continued to cling to discredited ideas and treat reality as the exception, not the core. While Sraffa's paper described a reality recognizable to anyone who has ever had management or marketing responsibility in a real business, and Wright's experience curve, reincarnated as the BCG matrix, features in every management course, the majority of academic economists persist with the elaboration of theories with no visible connection to reality.

A minority of economists attempt to develop theories without the most egregious departures from reality at the heart of neoclassical competition theory, but few indeed match Sraffa in their breadth of view or real-world relevance.

IO Economics

The American economist Edward Chamberlin (1899–1967) and the English economist Joan Robinson (1903–1983) worked through the implications of not-even-almost-perfect competition in the 1930s. Robinson did not continue in this direction, choosing to work on developing Keynes's macroeconomic ideas instead. Chamberlin focused almost exclusively on monopolistic competition, leaving others, notably Edward Mason, to develop the theories underlying what became known as "imperfect" competition. This discipline became known as Industrial Organization economics; the Orwellian implications of the study of "imperfect" competition ensure that such economists are a minority of the profession.

Some economists justify the assumption of "almost-perfect" competition even when only a handful of firms are competing by referring to the Cournot-Nash equilibrium. They come to this conclusion by assuming that if a small number of firms are supplying an identical product (Cournot's example was mineral water from the same spring) and that they must set their output quantity once and observe it forever, the "excess" profit that each firm can extract will be inversely proportional to the number of firms. Later economists built on the work of Cournot and Nash to develop the concept of conjectural variation: each firm in an oligopoly estimates how other firms can improve their profitability by increasing or decreasing their output, and chooses a level such that no other firm can increase its profits by producing at a higher rate. By symmetry, all the firms in the oligopoly will choose the appropriate level of output.

Leading IO economists recognize that a Cournot-Nash equilibrium is a limiting case. Real competing firms can generally find some way to differentiate their product offering; and even when they can't, they get frequent opportunities to adjust their prices. Many oligopolies will arrive at a joint profit-maximizing price with "noise": if one member reduces its prices and the others follow immediately and there is adequate spare production capacity, the initiator of the price cut will be worse off than before. Its increased sales will not offset its reduced margins, and the price may return to the joint profit-maximizing level reasonably rapidly. A well-known theorem in IO economics suggests that an oligopoly with four or fewer "core" members will generally observe a joint profit-maximizing strategy.[21]

Empirical studies such as that of Uslay and his colleagues[22] suggest that if there is an oligopoly with more than four members, competition, possibly including price competition, will force the weaker members into mergers or bankruptcy until there are only three large firms (with a market share of over 15 percent) left. Small firms, with a market share of less than 5 percent, can survive in such a market under the price umbrella set by the larger firms by specializing in market niches; but firms with a market share between 5 and 15 percent struggle to survive.

A number of well-regarded economists have developed explanations for the prevalence of competitive imperfection. There has been little if any attempt made by the economically orthodox to refute these explanations; rather, the leading academic journals and economics departments simply ignore them and persist in the assumption that real competition may be treated as if it were perfect, or at least that papers and arguments that implicitly assume the prevalence of perfect competition may be treated as both descriptive of the real world and the basis of policy advice to governments.[23]

The business historian A. D. Chandler (1915–2007) and the economist Edith Penrose (1914–1996) are associated with a small "realist"
school of economics; but while their work is a crucial part of the foundations of modern management theory, it has little recognition among
the generality of academic economists.

Monopolistic Competition

When consumers can differentiate between suppliers and form preferences, the basic conditions for perfect competition are breached. When
there are numerous suppliers offering products that are at least partial
substitutes the industry cannot be fairly described as an oligopoly. The
law in most jurisdictions specifically grants every firm an exclusive right
to its own name, and in general these rights are extended to a firm's
brands and trademarks. Even without the use of brands and trademarks,
firms necessarily operate from different premises, and consumers will
face different travel costs if they patronize different suppliers.

One of Chamberlin's more easily appreciated models of monopolistic competition was spatial. Gasoline retailing is a good example of
monopolistic competition: there are usually several miles between
gasoline stations on any road, so a decision to pass one gasoline retailer
and stop at the next involves some time and operating costs. Even if a
distant gasoline retailer offered slightly cheaper fuel, a motorist who
drove out of his way to travel to it would be worse off if the cost of
traveling the extra distance was greater than the saving in the price.

By generalizing this spatial example, neoliberal polemicists assume
that only delivery and search costs separate perfect from imperfect
competition, and where these costs are relatively small, the assumption of perfect competition seems to involve only a minor departure
from reality. There are, in fact, many other forms of differentiation, and
these have in aggregate the effect of ensuring that competition in wide
sections of the economy is not even nearly perfect.

Economists teaching at the undergraduate level tend to take a very
simplistic view of monopolistic competition, starting from the assumptions, firstly, that apart from a single differentiating factor (often location along a single road) all the firms in an industry are identical; and
secondly, that there are no sunk costs of entry to an industry.

When and if these conditions apply, entry to the relevant market will
be easy, and any abnormal profits will be competed away by entrants.
Although serious economists make neither assumption, it is the simplistic model that inspires neoliberal polemicists and their political

allies. Elementary economics textbooks may describe monopolistic competition as a rare deviation from perfect competition; marketing textbooks describe it as the normal state of most markets.

A little more thought shows that the idea of even a spatial monopoly being "competed away" by entrants is a mirage. In practically every industry, there will be a minimum operating scale. A gasoline retailer, for example, must have a site to operate from, which must be owned or rented; and if owned, the cost of the site must be justified by the profits earned. The site must have improvements—tanks, pumps, and buildings—and again, there must be a return on this investment. There must be an attendant or a remote supervisor; and even in countries without a minimum wage, attendants and supervisors must be paid at least a Malthusian minimum wage. In practice, since attendants are in charge of a valuable asset and valuable stock, they must be paid, as Manove showed, a "responsibility premium."[24]

A simplified model of gasoline retailing in Australia illustrates the difference between monopoly and monopolistic competition. Australia provides an appropriate example because of the way the term "remote" takes on a meaning unknown in most other countries. During the 1990s an international consortium proposed establishing a small satellite receiving station at a particularly remote location in Western Australia. The consortium was shocked when quoted a price of over $10 million to establish the base and over $1 million per year to operate it. "We only need a domestic power point," they protested. "And a five-hundred-mile-long extension cord," the Australian contact responded.

Geographic data	Metropolitan	Country
Number of motor cars	10,560,000	2,640,000
Settled area (sq. Km)	17,600	4,614,000
Service stations	2,400	5,600
Average SS separation (Km)	2.44	275
Equivalent cost ($)	1.71	192
Business statistics	Metropolitan	Country
Motor cars in catchment	4,400	471
Annual fuel sales (liters)	6,367,000	682,000

The typical cost of a new gasoline retailing station in Australia will be about $5 million in metropolitan areas (where land is expensive) and $3 million elsewhere. This amount covers land, buildings, and initial trading stock; and there will be an additional $250,000 a year to pay the attendants' wages and on-costs and local authority rates and taxes before any fuel is sold. Motorists' costs are of the order of $0.70 per kilometer once traveling time is added to vehicle operating costs when standing costs are ignored, and a typical fuel purchase is forty liters, made once every ten days. The wholesale price of fuel fluctuates, but $1.20 per liter, including transport, refining, and taxes is not out of line with recent trends.

Typical motorists in an Australian metropolitan area who decide to buy fuel when they are close to a particular service station will find it worthwhile to drive past if they think that they can save $1.71 by filling up at the next one; but the same motorists in the country would not go past a service station, even if they are not concerned about being stranded without fuel on an isolated road, unless they expect to save almost $200. With a typical purchase of forty liters, a metropolitan service station where the prices were 4.3 cents per liter higher than its neighbors might sell no fuel at all. In contrast, a country service station could charge almost $5 per liter more than the station down the road without forcing its potential customers to pass it by.

In practice, average margins on fuel in metropolitan Australia are in the range 4 to 8 cents per liter, so when the wholesale price is $1.20, a typical pump price will be $1.24 to $1.28.

Service station operators in the "bush" are not concerned about their neighbors, but they do know that if they charge too much their customers will limit their purchases and even buy more fuel-efficient vehicles. A margin much over $0.80 per liter will start to affect their customers' behavior. A typical remote service station will mark up a $1.20 wholesale price to between $1.80 and $2.00 per liter; less than 20 cents of this will be transport costs. With these margins fuel sales will comfortably cover operating costs even though the absolute volume sold is much lower.

These high profits on low volumes might, of course, attract a competitive entrant and bring margins back to the metropolitan level of 5 cents or so; but with two retailers dividing a market of only 680,000 liters, they would each earn a gross profit of no more than $15,000 and a thumping loss once the cost of capital and fixed operating costs are taken into account; one or both would rapidly go broke and exit the business.

The metropolitan automobile fuel market in Australia is monopolistically competitive; each operator in the remote area fuel market is a monopoly *tout court*.

Price in the Real World

The discussion above is not the whole story; it is only a snapshot view of the situation at a single point in time. In the real world, physical distance is seldom the only issue and often not the main one. Some people will shop at Wal-Mart, others at Costco. Sometimes they will shop at the closest outlet; on other occasions they may travel a significant distance or even ignore the bricks and mortar stores altogether and shop on the Internet.

Brands can justify a major price differential in consumers' eyes: given the alternative between "brown, sweet, fizzy drink" and Coca-Cola, the typical consumer is prepared to pay at least twice as much for the latter as for the former.

Economists use the term "elasticity" as a measure of how a small change in the price of something affects the quantity sold.[25] For example, if reducing the price by 1 percent raised the quantity sold by 3 percent, the elasticity is three. Elasticity is not a constant; it tends to rise as prices rise and the available quantities fall; but for very small changes in the ruling price level, treating elasticity as a constant does not introduce unacceptable errors. A little simple manipulation assuming (as most firms do) constant direct unit costs shows that a firm's contribution margin (or gross profit) is at its maximum when the gross margin (expressed as a fraction) is the reciprocal of the elasticity at that price level.[26]

If a shop selling into a market with an elasticity of three buys 100 units of a product for $60 each and sells them for $90 each, its gross profit is $3,000. If it reduces its price by 1 percent to $89.10 and this increases its sales by 3 percent to 103 units, its gross profit will be slightly less at $2,997.30; if it increases its price by 1 percent to $90.90 its sales will drop to 97 units, and its gross profit will be slightly less, again at $2,997.30.

The price where the gross profit is at its maximum is the "monopoly" price, and statistical studies suggest that real firms charge a little less than this figure; but the practice of mark-up pricing[27] is almost universal, which suggests that most firms regard themselves as quasimonopolists when it comes to working out a price list. For markets like gasoline with many suppliers offering almost identical products, the elasticity as perceived by any individual supplier may rise sharply as the price rises; under these conditions the most profitable prices will be only slightly larger than direct costs, and this is close to the result expected under perfect competition. When suppliers offer strongly differentiated products, each attracting its own cohort of customers, it may become possible to set prices to a point where they greatly exceed direct cost without any loss of profits.

Where there are markets with many suppliers and weakly differentiated products, the twin effects of fixed costs and economies of scale and experience mean that the firms with the lowest sales are at a permanent and growing disadvantage and are forced to seek acquirers before they get overtaken by bankruptcy. The surviving firms can then afford to add unique features to their products and to promote them with extensive advertising and other means, thereby achieving a level of differentiation where substantial profits are possible (if not easy) to earn in spite of substantial fixed costs.

Copyrighted software and patented pharmaceuticals are two examples of products where prices are a large multiple of variable cost. High mark-ups over direct cost are typical of recorded entertainment, luxury goods and services, private medical care, and in general all goods and services where the reputation of the supplier and/or the unique attributes of the product take precedence over the price.

Apple Inc. (formerly Apple Computer) has an incredibly strong brand: not everyone is a fan, but those who are, are prepared to pay prices that give Apple a gross margin of 39 percent, and a net margin of 22 percent.[28] Medtronic Inc. is not as well known as Apple, but as a medical device supplier, it trades behind a battery of strong patents, keeping its products unique. Its gross margin is 75 percent—that is, the price of a typical Medtronic device is four times its supply cost. Even after all other costs, its net margin is still a very healthy 18 percent.[29] By contrast, the major US conglomerate General Electric earned a gross margin of 23 percent excluding the finance arm, and a net margin of 9.1 percent.[30]

A variant on product differentiation are certain "winner takes all" markets, often in personally delivered services like surgery, legal advocacy, and professional sports team membership. People facing surgery for a life-threatening condition do not seek out the cheapest surgeon, but rather the one with the highest reputation for success in that field. The top performer has only a limited time available to practice in any period, and so in an uncontrolled market must set prices high enough to limit his or her patronage to the performer's capacity. Such markets are not quite "winner takes all," since those who cannot afford the fees charged by the performer with the best reputation must settle for someone further down the scale. But at any given time in such markets, there will be a few highly paid and highly regarded "stars" and many who from youth or misfortune lack the stars' reputation and must settle for much less.

Endogenous growth theory (Chapter 9) makes no economic sense except in an environment of imperfect competition, as perfect competition necessarily eliminates the economic incentive to innovate. Some of the critics of endogenous growth theory seem to have been motivated almost entirely by their authors' desire to reassert the primacy of perfect competition or at least "as if" or "almost" perfect competition. Paul Romer, in particular, has been responsible for a devastating refutation of several of these attempts.

Representative Consumers?

Automotive fuel is readily amenable to a standard economic analysis: consumers are well aware that there is little or no practical difference between the fuel sold at differently branded outlets. When modeling automotive fuel purchasing behavior, it does no harm to assume that all motorists are identical.

Many significant markets are more complex than automobile fuel retailing. The IO model adds considerable reality to economics by acknowledging that there is more than one product (alternatively, that all products are not perfectly interchangeable) and that most industries involve a finite number of firms each of a finite size. There are, however, important aspects of a modern economy where IO economics has little to say.

IO economists generally continue to use the concept of the representative consumer in their analysis, replacing a diverse real consumer population with an equal number of identical "representative" consumers. It may be reasonable to treat all buyers of automotive fuel identically in economic modeling, but it is far from reasonable to apply the same logic to the cars that they are driving. When they do depart from the model of a single representative consumer, they tend to divide the consumer population into a few discrete groups, with each group assumed to be internally homogeneous.

There are clearly some objective factors at work in the purchasing choices made by car owners: a family with four children may need a large sedan or station wagon just to accommodate everyone, while a single young person may be satisfied with a small, two-door car. But such objective factors tell only part of the story: many American families buy large, "off-road" (or "soft-road") sports utility vehicles even though they are more expensive and cost more to run than a large sedan or station wagon. Many young people and a few older ones buy a two-seat sports car at a multiple of the price of a small sedan, even though the actual travel times on crowded urban road networks are indistinguishable.

Reliance on the idea of the representative consumer blinds most economists to one of the most common marketing techniques, that of segmentation. Marketers strive to identify segments of a consumer population with distinct needs and wants, and then seek to develop products specifically addressed to consumers in that segment.

Segmentation can be based on solid differences: some manufactures make gluten-free food products suitable for sufferers from celiac disease; others manufacture sugar-free confectionary for diabetics. Sometimes the difference is hard to quantify except in money terms: for example, the linen manufacturer Sheridan used an advertising poster in the London Underground showing an extremely handsome young man asleep in a partly made bed with much of his upper body exposed. London's gay community identified with the young man and began replacing their existing bed linen with Sheridan products. To invite someone to share a bed not fitted with Sheridan sheets would be considered an insult. The boost to Sheridan's profits was considerable.

Representative Firms?

Adam Smith could not think of a good reason for a gentleman to become a manufacturer, but wrote that if any gentleman felt and surrendered to such an urge, he could find all that he needed to know about any branch of trade in a copy of M. Diderot's *Encyclopedia*. It is one of the great ironies of history that in the same year that Smith published his *Wealth of Nations*, Boulton and Watt obtained a patent for the steam engine incorporating a separate condenser, and they fired the starting gun on a race for innovation in energy delivery that hasn't ended yet.

Undergraduate students of IO economics are taught that any investment necessary before a firm can enter a market can be recovered on exit. More sophisticated IO economists consider cases where entry costs are sunk and cannot be recovered. The undergraduate model is deeply misleading; the sophisticated models are not much less so.

One simple issue is the question of entry: in the absence of collusion, tacit or otherwise, the ability of firms in a state of monopolistic competition to extract a profit is supposed to be limited by the entry of further competitors until long-run excess profit has been reduced to zero.

The work of Dixit and Pindyck (see Chapter 10) shows that, in the presence of uncertainty, rational investors will not commit funds except in the expectation of a return substantially above the "riskless" rate. It follows that the mere fact that some firms in an industry earn a comfortable profit will not be sufficient to induce entry; but the prospective profits must be quite substantial, sufficient for the prospective profit to remain substantial even after allowing for the impact of the extra capacity that an entrant will introduce on prices.

Oligopolies form when larger firms enjoy cost and other advantages over smaller ones, and entry to the ranks of the core firms is all but impossible unless an entrant has the benefits of a significant innovation. Without such an innovation, the "ditch" separating a market share of 5 and 15 percent is almost impossible to cross.

In the standard model, firms will leave an industry when they can no longer cover their cost of capital; but Dixit and Pindyck demonstrate that, in the presence of uncertainty, firms may remain in a market while absorbing significant losses. In a growing economy, the Dixit and Pindyck results suggest that many firms will be able to charge prices well in excess of their long- run costs and so enjoy consistent profits.

Unique Attributes

The economics of entry and exit are only the start of the process of differentiation between firms.

Entrepreneurs and conscientious managers go beyond finding a segment of consumers (or other businesses) to whom they can market a product particularly attuned to their needs: they attempt to build an organization peculiarly adapted to producing that product and delivering satisfaction to their customers. Edith Penrose is generally credited with a redefinition of the firm as an assembly of resources controlled by a more or less purposeful management; Penrose referred to management competence, and she probably originated the concept of diffused capabilities, which Gary Hamel and C. K. Prahalad named "core competence."[31]

Penrose was building on the work of the business historian Chandler, who had demonstrated quite conclusively that real firms differed significantly from each other and that the concept of the representative firm was inadequate to explain real firm performance. Hamel and Prahalad took Penrose as their starting point.

The core competencies described by Hamel and Prahalad are not tradable resources; neither are they skills embodied in particular people. They may best be described as emergent properties—"the way we do things here." When tasks are aligned with embedded competencies, they are completed faster, with fewer errors in development and production and fewer faults in the finished product than tasks not so aligned. Competencies are often based around an informal structure within a firm that may bear little relation to the formal hierarchy. Tsun-Yan Hsieh and Dominic Barton interpreted core competencies in terms of leadership,[32] but their discussion is more about informal hierarchies than leadership in either the US or British sense. (US authors tend to write about leadership as a set of techniques for ensuring subordination—"keeping the galley slaves rowing after downsizing the man with the whip." Other cultures follow Lau Tse: "When the best leader's work is done, the people say, 'it happened naturally.'")

A firm with a deep understanding of the customers in its chosen market segments and highly competent in delivering products that meet or exceed its customers' expectations will generally outperform firms with a weaker understanding of their potential customers or a less competent approach to production, much as Toyota has outperformed General Motors.

Change and Continuity

The apparent stability of oligopolies is, as Schumpeter noted, a mirage. Tacit collusion to maintain prices is only a rational strategy among firms with a common cost structure; but a firm that makes a breakthrough innovation in either cost reduction or quality improvement is freed from any need to continue tacit collusion and can and usually will use its advantage to gain market share. If the innovation is sufficiently disruptive and the competitors sufficiently slow to respond, they may be driven into niches or out of the industry entirely.

Henry Ford, with assistance from Frederick Taylor, applied mass production techniques to the T-model Ford in 1908, and for the next fifteen years enjoyed unchallenged dominance of the US motor car market. In 1923 Alfred P. Sloan was appointed president of General Motors, at that time an arbitrary collection of eight more or less bankrupt motor manufacturers. By the vigorous use of product differentiation and the invention of consumer finance, General Motors drove the Ford Model T off the market in only three years, achieved global dominance of the motor car manufacturing industry, and held that position until overtaken by Toyota in 2008.

Even in the absence of a breakthrough cost or quality innovation, a modest gain in market share can lead to a significant cost advantage through the gains resulting from experience; in an oligopoly a firm with sales consistently 10 percent higher than a rival would have variable costs about 2 percent lower. If this cost advantage is used to increase marketing effort rather than paid out as dividends, the larger firm's market share would continue to increase, and the cost advantage with it.

It can be correctly objected that this sequence would have reduced a capitalist system to a series of monopolies, and in the second half of the nineteenth century, Marx was far from the only observer who thought that this process was underway. The passing of the Sherman Anti-Trust act in the United States and its active enforcement by "trust-busting" president Theodore Roosevelt at the start of the twentieth century reflected a wider concern about the tendency to monopoly observed in nineteenth-century capitalism.

Roosevelt himself may not have taken a simplistic "Big is bad; small is good" approach, but the activities of the "robber barons" in the late nineteenth century had predisposed the US electorate to support antimonopoly laws and actions.[33] Procompetition legislation was not even introduced to the United Kingdom and Europe until the 1970s.

Schumpeter observed that disruptive product innovations could destroy the apparent stability of an oligopoly: the ability of corporate quasimonopolies to bring forward cost and quality innovations could not protect them from product innovations that made their core products obsolete. He wrote that

> new combinations are, as a rule, embodied, as it were, in new firms which generally do not arise out of the old ones but start producing beside them; . . . in general it is not the owner of stage-coaches who builds railways.[34]

Schumpeter's observation is truer of the United States and Britain than it is of Japan or Germany: it may be that the relative freedom from hostile takeover enjoyed by companies in the latter two countries allows top management to be more relaxed about projects with a longer-term payoff and less concerned with short-term results.

Notes

1. Keen (2001, 2011).
2. Denicolò & Zanchettin (2012).
3. Clark (1940).
4. Sosnick (1958).
5. P=MC=AC.
6. Ezekiel (1938).
7. Gleick (1987), Waldrop (1992), Legge (2012).
8. Schumpeter (1942).
9. Students who study IO economics will be taught that firms maximize the discounted value of their future income, which P = MC pricing will certainly not achieve.

10. $MC = \dfrac{dC}{dQ} = MR = \dfrac{d(PQ)}{dQ}$.

11. Using lower case to represent a single firm: $\dfrac{dp}{dq} = 0$.

12. Using lower case to represent a single firm and upper case to represent an industry: $P = p; Q = \Sigma q; \dfrac{dP}{dQ} \neq 0$.

13. Keen & Standish (2006, 2010).
14. Mark 10:19–21.
15. Samuelson & Nordhaus (1995).
16. A leading economist commented on this section: "This is a statement about the technology that is used in an industry (about the production function or equivalently, by duality theory, about the cost function). No doubt it is true for some industries, not true for others. Some very old debates about antitrust policy are between people who assume returns to scale are usually constant and people who assume returns to scale are usually increasing." Keen (2011: pp. 121–126) presents the empirical evidence that shows that the great majority of firms experience increasing returns to scale.
17. Hysteresis: a term from physics originally applied to magnets: it takes some power to magnetize a piece of iron, but it then stays magnetized. Reversing the magnetization takes more power.
18. Dixit is by no means a "heterodox" economist, but he is both extremely capable and willing to explore deviations from the standard neoclassical assumptions. His contribution is discussed further in Chapter 10.
19. Sraffa (1926).
20. C_i is the variable cost of the ith item:

$$C_n = C_m \left(\dfrac{n}{m}\right)^{\log_2(1-k)} ; \; 0 < k < 0.3$$

An alternate statement of the Experience Curve is known as the Law of Records: instead of decreasing variable cost it tracks the increase in the time between new records being set in a particular sport.
21. Martin (1993).
22. Uslay, Altintig & Winsor (2010).
23. A leading economist commented: "This paragraph accurately describes the hard-core Chicago approach; if it was ever true of (American) academics that would have been in the early 1980s. It is no longer accurate." I hope that he is correct.
24. Manove (1997).

25. $e = \dfrac{P}{Q}\dfrac{dQ}{dP}$.

26. $\dfrac{P}{P-v} = |e|$ where v is the constant variable cost.

27. $P = (1+m)v; m \leq \dfrac{1}{|e|}$, Shapiro & Sawyer (2003).

28. From 10-K SEC statement for 2014.
29. From 10-K SEC statement for 2014.

30.   From 10-K SEC statement for 2014.
31.   Prahalad & Hamel (1990).
32.   Hsieh and Barton (1995).
33.   Josephson (1934 [1962]).
34.   Schumpeter (1934).

4

Money and Banking

We reward people for making money off money, and moving
money around and dividing up mortgages a thousand times
over, selling it to China . . . and it becomes this shell game.
—Michael Moore

Economists have found money a surprisingly elusive concept.[1] Money does not appear in the simplest forms of trade: "I will trade you a brace of rabbits for a bag of apples." And trade with intrinsically valuable coinage can fit into the same model: "I will sell you this brace of rabbits for two bronze coins, which I can then use to buy apples or anything else that takes my fancy at the market." This leaves open the question of how much the coins are worth as objects of use rather than exchange.

Keynes[2] followed Ricardo (and Marx) by equating value, at least in a primitive economy, with labor power: if it takes one hunter one hour to catch two rabbits and one gatherer one hour to collect a bushel of apples, then the exchange of two rabbits for one bushel of apples can be considered a fair trade.

Keynes suggested that money then enters the system as a "store of value"—if the hunter sees nothing that he wants at the market today, he can keep the two bronze coins until he has an opportunity to spend them buying something that he does want. More importantly in Keynes's view, someone may not know what he wants, but he does know that he is likely to want something. Holding money allows the hunter to postpone a purchasing decision until he has a clearer view of how he wants to spend it. Dixit (see Chapter 10 below) built on this insight to develop the theory of investment under uncertainty.

Bronze (or silver, or gold) coins are tangible enough, but what about our modern customer who simply "flashes the plastic"? Before the transaction there was no money; immediately after it the merchant's bank account has been credited and the purchaser's card account debited: the money, or money substitute, has been created as required.

Note that the credit to the merchant's account is money and can be spent or saved as the merchant's needs dictate. The debit to the customer's credit card account is *not* money: it an asset of the card issuer and can't be used to buy anything. The credit card issuer may sell the asset to another entity for cash, but that merely changes ownership of the asset; it doesn't change the total amount of circulating money. The level of the money supply is restored when (or if) the credit card holder discharges the debt.

When Friedman wished to popularize his theory that inflation could be controlled by controlling the money supply, he had himself filmed beside a printing press in the US Mint; he pressed the "Stop" button and the press duly stopped. "This," he told the camera, "is how to stop inflation." This was a fairly typical Friedman publicity stunt; neither he nor the central bankers actually responsible for monetary policy believed that money only took the form of notes and coins.

Keynes's work on money in the 1930s had established that the quantity of money available affected output and employment. Businesses needed money to maintain their premises, plant, and equipment, and they needed circulating capital to fund their debtors' ledger, inventory, and work in progress. If there was too little money available, or interest rates were too high, businesses would be forced to contract their operations, and unemployment would rise.

If, argued Keynes, exactly the right amount of money was available, there would be full employment and low inflation; but if more than this amount was circulating, inflation would rise. Keynes concluded that governments and central banks should control the money supply so as to maintain full employment and low inflation, and should do so directly. The British and United States governments accepted Keynes's advice during the Second World War and were able to raise and supply large armies, navies, and air forces on the back of unprecedented levels of public debt without significant inflation.

Keynes died in 1946 and was not around to supervise the peacetime application of his theories. His influence remained strong, and during the "long boom of the West" from 1948 to 1972, there was full employment, strong economic growth, generally low inflation, and reduced inequality. The measures used to control the money supply were effective but not very popular. First-home buyers were expected to demonstrate a savings record and provide a substantial deposit before obtaining a mortgage. Banks were kept in line by being forced to maintain "statutory reserve deposits"—low-interest loans to their supervising central bank—which could be and were increased or decreased if the central bank considered that the clearing banks' loans were adding too much or too little to the money supply.

Friedman did not dispute Keynes's analysis, but he did argue that direct regulation could be replaced by pure market mechanisms. Instead of limiting the amount that banks could lend by regulation, Friedman proposed to deregulate lending but control the money supply by varying the short-term interest rate.

Instead of banks being forced to make loans to their central bank, they would be enticed to do so by the interest rates on the money market. Since this interest rate acted as a floor for all lending rates, raising it would raise the cost of money and deter borrowers. Central banks should, Friedman argued, set and publish monetary targets and raise interest rates should these targets be exceeded and lower them when it was necessary to increase the money supply.

Both the Reagan administration (1981–88) in the United States and Thatcher ministry (1979–90) in the United Kingdom attempted to apply Friedman's theories to their real economies, and the consequences were disastrous for both. One of the more obvious problems was that even measuring the money supply accurately was difficult: deregulating the finance industry released a flood of innovation in the form of new instruments and new ways of trading them. The crucial problem was that the money supply was far less sensitive to the cash rate than Friedman had assumed.

These attempts to run monetary policy by managing aggregates were abandoned after two to three years. Because both governments had rejected Keynesian (or more properly, Hicksian) policies to follow Friedman's monetarism, a return to the earlier policy mechanisms was politically unacceptable and administratively impossible. The US and UK central banks and their imitators did not reinstate quantitative credit controls, continuing to rely on setting short-term interest rates. They did so solely in response to perceived or actual inflation.

Friedman had also persuaded many politicians and central bankers that the only cause of inflation was wage rises. As long as it was considered that competition between businesses was "perfect" (see Chapter 3 above), it was possible to argue that businesses only adjusted prices in response to wage changes. As a necessary corollary, central banks abandoned attempts to maintain full employment and instead set out to keep unemployment above a more or less arbitrarily determined minimum level as a way to deter wage increases.

Fiat Currencies

Physical money may or may not be intrinsically valuable. The right of seigniorage, the power to declare some instrument legal currency, is jealously guarded by governments throughout the world; and to the extent that there may be a difference between the cost of the instrument, whether a metallic coin or paper, and the nominal value, this difference represents a source of profit to the issuer. When a government declares that some instrument or family of instruments may be used to settle debts and pay taxes, it has created a fiat currency, one that derives its value from the law rather than from its intrinsic value.

All currencies are essentially fiat currencies, since the law establishes them as a sufficient way of settling debts. A modern Shylock must be satisfied with a sum of money to settle Antonio's debt since pounds of flesh are not legal tender. A very few countries go one step further and guarantee that their currency notes are exchangeable for precious metal on demand; the last major economy to do so was the United States, and its currency ceased to be convertible in 1972.

A limited political movement in the United States calls for a return to a gold-backed currency; few economists of any persuasion take them seriously. One of its adherents is Paul Ryan, the Republican candidate for vice president in the 2012 elections, and an admirer of the theories popularized by Ayn Rand.

Banking in Theory and in Practice[3]

People don't need banks in order to lend each other money, and such loans do not affect the total amount of money in circulation or the aggregate spending power of the population. If Bill lends Bob $100, that is now money that Bill can't spend but Bob can. To some economists at least, banks make no real difference to the picture: they are just intermediaries. Bob deposits $100 in the bank and Bill borrows $100 from the bank, and again the aggregate money supply and community spending power has not changed.

Reality is more complicated. When an entrepreneur secures an advance from a bank, there are no bags of coin handed over. Rather, the entrepreneur is given a bank account number and permission to draw on the account up to the agreed limit. The entrepreneur offers a check or draws on the account electronically in exchange for the goods and services required by her business, and after processing, an amount will be added to the vendor's balance and deducted from the entrepreneur's. As with the credit card example, the loan to the entrepreneur is an asset of the bank, not money, while the deposit to the supplier's accounts is money, created as it is needed.

Fractional Reserve Banking

Modern banking goes back to the foundation of Amsterdam Wissel-bank in 1609 and its English imitator, the Bank of England, in 1694. Prior to 1609 money meant specie: gold or silver. A moneylender lent a quantity of gold or silver to a debtor and expected it to be returned, plus interest, on a defined date or under particular circumstances. The debtor took physical possession of the money from the lender, or in the most sophisticated markets, took possession of money held by a third party and owed to the original lender, transferring the debt. Direct or indirect, the money was lent and could not be lent a second time.

The Wisselbank and its successor banks did not give its borrowers gold or silver; rather, it gave them paper on which was inscribed a promise to pay the bearer a certain amount of gold or silver. These notes could then be used to purchase goods and services. When the businesses or persons who had accepted the paper in return for supplying goods or services presented the paper, the bank would, if pressed, honor the promise. However, it would try, generally successfully, to persuade the claimant to become a creditor of the bank.

The Wisselbank, and even more so the Bank of England, had a strong argument in their favor: the depositor's gold would be held in a fortified vault in a secure banking chamber in a country protected by a strong fleet and, in the Dutch case, a formidable army. Quite early the Dutch discovered that at least half the paper money presented to the Wisselbank could be converted to deposits, and so each guilder of the bank's capital could become at least two guilders of circulating currency.

Theories of monetary neutrality lay far into the future; the pragmatic Dutch simply observed that more money meant more economic activity, and more economic activity meant higher profits. If anyone objected to the practices of the Wisselbank, they kept their concerns to themselves. As they do today, banks charged interest on loans and paid interest, at a lesser rate, on deposits. As long as the creditors of those who received loans from a bank could be persuaded to become depositors, the bank's own capital was untouched.

Until the early twentieth century, banks in most countries were permitted to print their own banknotes; and while the Bank of England limited the value of its notes in circulation to the value of the gold in its vaults (except in times of great crisis), the private banks were under no such restraint. At times of general confidence, depositors were happy to leave their gold in the bank, and suppliers were happy to accept bank notes or checks from their customers. As long as very few borrowers defaulted, banks were extremely profitable.

In the nineteenth century, US banking regulation was extremely lax, and many small-town banks accepted deposits and made loans, relative to their resources, that would be considered wildly reckless today. For many small Western and Southwestern communities, their local bank, and its survival, made the difference between poverty and relative affluence. The fable of Dustytown may make this easier to understand:

Dustytown, United States

Dustytown was a typical (if fictitious) little settlement serving a small farming community in the US Midwest in the third quarter of the nineteenth century. It suffered from a deeply depressed economy. Farmers sold their crops through agents who took months to pay, while suppliers of essential equipment demanded "cash on the barrel": no sooner did any money enter the town that it rushed out again. Old timers remembered the days of the silver mine, now worked out: there was plenty of money around then. None of the town's buildings had seen a coat of paint in years; the saloon charged ten cents a shot for its rotgut and was still half empty, and the bar girls had few offers even at fifty cents a trick. Some of the farmers' daughters were lucky enough to own third-hand clothing; most wore clothing sewn out of flour sacks most of the time. All this was about to change.

One day a man in a smart suit driving a pony trap with a big chest in the rear drove into town, rented the least dilapidated of the empty shops, and hung out a sign announcing the "First Bank of Dustytown." It didn't take long for a farmer to knock at the door.

"Do you lend money?"

"That's what I do. How much do you need?"

"I need twenty dollars to buy seed for my next crop."

To the farmer's surprise, the banker didn't open the chest and draw out twenty silver dollars. He wrote "Twenty dollars" on a piece of paper and handed it over. "Take this to the seed merchant," he said. Half an hour later, the seed merchant knocked on the door

---

and presented the piece of paper. "Joe Farmer said that this is worth twenty silver dollars," he said. "Give it to me."

"You don't really want to carry that much silver down the street, do you?" asked the banker. "Some of those varmints outside would knock you down for half of it. Let me open an account for you, and any time you really need the silver, you only have to ask. Come to think of it, your roof is leaking and rats are getting into your store through the holes in your walls. Let me lend you fifty dollars to fix your place up." The bemused seed merchant left the bank carrying a check book.

A year later the town was unrecognizable. Every building was repaired and freshly painted, and new ones were going up everywhere. The saloon was rebuilt into a hotel and served good beer, fine wine, and honest whisky in its bars. The bar girls quit the oldest profession and set up a seamstress business supplying pretty frocks to the many farmers' daughters in the district and sturdy work clothes to the farmers and their sons and wives. The layabouts who used to hang around the street were now smartly dressed cowboys riding sleek horses as they went purposefully about their business. The bank had new premises and employed a teller and a clerk. The town had a council that collected taxes and paid a schoolteacher and a sheriff.

And what was in the banker's great chest when he drove into town? Absolutely nothing.

A bank's deposits are liabilities, and its loans are assets. The basic balance-sheet equation states that any company's assets should equal its liabilities plus its equity. Reserves are simply that part of a firm's equity held in liquid or near-liquid form as a precaution against contingencies: in the case of a bank, the risk of a loan "going bad."

The First Bank of Dustytown, like all banks, charged interest on its loans and paid little or none on its deposits, and this "spread" was the bank's main source of income. Some would be paid to the bank's owner or shareholders as dividends, some to its employees as wages and its trade creditors as expenses, some spent on purchasing fixed or negotiable assets, and the rest accumulated as reserves.

A banker like the man in Dustytown could, given reasonable prudence in lending and no sudden economic crises, build substantial wealth on top of his empty chest, and founding a bank became a well-known way to wealth (and occasionally ruin) for middle-class families in the developed countries.

The Dustytown fable reflects nineteenth-century reality in many small Midwestern communities; but in many places, there was more than one bank, leading to the certainty that money borrowed from one bank would be deposited in another. In normal circumstances banks would receive deposits roughly in line with their advances, but because the advances would be a multiple of each bank's capital, even a small discrepancy could have a relatively large effect on the value of a bank's equity. This led banks to make clearing arrangements such that banks with a temporary surplus of deposits would make balancing loans to those in deficit.

In England and Holland, the central bank became a "lender of last resort," accepting deposits and making loans to banks that could not find another corresponding partner. Today practically every country has a central bank that fills this role, administering an overnight money market and incidentally fixing short-term interest rates for each country's banks.

Banks could crash. Not all bankers were prudent, and many would be proven to have had inadequate reserves when an economy entered a crisis (as recessions were called before the term was replaced, initially by "depression" and later by "recession," to avoid arousing unhappy memories). A bank failed when its liquid reserves were exhausted by demands from depositors for silver or central-bank currency notes and no other bank would lend it sufficient money to make up the short-fall. Those depositors, inevitably the majority of them, who could not withdraw their money before the crash became creditors of a bankrupt institution, and many of them would be unable to meet their own obligations and so would follow their bank into bankruptcy.

The failed bank's debtors—those holding loan balances with it—would obviously not be able to draw more money; but worse, they would be pursued by the failed bank's receivers to repay their loans or forfeit their security: they, too, could be forced into bankruptcy. Reverting to Dustytown: just as the arrival of a bank could turn despair into prosperity, its collapse could restore the *status quo ante*.

Reality Turned Upside Down

There was no central bank or centralized monetary authority in the Dustytown story, or in the United States at all between 1836 and 1865, and the present Federal Reserve System was not established until 1913.[4] This inconvenient fact is ignored by many textbook authors and even by some chairmen of the US Federal Reserve.[5] In their account the deposit precedes the loan: a textbook bank accepts deposits from savers and only then offers loans to borrowers; and the size of the loans it can make is constrained by the total value of the deposits it holds; its "reserves" are a fraction of its total deposits.

The persistence of this error suggests a total ignorance not merely of actual banking practice, but also of the most basic rules of double-entry accounting and of the legal obligations on any business that accepts money from the public. A bank's reserves are comprised of cash and other assets owned by the bank; its depositors' balances are the bank's liabilities. Corporate criminals regularly treat liabilities as equity. "It's what they do," but for economists to treat this crime as ordinary banking practice is taking criticism of banks too far.

Political Consequences

Banking was proved to be a great way to make money and to encourage economic development in the US West and Midwest; but unregulated "free banking" as practiced in the American West did not suit the financiers of New York, who have never seen a profit that they were prepared to share. The resulting political conflict came to the forefront in the 1896 presidential election, with William Jennings Bryan and the Democratic Party campaigning for the status quo under the rubric of bimetallism, and their crushing defeat by the forces of finance and the Republican candidate William McKinley. (Bryan may have been the last ever major party candidate nominated as the result of a speech to his party's convention: the "Cross of Gold" speech. It is not entirely clear that Bryan understood much about the subject, but his campaign called for preserving the right of states and even cities to mint their own silver coinage. The Federal Government would maintain its monopoly over gold coinage and gold-backed notes.)

In due course the Federal Reserve, owned by a consortium of the largest New York banks, was created under federal law. It became the official lender of last resort and the unofficial regulator of the US banking system, although initially many of the smaller, single-community banks were left to the various states to regulate—or not.

At the start of the Great Depression in 1929, over 30 percent of small, state-regulated banks failed, as did over 10 percent of larger, federally regulated ones. The effect on the US economy was devastating, and the Roosevelt administration, elected in 1932 and taking office from the beginning of 1933, introduced laws and regulations that established strong banking regulation intended to prevent banks from taking undue risks. The administration also established the Federal Deposit Insurance Corporation (FDIC), with the power to take over failing banks and to reimburse their depositors up to a fairly generous limit.

Regulated Banking

Modern banking regulation is based on the rules set out by the Bank of International Settlements (BIS) and generally referred to as the Basel Accords. These are maintained by the Basel Committee on Banking Supervision.[6] The actual supervision of banks is carried out by the central bank in each country, but rules and regulations administered by each central bank are generally compatible with the Basel Accords.

If a country's banks are believed to be operating outside the accords, they will be restricted in their ability to negotiate international deals. Companies that use such nonconforming banks will find it difficult to conduct international trade.

In broad terms the accords require banks to limit their lending to each of several classes of possible borrowers to a prescribed multiple of their capital. In detail, the accords set out criteria for judging the creditworthiness of borrowers and the security offered and apply different multiples to each class of loan. Multiples range from twelve, for loans to AAA-rated governments and first mortgages on domestic property, to one, for the riskiest classes of loans.

The Accords also specify how each bank's capital base must be managed, and in particular, how much must be "Tier 1" consisting of cash in the vaults and deposits with the bank's country's central bank. Since cash earns no interest and the central bank's cash rate is lower than any commercial interest rate, banks keep as much of their capital as they are permitted to outside Tier 1 in the form of securities such as government bonds and even high-rated private debt securities. This raises the possibility that the a bank's Tier 1 capital base might fall below its minimum level, possibly because of unusual or seasonal demands from its depositors for cash. To enable clearing banks to restore their Tier 1 balances to the statutory minimum, central banks will lend them cash against security, such as part of their holding of government bonds.

Contrary to widely held opinion, the clearing banks do *not* need access to central bank funds in order to write new loans; banks could operate perfectly well, if somewhat less profitably, if all their capital was held in cash or central bank deposits and there was no "discount window" where they could borrow from the central bank against security drawn from their Tier 2 and Tier 3 capital.

At the onset of the Global Financial Crisis, the ruling accords were known as Basel II, and many banks were shown to be in deep trouble in spite of their previous conformity to the regulations. In consequence, the Basel Committee prepared a stiffer set of accords known as Basel III, and these were implemented globally in 2013.

Saving and Investment

Keynes pointed out that there were certain broad constraints on any economy: there were only a certain number of people available to work, and they could produce goods and services for immediate consumption or goods and services to be used to support future production, but not both at the same time. Keynes described the production of goods and services intended to support future production as investment, and the diversion of resources from the production of consumption goods and services to the production of investment goods and services as saving. When measured by the labor hours involved, Keynesian saving is mathematically equal to Keynesian investment.

Keynes was quite clear about his meaning. Unfortunately many economists have chosen to reverse his causation. They assume and assert that money that is not spent on consumption is necessarily spent on investment. Rather than investment leading to saving they say that saving causes investment. Economists who retained Keynes's meaning refer to this reversal as "hydraulic Keynesianism." The idea that saving drives investment is one of many economic dogmas that only someone with no experience of owning or managing a business in the real economy could believe.

One of the major sources of funding for investment comes from the retained profits of large corporations. It is "saved" in the sense that it is not paid out to shareholders as dividends. It is only a fraction of the actual investment expenditure by corporations, however, since it is usually "geared" by loans from banks and the issue of debt securities. Corporate net profit margins are of the order of 5 percent of sales, and dividends typically take 40 percent of this, so a company with fixed assets of a typical 60 percent of annual sales planning a 10 percent expansion must raise half of the required money through some combination of debt and the issue of new shares.

Large corporations represent the climax state of capitalist development, but most economies also have small and medium business sectors, mostly in fields that corporations find unattractive. A few of these small and medium enterprises will be entrepreneurially managed, rapidly growing businesses that will, if unchecked, become major corporations in the future. In the Anglo-Saxon economies, a supply of such growth businesses is essential to replace those older corporations that succumb to mismanagement, as up to 5 percent do each year.

As Keynes and Schumpeter were well aware, the actual money that entrepreneurs use to pay for the resources that will become their investment comes from commercial banks where it is created as required; and whether households put money into savings accounts, under the mattress, or into stock-market speculation has a negligible effect on the ability of banks to support entrepreneurs. The two critical issues controlling the level of investment are the availability of entrepreneurs with realistic proposals, and the optimism or otherwise of banks and other investors when presented with such proposals.

Ambitious small firms and individual entrepreneurs in the Anglo-Saxon countries, even those with a highly profitable business model, cannot generate enough cash to fund their expansion from their operations and don't have the assets needed to pledge as security if they wish to secure an advance from a clearing bank. They are forced to rely for their funding on wealthy individuals (informal venture capitalists, sometimes referred to as "business angels"), professional venture capital firms, and merchant banks.

Because these advances are unsecured and the returns are uncertain, investors in early stage entrepreneurial ventures expect terms that promise them substantial gains if the venture succeeds as planned: an expected return of 60 percent per year is not uncommon. A more complete explanation of the venture capital process is in Chapter 10 below.

The German finance and management model, also used in Japan, supports longer-lived corporations than the Anglo-Saxon one, and so the need for the financial nursery services upon which entrepreneurial growth businesses in the Anglo-Saxon world rely is less urgent. While there are large corporations in Germany and Japan (like Siemens and Toyota), there are also many medium-sized businesses that supply them and have a common banking relationship. Innovative ideas, if endorsed by the major corporation in a group, are supported by the group's core bank. This process leads to more innovations but fewer millionaires. American commentators often describe this as a weakness; in the wake of the Global Financial Crisis, it looks like a strength.

Interest

In simplistic neoclassical models, interest rates are set by the balance between entrepreneurs' desire for cash to invest and households' willingness to defer consumption, but these effects are not visible in the real world; rather short-term rates are set by the relevant monetary manager: the Bank of England for Britain, the European Central Bank for the countries of the Eurozone, the Federal Reserve in the United States, and equivalent bodies in other countries.

Under most circumstances this cash rate is the floor for all other loan rates: if a bank can earn the cash rate by depositing money with its reserve bank, there is no need to earn less on riskier loans to entrepreneurs and households. The exception is when it is widely believed that the cash rate is about to be reduced sharply: a prudent banker might want to "lock in" a higher rate even if it involves a slightly higher risk.

Since deregulation became general in the 1980s, banks have almost complete freedom in setting interest rates; but as with all pricing decisions, they are aware that raising rates too far will deter borrowers and reduce their gross profits. At the margin they will also consider the loss of customers to a competitor if their rates drift too far from the average for any class of borrower, and in public they will claim that their rates are determined by the magical forces of competition. The overall effect is that there will be an average rate of interest at any one time, and this will affect the average borrower's incentive to increase or decrease their debt.

Keynes[7] suggested that the prevailing interest rate would set a limit on investment, in that no rational investor would invest in a business if the cost of funds was the same or higher than the prospective return. In reality (see Chapter 10) the hurdle rates used by businesses considering investments are substantially higher than the expected interest rate to account for the risks implicit in any investment; but an increase in the general level of interest rates will lead to an increase in typical hurdle rates and a reduction in investment. This will, in turn, affect consumption and employment.

In the immediate postwar period, it came to be believed that monetary policy, involving the regulation of interest rates and bank lending, could be used to keep an economy in a state of full employment with minimal inflation. There were two obvious limitations on the effectiveness of monetary policy: the first was that if an economy was deeply depressed, even an interest rate of zero might not be enough to restore full employment; and the second was that loose fiscal policy, as described below (pages 113 ff.), could overwhelm monetary policy as government deficit spending flooded the economy.

The "stagflation" of the later 1970s was widely held to have discredited Keynesian economic management, and after a brief flirtation with attempts to manage monetary policy by controlling the monetary aggregates, the various central banks now manipulate short-term interest rates in order to control demand and so avoid excessive inflation. At the macroeconomic level, this appears to be a straightforward process; but in the real economy, rising interest rates restrict demand by causing business and household bankruptcies, rather than bringing about a uniform and generally modest reduction in demand. China still follows a Keynesian approach, controlling demand and the money supply by restricting credit and, if necessary, raising marginal tax rates to achieve the same effect with far fewer business and household casualties.

Notes

1. See Rochon & Rossi (2013) for a more formal discussion of money and the contrast between the orthodox or exogenous view and the Keynesian endogenous view, espoused here.
2. Keynes (1936 [1961]: p. 41).
3. Lindner (2015) offers a very formal critique of the loanable funds theory accepted by the majority of conventional economists.
4. http://www.federalreserveeducation.org/about-the-fed/history/.
5. Keen (2011: pp. 306–12).
6. http://www.bis.org/bcbs/.
7. Keynes (1936 [1961]: pp. 136–137).

5

Macroeconomics

What made the General Theory so hard to accept was not its intellectual content, which in a calm mood can easily be mastered, but its shocking implications. Worse than private vices being public benefits, it seemed that the new doctrine was the still more disconcerting proposition that private virtues (of thriftiness and careful husbandry) were public vices.
—Joan Robinson

The early (or classical)[1] economists looked at single markets and industries: they tried to work out how a merchant or artisan set his prices and how a farmer decided which crops and how much of them to plant. If asked how this affected the broader economy, they assumed that it was simply a matter of multiplication and competition: ten farmers would plant ten times as much as one farmer. The market would set the price: ten merchants would quote the same prices in any given market as one merchant would.

Smith and his immediate successors considered a national economy as simply the sum of many local economies, and assumed, rather than arguing, that any action that improved the operation of any local market would also improve the national economy. They were aware of the frequent occurrence of "distress" due to crop failure or demobilization at the end of one of the many wars that filled the history books, but such problems were, in present-day terms, exogenously caused. Wars and famines affected the economy, but the economy did not cause either.

As the nineteenth century progressed, there were recurring crises with no obvious external cause. Marx asserted that these crises were endogenous, arising from the normal operation of the economic system; but his explanation, the declining rate of return on capital, was flawed, to put it kindly.[2]

As Walras and Jevons set out to redefine economics as a branch of mathematics, they started from the idea of a static equilibrium, a point at which an economy had reached an ideal state and from which every change would make things worse. This approach did not explain crises but did give mainstream economists an excuse for ignoring them.

When economists were forced to comment on a crisis, the standard response would be that some vested interest was selfishly preventing the economy from reaching equilibrium. There were three possible sets of vested interests to blame: greedy monopoly capitalists, holding back production to keep prices high; or greedy industrial workers and their unions, keeping wages too high; or incompetent governments, buying political favor with regulations that prevented the economy moving toward an ideal equilibrium.

By and large, mainstream economics has not moved beyond this position. Most developed countries have procompetition authorities, vigorously suppressing monopoly behavior whenever and wherever they can find it or even imagine it. Trade unions have been greatly weakened by institutional changes and by globalization. Governments even have ministers of deregulation. In spite of all this activity, 2007 saw the onset of the greatest depression since the 1930s, and in some countries, the greatest depression since the 1890s.

Mainstream economists keep chanting the same mantras, the only difference being a politically influenced choice of which evil to denounce most loudly. Unions now represent less than an eighth of the US labor force, but economists engaged by employer organizations call for even more "flexibility." Even when regulations are not explicitly repealed, cuts to the public service in many countries and repeated calls for "efficiency dividends" mean that regulations are weakly enforced at best.

In Europe the Competition Directorate of the EU goes on periodic rampages, recently fining Microsoft €561 million for not promoting its rivals' browsers with sufficient enthusiasm.[3] The recession/depression continued.

Crises Are Endogenous

In a world populated by econs[4]—hyperrational, wholly egocentric creatures producing and consuming a single, universal product—crises might be avoided, and if they occurred, the mainstream economists' remedies might work.

When Keynes sought to explain the Great Depression, he returned, somewhat indirectly, to Marx's position though not his explanation: economic crises were endogenous, arising out of the normal operation of a market economy, and no external shock was required to explain them. One of his critical observations was that observing the behavior of an individual in isolation was not a sufficient way of predicting the behavior of that same individual when interacting with others. Keynes was very familiar with the financial markets. He commented that if there was only one trader, he would buy or sell at a price that reflected his best estimate of the value of the various securities on offer; but if there were many traders, they would each observe and react to what other traders were doing.

Suppose a trader, after careful research, decides that shares in the XYZ Company are worth $10, which happened to be their current price: if he was the only trader, he would sit on his hands, neither buying nor selling. If, however, he learns that another trader believes that the shares are worth $12 and is prepared to pay that much, our first trader's rational decision is to buy, even if he has to pay more than his estimate of the value until the price reaches $12 because he is confident that he will be able to sell to someone else at that price. This is sometimes referred to as the "greater fool" theory of stock-market trading: during a bull market, no matter how ridiculous a stock price may be, you should buy it, because a greater fool will come along and buy it from you at a still higher price. Eventually the price will reach a level so ridiculous that even the greatest fools will decide to sell, and the price will crash, possibly to a level below its realistic valuation.

On December 10, 1999, at the height of the dot-com bubble, shares in Amazon.com Inc. traded for $106.69; less than two years later, on September 28, 2001, the same shares traded for $5.97. Amazon proved to have a sound business model, unlike many of the other dot-com ephemera, and in December 2009 its shares once again traded for over $100, peaking at $246 in October 2011; but the 2011 price does not justify the 1999 mania. An investor who bought at the 1999 peak and sold at the 2011 peak would have only earned 7.11 percent on her money, before tax and ignoring inflation—a very poor return, given the risks involved. Had an investor bought at the 1999 peak using borrowed money, the interest costs would have wiped out any conceivable gain; had such an investor bought "on margin," the margin would have been called long before the price recovered, inflicting heavy losses and possible bankruptcy for the investor.

Stock prices do not reflect the calm evaluation of a single analyst; rather, they reflect the frenzied efforts of many traders to make money by forecasting the reaction of other traders. For this reason, studying how a single individual reacts to challenges does not make it possible to predict how a number of individuals will react if simultaneously exposed to that challenge.

Work on chaos and complexity theory, mostly since the death of Keynes, has shown that even the slightest relaxation of the standard microeconomic assumptions is sufficient to make arrival at an equilibrium state almost impossible and remaining in that state, as long as life continues, quite impossible.[5] I discuss this further below.

Stock markets are only one aspect of a modern economy, but similar effects may be observed in all its sectors. Keynes decided that trying to predict the course of a market or an economy by studying the behavior and motivation of isolated individuals was both futile and deeply misleading: a regional, national, or global economy had to be studied as a system. Following Keynes, terminologically at least, the study of economies as systems has come to be known as macroeconomics, while the traditional form of economics has become known as microeconomics.[6]

Counterattack

Traditional economists were (and are) heavily invested in their models and were deeply disturbed by Keynes's suggestion that there were economic phenomena that their traditional models could not explain. The omnipresent fact of the Great Depression at the time that Keynes wrote his *General Theory*[7] revealed a deep flaw in traditional economics, since using the traditional assumptions, there was a logical proof that lasting depressions and persistent unemployment could not occur. This divergence from reality was very hard to ignore.

There was one widely respected if utterly surreal attempt to explain depressions without referring to deficiencies of demand, and that was the "Austrian" theory of capital, now associated with Hayek.

Unfortunately Austrian capital theory is completely impenetrable to anyone not both fluent in German and entitled to use "von" before his or her surname. To the extent that it uses words that have a commonly understood meanings, it makes anyone with actual experience of managing businesses or evaluating investment proposals dizzy.

Even before the first edition of Keynes's *General Theory* was printed, there were attempts to absorb macroeconomics into the traditional form: economics looked at reality and stumbled back. The attack on Keynesian macroeconomics generally focuses on its lack of "microfoundations." It is impossible to derive Keynes's conclusions starting from standard microeconomic assumptions—that is, a world populated by identical, egotistical, perfectly rational econs. To ideologically committed economists, this counts as a damning indictment of Keynes's work; to less ideologically committed enquirers, it seems to be an advantage.

Microfoundations

The physical sciences went through a period of extraordinary intellectual ferment in the late eighteenth century that continued well into the nineteenth. This is clearly among the factors that inspired Walras and Jevons in the development of General Equilibrium Theory, a mathematical *tour de force* that began the process of putting the study of economics on a par with celestial mechanics. I mentioned Herschel's feat of prediction in Chapter 3; the logical conclusion of Walras's program was the achievement of a similar level of predictive accuracy in the study of human affairs.

The French philosopher, astronomer, and mathematician Laplace[8] built on Newton's laws of motion to assert that a superhuman being, if equipped with information about the mass and velocity of every particle in the universe, would be able to both overlook the entire past and foresee the entire future. Walras's program looks positively modest in consequence.

Modern orthodox economists have made valiant efforts to extend the work of Walras and Jevons into macroeconomics. To do so they attempt to demonstrate that the aggregate behavior of real economies can be explained by knowledge of the behavior of individual economic agents, or at least, that a consistent theory about the behavior of economic systems can be built on a set of assumptions about the behavior of individual agents.

Unfortunately for both the Laplace and Walras programs, the French mathematician Henri Poincaré (1854—1912) dealt their program a fatal blow with his work on the three-body problem.[9] Newtonian mathematics showed that a system of two bodies subject to gravitational attraction would orbit each other in ellipses, as the moon does the Earth or the Earth does the sun. No mathematician or astronomer until Poincaré had been able to produce an equally clear result for three bodies; and Poincaré proved that there was no solution to the three-body problem with the predictability and elegance of Newton's two-body solution. Worse for the followers of Laplace, Poincaré showed that even careful observation of the actual orbits of three bodies would not, in general, allow a reliable prediction of their future trajectories. (Newton and his successors, including Herschel, calculated the orbits of the planets as if each was on its own orbiting the sun; and then worked out how the planets would influence each other's orbits. This only works because the sun is far more massive than any of the planets.)

The larger ramifications of Poincaré's work were not explored in depth until the availability of reasonably powerful but inexpensive computers. Waldrop[10] provides an accessible account of the early development of chaos and complexity theory. Among the conclusions drawn by students of complexity is a comprehensive proof that it is not, in general, possible to predict the long-term behavior of any assembly of more than two interacting objects. People and markets are sufficiently complicated to meet the conditions for complex behavior to emerge,[11] and so the medium and long-term behavior of human systems cannot be predicted from studying—or making assumptions about—individual behavior.

The American economist Paul Krugman is a well-known critic of the attempt to rebuild macroeconomics on microfoundations. He wrote:

> In the hard sciences, when dealing with complex systems people have often used higher-level, aggregative concepts that seem to work empirically long before they have a full derivation of effects from the underlying laws of physics. Read *Air Apparent*, a nifty book on the history of meteorology: meteorologists were using concepts like cold and warm fronts long before they had computational weather models, because those concepts seemed to make sense and to work. Why, then, do some economists think that concepts like the IS curve or the multiplier are illegitimate because they aren't necessarily grounded in optimization from the ground up?
>
> And when making such comparisons between economics and physical science, there's yet another point: what we call "microfoundations" are not like physical laws. Heck, they're not even true. Maximizing consumers are just a metaphor, possibly useful in making sense of behavior, but possibly not. The metaphors we use for microfoundations have no claim to be regarded as representing a higher order of truth than the ad hoc aggregate metaphors we use in IS-LM or whatever; in fact, we have much more supportive evidence for Keynesian macro than we do for standard micro.[12]

Since Keynes's death, and even more aggressively since the ascendancy of neoliberalism from the mid-1970s, academic macroeconomics has been hammered into a shape conforming to traditional economics if not to reality, and advanced macroeconomics students and practitioners use DSGE (dynamic stochastic general equilibrium) models in their learned papers and their economic forecasts.

The attempt to recreate macroeconomics on microfoundations was misguided from the beginning, and the conclusions of any studies based on these assumptions are, at best, irrelevant to the actual behavior of market economies. It can be persuasively argued that DSGE modeling leads to policy conclusions that do far more harm than good.[13] The Global Financial Crisis starting in 2007 is just as impossible to explain by DSGE models as the Great Depression was impossible to explain using traditional economics. John Quiggin explains the failure of DSGE in his popular book *Zombie Economics*[14] but, as the European Commission's and the European Central Bank's response to the sovereign debt crisis in Europe shows, the zombies are still in charge of major sections of the global economy. The authors of the proposed new Eurozone treaty in 2012 were sublimely unaware that their proposals were not merely arithmetically impossible but based on utterly discredited theories. The treaty requires all Eurozone members to run trade surpluses with no one to run deficits and absorb them.

The logic of the "Troika" of the International Monetary Fund, the European Commission, and the European Central bank is a canonical example of failing to see the wood for the trees or, more technically, being so focused on micro issues that they refuse to see the macroeconomic impact of their policies. Greece owes Germany a lot of money for past imports, so the Troika have ordered Greece to cut its minimum wage and slash government spending so with nobody in Greece able to buy its firms' products, they will export them, paying down the debt. Germany is the only Eurozone country with a substantial surplus and therefore the only one that can buy Greece's exports without itself building up an external debt. Unfortunately, Germany is also holding down its workers' wages and limiting its government spending in order to ensure that German firms have a surplus to export. No matter what Greece does, it can't export a surplus if there is no one to buy it.

The only possible result of implementing the Troika's policies will be universal depression as every Eurozone country suppresses domestic demand in a vain attempt to increase exports.

Drivers of Employment and Unemployment

Keynes pointed out that everyone needed some sort of "rainy-day" money, and the more scared they were of future unemployment or other serious expenses, the more they would save out of their current wages and hold as cash or highly liquid bank deposits.

People who fear civil strife or arbitrary confiscation will have an additional urge to save some ready money, preferably out of the reach of the bandits or corrupt governments that might prey on them. Entrepreneurs in the transition economies of Europe, particularly those of the former Soviet Union, have every reason to fear extortion, official as well as criminal, and will not merely hoard their cash; they will place it out of reach of the bandits and corrupt officials that they fear. In whole suburbs of London, Russian accents, and Russian-owned property, seem almost as common as English and local owners.

Orthodox economists recognize that households might choose to save part of their income but assume that this is only so that they can invest it; and they will only save and invest part of their income when the prospective returns from the investment are sufficient to compensate them for the loss of current consumption.

Keynes saw two critical flaws in this argument:

- Investments are inevitably illiquid to a greater or lesser extent, and since the future is uncertain, nobody can be sure of when they will need cash or how much they will need: "rainy-day" money must be held as cash or at call deposits while money entrusted to an entrepreneur will be accepted on the basis that it does not have to be returned before some future date.
- There is no reason why entrepreneurs' demand for investment funds would exactly match householders' desire for savings.

Keynes pointed out that a change in liquidity preference could lead to an increase or decrease in economic growth and hence employment. This effect was, Keynes wrote, amplified by the division of industry into two major sectors: some firms produced consumer goods and services for immediate use; but others produced capital equipment and built structures for use by firms producing consumer goods and delivering consumer services.

Only part of the labor force was employed in the production of consumer goods and the delivery of consumer services; the rest was employed making capital equipment and building structures to be used in the production of consumer goods and services. Total economic demand and therefore the production of consumption goods and services consisted of the wages and profits of both the consumption and the capital-goods industries, adjusted for any changes in liquidity preference and household, government, and business debt levels.

If firms in the consumption-goods industries believed that demand was about to rise, they would place orders for new equipment and structures in order to meet it, as well as engaging more workers. Their orders for capital equipment would encourage increased employment in the capital-goods industries, and the newly hired workers in both sectors would spend most of their income on consumption goods, causing an increase in sales by the relevant industries. This increase would confirm their original judgment, and they might hire even more workers and place more orders for capital equipment, leading to an economic boom.

If firms in the consumption-goods industries believed that demand was about to fall, they would lay off workers and defer or cancel orders for new capital equipment, forcing firms in the capital-goods industries to lay workers off. Demand would continue to fall, thus confirming firms in their judgment, and the economy could enter a slump, with unemployment among those willing to work.

If, as in the countries of the former USSR, many entrepreneurs and successful professionals move their surplus income to a different country, rather than either spending or investing it in their own country, the consequence may be continuing depression. The economists and other advisors upon whose recommendations the Yeltsin government of Russia destroyed the command economy in order to allow the spontaneous emergence of a prosperous, Western-style consumer economy are now safely at home. They fail to acknowledge that, by encouraging the theft of state assets in order to create an oligarchy determined to prevent the return of communism or anything like it, they dignified theft as a normal entrepreneurial activity.

If the owners and managers of a privatized Soviet enterprise consider making an investment as distinct from moving the cash flow to a foreign jurisdiction, they may well feel inhibited by the prospect of a state-sponsored thief seizing their enterprise. Many ordinary Russians now look back on the stagnation and petty corruption of the Soviet era with nostalgia.

Traditional economists argued in Keynes's day, and some still argue, that involuntary unemployment is impossible, and those who claim to be unemployed are exercising a "leisure preference." They quote Say's Law, which, briefly put, asserts that supply creates its own demand.

In a primitive economy, this may be so: in such economies workers produced goods that were immediately consumed, and the wages and profits earned from production created sufficient demand to absorb all that production. In such an economy there is no liquidity preference, since workers are paid a subsistence income and must spend all their wages to live; and there is no sector producing capital goods.

Say's Law clearly applies in a hunter-gatherer economy without money or refrigerators: if a hunter returns with a kill, anything that the tribe does not eat will rot; when members of the tribe feel hungry, they will hunt and forage and then consume the proceeds. Nothing will be saved because nothing can be saved. Once money and markets enter the picture, the direct link between production and consumption is broken: a hunter may sell excess game at the market for money. It is possible that the hunter will immediately spend the money on consumption, as assumed by Say's Law; but it is also possible that he will save some of the money with a view to spending it at some future time when game may be harder to find.

Keynes pointed out that money served as both a medium of exchange and as a store of value. It is in this latter role that it affects the real economy.

Say's Law was rendered obsolete by Boulton and Watt when they started producing steam engines at their Soho plant in Birmingham in 1776: nobody consumes steam engines.

Instability

Keynes anticipated modern systems theory by pointing out that booms and slumps could arise within an economic system: such events needed no external cause. Hyman Minsky and, more recently, Steve Keen[15] have demonstrated a second endogenous route to instability in a capitalist economy. During a boom consumption-goods firms invest to expand production, and capital-goods firms invest to meet their orders. As Keynes and Schumpeter followed Adam Smith in pointing out, the necessary money is created by banks as it is required; and to the extent that the banks are acting "responsibly," their advances are secured against valuable property and equipment. At the same time, the stock prices of firms in both the consumer- and capital-goods industries will rise in anticipation of higher profits.

This presents an opportunity for speculators to borrow money with which to buy shares in the expectation of trading profits as the stock prices rise further. "Responsible" banks are happy to lend money secured against these shares, which, since they are traded on a minute-by-minute basis, seem to be an even better asset than the buildings and machinery used by productive firms.

As a boom develops, speculators take an ever-more-optimistic view of the prospects for stock prices, and banks become ever-more-sanguine about the security that they are offered. While in normal times, a responsible bank would not advance a speculator more than half of the price of the shares offered as security (these advances are referred to as margin loans), in boom times banks may advance much more: up to 80 percent in the months leading to the Great Crash of 1929 and over 90 percent (through the use of derivative instruments) before the crash of 2008.

In the years before the crash of 2008, American and several European banks also financed reckless real estate development, offering mortgages up to and sometimes in excess of the assessed value of a property, relying on the cheerful assumption that real estate prices always go up and even the so-called NINJA (no income, no job or assets) borrowers could repay their loans out of the increased value.[16]

Under these circumstances only a small fall in share or property prices can have a major effect. Financiers describe the practice of acquiring an asset using borrowed funds to cover part of the price as gearing because it amplifies the possible trading profit. Suppose a stock trader has a million dollars to invest, and he believes that XYZ Company shares, currently worth $10, are about to rise in value by 20 percent. He could buy 100,000 shares, and when they rise to $12, sell them for a profit of $200,000. Alternatively, he could borrow $9 million and buy a million shares, and when the stock price rose to $12, sell the shares, pay back the loan, and make a profit of $2 million, less a small interest payment. Of course, if the speculator was wrong in his prediction and the stock price fell by 20 percent, he would have no money, stock worth $8 million, and a debt of $9 million. The bank would force him to sell the shares and then seize his assets and possibly bankrupt the trader in an attempt to cover its loss.

In this example the loss fell mainly on the trader, but suppose as with Amazon.com Inc., discussed above, the stock price fell by 95 percent? (Since it took a couple of years for the Amazon.com stock price to fall that far, a succession of speculators were probably ruined, but the net loss to the banking system would be the same as if a single speculator had been involved.) The banks that had financed the speculators would have to write off nearly all these loans; and since banks' advances are a multiple of their reserves (as described in Chapter 4) the bank would be forced to reduce its other advances by up to twelve times as much as it lost to the defaulting borrower in order to maintain its regulated capital adequacy ratios.

Banks suffering from losses in speculative loans will refuse to extend loans to even the most rock-solid borrowers until they have rebuilt their balance sheets. The frustrated borrowers will include the capital-goods suppliers trying to meet demand from the consumer-goods industries, and the consumer-goods industries needing loans to buy the capital goods needed to expand or perhaps just to maintain their production. As Minsky predicted and Keen's modeling confirms, the speculative losses in the bubble economy will damage the real economy, turning a "Keynesian" fluctuation into a full-scale recession.

Irving Fisher was an economist who bankrupted himself by assuming that the Great Crash of 1929 was merely a short-term correction; and with the leisure to repent, he developed the debt-deflation hypothesis to provide an additional explanation as to why the Great Depression was so intractable.

The Fisher hypothesis has two legs: firstly, if there is deflation, prices and incomes are falling, but commercial bank interest rates can't fall below zero and seldom fall that far; so low nominal interest rates become higher effective rates, discouraging investment. Worse, while prices may fall, the principal amount of any debts owed by a business does not, and neither does the interest due. During the Great Depression, both prices and output fell, so even businesses that survived the initial shock were forced to meet interest bills that had seemed reasonable before the crash but were increasingly onerous after it because of their drastically reduced revenue. Firms caught in such a trap struggle to survive and certainly don't plan ambitious investments.[17]

Steve Keen's great achievement has been to combine the insights of Keynes, Fisher, and Minsky and incorporate them into dynamic models that have proven to have great explanatory and some predictive power. Keen was one of the very few economists who predicted the crash of 2007 and the onset of the Great Recession.

Monetary Neutrality

In traditional economic theory, money is an illusion: the only value of money is what it can buy, and rational agents will spend their money, partly on consumption goods and services and partly on investments. Since consumers are assumed to have perfect foresight (either individually or in aggregate), there is no reason to hold cash or at-call deposits, since they offer neither the pleasure of immediate consumption nor the benefits of increased future consumption when investments mature. Money, in this view, is neutral in that the absolute quantity of it does not affect the real economy. If there was a lot of money around, the hunter from Chapter 4 might have sold his brace of rabbits for four copper coins rather than two, while if there was less money, the brace of rabbits might have been sold for a single penny; but still one brace of rabbits and one bushel of apples would be brought to market.

Keynes made few friends among traditional economists when he ridiculed the assumption of monetary neutrality and the related assumptions as being appropriate only in economies where money took the form of fresh fish or ripe bananas: unless used at once, it would rapidly lose its value. In reality consumers did not have perfect foresight and so would want to hold some money as a precaution against unforeseen events.

The Politics of Trade

The early years of the nineteenth century were not kind to Portugal; the country fell rapidly to a Spanish-French invasion in 1807, forcing the royal family to flee to Brazil, at that time a Portuguese colony. Various pockets of resistance survived in Portugal until in 1808 a British army under Sir Arthur Wellesley (later first Duke of Wellington) arrived and forced the French to agree to being evacuated. Wellesley himself was evacuated after a dispute over the command and the terms under which the French had been allowed to evacuate but returned as unchallenged commander later in 1808 ahead of a renewed French offensive. After some ferocious and bloody battles, Wellesley cleared Portugal of the French by 1811, earning the title Earl Wellington. He began, in support of a Spanish insurrection against Napoleonic rule, to evict the French from Spain as well.

In 1809, with the French still a major threat and the Portuguese government split between Lisbon and Brazil, the British dictated a treaty giving Britain control of Portuguese finances. British manufactures had enjoyed low-tariff entry to the Portuguese market since the Methuen Treaty of 1703, and in 1810 Britain dictated a supplementary treaty allowing British merchants to trade freely with Brazil. The loss of customs duties and the levies on trade with Brazil had a devastating effect on the Portuguese economy, although opening Brazil to British trade proved very beneficial to Brazil—and Britain.

In 1817 the British politician and banker David Ricardo published a book in which, among other matters, he presented what has become the standard argument in favor of free trade, and used Portugal as his primary example. He enunciated the Theory of Comparative Advantage, in which he argued that, as long as Portugal (and implicitly Brazil) was more suited to making wine and other agricultural commodities than textiles and other manufactured goods, it should concentrate on agricultural commodities, exporting its surplus, and buy its manufactured products from Britain. He argued that Portugal would be better off by agreeing to these arrangements even if the Portuguese could have set up their own manufacturing industries.

Ricardo's counterintuitive but profoundly influential conclusion even covered the case where Portuguese manufacturing was more efficient than British manufacturing. Ricardo asserted that as long as Portugal's advantage over Britain in raw material production was greater than its advantage in manufacturing, it should stick to raw materials.

Ricardo may well have believed his own theory, and his principal target was the English Corn Laws, not the Portuguese tariff; but it was morally convenient to demonstrate that, in imposing the treaties of 1809 and 1810 on Portugal, England was acting in Portugal's interests as much as in its own. Ricardo was properly cautious in setting out the main assumptions hedging his theory, and certain implicit assumptions can be found in his work. Three of the most important were that

- wages were at or close to subsistence level in each country involved in trade;
- demand for all forms of product was infinite, or, at least, greater than the entire potential output of either the British or Portuguese economies;
- capital was immobile: capital in the form of land is obviously not portable, but Ricardo thought that men who owned an investible surplus of gold and silver or an equivalent value in tradable goods would not let it far out of their sight.

In the early nineteenth century, before the introduction of the electric telegraph or the railway or of reliable steamboats, a man who invested his money abroad without following it was very unlikely to see it again; and the man who did follow it would be sacrificing his family ties, his familiar acquaintanceships, and the social and legal rules with which he was familiar.

In the twenty-first century, the constraints on capital mobility are largely erased: an investor can move from practically any point on Earth to any other point in thirty hours or less, while modern communications technology can provide second–by–second oversight from any point on Earth to plant, mine, or market operations at any other point.

The assumption that all laborers earn subsistence wages no longer applies either. The labor market in a modern economy leads to a complex structure of relativities (see Chapter 8) based on the minimum wage, which is, in most countries, set at a point above bare subsistence level by law or regulation. History and policy has led to a situation where the minimum and median wages differ from country to country.

With two of Ricardo's key assumptions knocked out, his demonstration of the mutual benefits of free trade also fails, and in spite of very great efforts, no reputable economist has been able to develop a plausible, much less a convincing, proof that the so-called Law of Comparative Advantage holds in a world of capital mobility and wage differentials.[18] This absence of proof has not stopped the majority of economists adhering to free trade with dogmatic obstinacy.

Trade in General

When an economy is exposed to international trade, some of its resources will be used to provide goods and services for export while the resources of other countries will provide goods and services for it to import. Trade implies reciprocity but has its temptations. Living standards are normally defined in terms of the consumption of goods and services; but a country that imports more than it exports is able to consume goods and services that it has not produced, and so to enjoy a higher average standard of living than its production of goods and services would appear to justify.

Before the first major globalization of the late nineteenth century, each country's imports and exports tended to balance; if a country imported more than it exported, it would run out of gold and silver and have to increase its exports and reduce its imports to avoid being stripped of precious metals entirely. The Opium Wars, in which England forced China to permit imports of opium, were deemed necessary because otherwise China's exports of tea to Britain would have been paid for in silver, reducing Britain's holdings of that important metal.

Britain's position as the globally dominant manufacturing nation in the nineteenth century created vast imbalances as the country's demand for raw materials and food was only a fraction, in money terms, of the value of its exports. The difference was made up by overseas investment on a massive scale, particularly in North and South America, but substantial amounts flowed to Australia, South Africa, and New Zealand.

This made the macroeconomic equation slightly more complicated: consumption now equals production minus investment plus net imports. There are additional financial transactions needed to achieve an accounting balance; but there is no direct connection between contra flows on the current account and actual investment. There are plenty of examples of countries with high levels of inward investment measured by accounting rules and negligible actual productive investment; the difference often consists of a combination of higher debt levels and corrupt transfers to members of the ruling elite.

The end of the twentieth century and the start of the twenty-first saw the rise of global banking on an unprecedented scale. The immediate beneficiaries included Britain and the United States, where the consumption of manufactured goods ran far ahead of their production. The contra funds were provided by the newly industrialized countries that supplied these manufactured goods, and in consequence these countries built up massive external balances.

In 1967 Britain was forced into a humiliating devaluation and ordered to undertake fiscal retrenchment by the International Monetary Fund because its trade deficit had risen to a fraction of the levels taken for granted in the early twenty-first century. The political repercussions of these events were a major factor in the loss of office by the Wilson Labour government in 1970.

Contemporary Issues

In spite of the United States' self-characterization as the world's most innovative and entrepreneurial economy, its enormous trade deficit suggests a drastic shortfall in domestic production capacity that must reflect an equivalent shortfall in productive investment and in the demand for funds to support such investments. Productive investment has apparently been replaced as the key driver of the US (and British) economy by consumer debt and debt-financed speculation; the proximate cause of the Global Financial Crisis of 2008 was that housing finance had been offered to many US households with no capacity to meet the interest payments, and their defaults made many financial instruments worthless. Increasing liquidity in the system can only drive still more attempts to increase consumer debt and various forms of speculation.

Animal spirits may indeed be liberated; but is the spirit of speculation, not productive investment, that now dominates. There are still many active entrepreneurs, many of them American; but most of their productive investment takes place in China, India, and certain other developing countries. Apple Inc. is, at the time of writing, the most valuable company in the world judged by its market capitalization. Its products are assembled in China, incorporating chips, screens, and other components manufactured in South Korea and Taiwan; only one major component is sourced from a US-based manufacturer.

Vast numbers of manufacturing workers in the English-speaking countries have seen their jobs outsourced to Asian countries. Free-trade advocates forecast that these manufacturing jobs would be replaced by even better-paying ones in the emerging "service economy." In practice most of the unemployment caused by the contraction of the manufacturing industry has been replaced by low-value-added service industries offering what Reich termed "in-person services."[19] In recent years many of these services, such as call center operation and basic accounting, have also been outsourced to low-wage countries; there has even been substantial outsourcing of high-value-added activities such as software maintenance and development.

Economic orthodoxy before the Global Financial Crisis was that "deficits don't matter," and either the imbalances can increase without limit or alternatively they are self-correcting or would be if exchange rates were permitted to float freely. This made it politically convenient to blame China and other developing countries for the imbalances; but when the correction occurred, the pain was felt more strongly in the deficit countries than the surplus ones. China addressed the political problems of the necessary correction and the fall in its external surplus by increasing domestic investment and promoting its people's consumption, a politically pleasant objective. The deficit countries will have to reduce their domestic consumption in order to restore balance, a process likely to cause a political backlash.

Trade and Investment

In a closed economy, persistent unemployment can occur if the entrepreneurial class lacks sufficient animal spirits or faces other barriers to innovation; but in an open economy, a surplus on the current account, if not offset by increased borrowing, can lead to a demand deficiency at any level of innovation. Wages must be paid to produce the exported goods, but the price paid for them is retained in the trade deficit country and so is not available to support economic activity in the surplus country. An accounting balance will be maintained by banks in the surplus country making loans to banks in the deficit country, and by firms in the surplus country making real and speculative investments in the deficit country.

Since the economically orthodox ignore speculation as being "irrational," they assume, and assert loudly, that all the money spent by firms from the surplus country in the deficit country are real, income-generating investments, the revenue from which will eventually restore a trade balance. This was largely the case under Keynesian economic management between 1946 and 1975; but speculation overtook real investment as soon as Keynesian regulations were abandoned. Economists familiar with the work of Adam Smith should not have been surprised at the explosion of speculation once capital movements were deregulated.

In a slightly different context, Smith observed:

> [Without regulation the] greater part of the money which was to be lent, would be lent to prodigals and projectors. . . . Sober people, who will give for the use of money no more than a part of what they are likely to make by the use of it, would not venture into the competition. . . . [In consequence a] great part of the capital of the country would thus be kept out of the hands which were most likely to make a profitable and advantageous use of it, and thrown into those which are most likely to waste and destroy it.[20]

The arguments preceding the Bretton Woods agreements at the end of World War II recognized the tendency for a transfer of employment from surplus to deficit countries and so mandated balanced trade; the major point of contention was whether the obligation to act to correct imbalances should be placed on surplus or on deficit countries. Keynes argued that countries in surplus should be obliged to stimulate their economies and so draw in more imports, while the American Harry Dexter White (1892–1948) argued that the obligation should be placed on the deficit countries to suppress domestic demand and increase their exports. The United States, as the dominant economic power at the end of the war, saw no possibility that it could ever be a deficit country, and so White's position won, and the burden of adjustment was placed on the countries in deficit.[21]

Notes

1. See page 21 ff.
2. Keen (2011: esp. Ch. 17).
3. European Commission (2013).
4. See page 33.
5. Legge (2012).
6. Robinson (1962, 1969 [2013]) built on Keynes's work to accommodate economic growth; Davidson (2009) offers a much shorter but identifiably Keynesian approach to twenty-first-century economic issues.
7. Keynes (1936 [1961]).
8. Pierre-Simon, marquis de Laplace (1749–1827).
9. https://en.wikipedia.org/wiki/Three-body_problem.

10. Waldrop (1992).
11. Even the behavior of a single living person often confounds predictions.
12. Krugman (2012).
13. Quiggin (2010).
14. Quiggin (2010, 2011).
15. Keen (2009).
16. Stiglitz (2010).
17. Keen (2011: p. 319).
18. For a recent critique of conventional trade theory, see Schumacher (2013).
19. Reich (1991).
20. Smith (1776: Book II, Chapter 4, p. 15).
21. Skidelsky (2000).

6

Inflation

A steady rate of monetary growth at a moderate level can provide a framework under which a country can have little inflation and much growth.
—Milton Friedman

Inflation occurs when the average prices of consumption goods and services rise without corresponding quality increases. Inflation has occurred at many times and for many reasons.

In Chapter 4 above, I mentioned that economists generally find money an elusive concept, and so inflation becomes elusive squared. If money is a mere lubricant making barter easier, then the amount of it available, and the price of any individual item offered for sale, are second-order issues of no great importance. Keynes attempted to break this fixation with barter by focusing on the difference between the real wage (an arbitrary amount of money that suffices to buy a given basket of goods) and the money wage (a definite amount of money that may or may not suffice to buy the same basket of goods).

Keynes noted that wages are nearly always defined in terms of money; payment in goods ("truck") is actually illegal in Britain and other common-law countries, and has been since the early nineteenth century. Wages are, of course, the employer's costs: and if prices rise while money wages do not, employers earn greater profits; conversely, if prices fall but money wages do not, employers will earn reduced profits and may even be forced into a loss. Keynes, and Irving Fisher before him, noted that loan contracts are practically always designated in money terms, and so employers who finance their business in whole or in part with borrowed money suffer a double squeeze if prices fall as a fixed amount of interest must be paid out of a diminished gross profit.

Keynes was a practical businessman as well as an economist, holding the position of bursar of Kings College, Cambridge, where he greatly increased the tidiness of its accounts and the value of its endowment.

He knew that a growing business *must* borrow money to meet its working (or circulating) capital needs; and if interest rates were too high, a business would have to reduce its working capital and, in the process, reduce its output and its workforce. If interest rates were too low, businesses might overexpand, bidding up wages and raising their prices, but this did not seem to be a major problem during the 1930s when prices were generally falling: deflation was a real, current problem while inflation was a mere theoretical possibility.

Friedman was the most "Keynesian" scholar in the neoliberal movement, and his contributions to monetary theory were valuable and may prove to be lasting. As a neoliberal Friedman saw inflation as something to be avoided because it transferred value from creditors to debtors, while as a monetary scholar, he knew that there had to be sufficient money available at affordable interest rates if an economy was to experience more or less steady growth.

The economist Phillips had observed that there appeared to be a negative correlation between inflation and unemployment in that unemployment was lower when inflation was higher. This led many economists in the post–World War II period to assert that a moderate level of inflation was necessary to ensure low unemployment. Friedman disagreed with this conclusion furiously and argued that any attempt to limit unemployment by tolerating inflation was futile because it would lead to hyperinflation and the complete collapse of the monetary system. Friedman's arguments have proved politically persuasive, and governments in most developed and developing countries now tolerate levels of unemployment and underemployment that would have been politically unacceptable in the 1950s and 1960s. They justify this approach by citing Friedman and the dangers of hyperinflation.

Keynes, and Friedman, developed a coherent macroeconomic explanation of money and inflation; but dealing with aggregates on a national scale necessarily obscures how inflation enters a system and how it may be controlled. In particular, as I explain below, the rate of innovation may be a critical link between inflation and unemployment, and very few economists have looked at how real firms set their prices. I look at reality below; one day theory may catch up with it.

Prices and Wages

In a purely hypothetical economy in a state of (almost) perfect competition, prices (almost) perfectly reflect costs, so if prices rise in such an economy, a reasonable presumption is that costs have risen.

Since wages are a major part of most firms' costs, a rise in prices can readily be blamed on excessive wage demands, and often is. As with many of the assertions made by believers in the prevalence of perfect competition, this one is much more solidly based in theory than in fact.

In an economy dominated by oligopoly and monopolistic competition, prices are set at the firm level and reflect each individual firm's demand conditions. Since these prices will be set at or slightly below the point of maximum profit, most (not all) of a cost increase will be absorbed by individual firms. Wages are an important part of overall economic demand, so if wages rise, so will demand; and if there is insufficient product innovation, this increase in wages might lead to increased demand at the firm level, encouraging price rises and increasing the measured rate of inflation. If the wage increases are paralleled by the introduction of new products, much of the increased demand will be for these new products, suppliers of established products will not experience an increase in demand, and their price rises, if any, will be less than the increase in wages. Wage increases may lead to inflation, but they may not.

Demand at the firm level can be divided into three components: the number of customers for a firm's products may change; the frequency with which established customers purchase a firm's products may change; and the willingness of a firm's customers to pay the ruling price for a firm's products may change. The number of customers for a firm's products will be affected, slowly, by demographic changes; or slightly more rapidly by the firm's sales and marketing efforts and those of its rivals; or dramatically, by the entry or failure of a firm's competitors. None of these circumstances necessarily imply that a firm should adjust its prices, although the entry of an ill-managed competitor launching a price war may require a firm to respond in kind. The frequency with which a typical customer purchases a firm's products will change with changes in the general level of affluence, with rising affluence increasing the rate of purchase of luxury and higher-quality products and leading to a relative or even absolute decline in the rate of purchase of basic products. At a certain level of affluence, households may satisfy their demand for cake by buying the basic ingredients and baking it themselves. As affluence rises, equivalent households may purchase manufactured cake, and the relative quantity of flour sold at retail will fall.

Firms may also affect these frequencies by repositioning themselves in the market in order to access less affluent customers (a "value" strategy) or more affluent ones (a "quality" strategy); such moves are more easily written about than executed. However they are driven, changes in purchase frequency do not necessarily imply substantial changes in price levels.

Quality improvements by a firm or its rivals can have an immediate impact on the most profitable price level. Fortunately for many firms, customers generally are slow to recognize changes in the relative quality of the products they use compared to those that their supplier's rivals may offer; and even when such changes are brought to their attention, many users will challenge their current supplier to match the supplier's rival's quality before changing suppliers. "Better the devil you know" guides many purchasing decisions.

Firms that can package their quality improvements into optional purchases, building on a core product with a stable or even slowly declining real price, can achieve an effective price increase without any specific price changes. When Ford introduced the Falcon to the US market in 1959, the car was very successful in revenue terms but only modestly profitable; the Mustang, which was launched in 1964, was essentially a Falcon with "sporty" styling. It was, in its basic form, no more profitable than the Falcon, but the typical buyer spent another 50 percent of the basic purchase price on immensely profitable optional accessories.[1]

Individual firms are part of a wider economy and are subject to a number of its effects. One is that unit labor costs fall (when measured as units produced per hour worked) as experience accumulates; the magnitude of this effect depends on labor turnover, the age of the technology in use, and, to some extent, pressure from rivals. The newer the technology and the slower the labor turnover, the faster the rate of decline in unit labor costs will be.

When unit costs fall, the most profitable strategy for a firm marketing differentiated products is to reduce its prices (but by less than the fall in costs) and so to profit both from increased sales and from higher margins.

Two other factors are less favorable to a firm: rival firms may offer higher quality products in direct competition with it; and firms not in direct competition with it may offer new products that attract its customers and divert part of their expenditure from the older to the newer product.

Innovation, Prices, and Employment

Innovative firms affect the rest of the firms in an economy in two ways: they take some fraction of the market served by other firms before the innovation appeared; and they force the general wage rates up by bidding workers away from less innovative firms. The second-round effect of the appearance of an innovation is that the survivors from the previously active firms will find their unit profits squeezed but the total demand for their products increased; the most marginal firms may now fail, and their market will be divided between the existing firms less the share captured by the innovative one.

Innovations, or a cascade of innovations, divide the firms in the affected economy into three main groups. The successful innovators will enjoy above average profits. Well managed but less innovative firms are caught in a profitless growth squeeze, with an increased volume of demand at reduced margins. Previously marginal firms will edge towards bankruptcy driven by shrinking markets and rising costs.

The extinction of the most marginal firms will cause their employees to lose their jobs. There is no automatic mechanism to ensure that the increased demand for the output of the innovative and surviving less innovative firms will generate a demand for labor that will absorb the displaced workers exactly. There cannot be too much innovation, at least from the immediate employment perspective, since a large and rapidly growing innovative sector will lead to accelerated wage rises and ample employment opportunities for the employees displaced by the extinction of the least viable firms.

There can, however, be too little innovation. The working of the experience curve and the adoption of new production technology and methods will reduce unit costs across an economy and the optimum price firms within the economy can charge. In the absence of an adequate level of innovation, real wages will stagnate and with them effective demand, leading firms to lay off redundant workers. Competition from the unemployed may lead to real wage decreases among the employed (as nominal wages fail to keep pace with inflation); but since such decreases reduce aggregate demand, while the wage decreases lead to real price reductions that are proportionally less than the fall in wages, there is no reason to expect the result to be an increase in total employment; rather, the reverse.

Demand increases can be real or nominal. Real demand increases follow higher aggregate productivity from innovation, from firms moving down the experience curve, and by the efforts of new entrants to employment. With more, or more valuable, output produced by each worker, the economic surplus will increase. This surplus may be partitioned between profits and wages, but in either case they become available for some mixture of investment and consumption.

Origins of Inflation

The easiest-to-explain form of inflation is the consequence of a supply shortage: for example, early in 2012 the wheat crop in Russia, Canada, the United States, and Argentina was affected by drought, with global supply falling 28 million tons short of normal demand.[2] Prices rose by almost 50 percent, forcing up the price of wheat-based products such as beer and bread and also raising the cost of animal feed, with a knock-on effect on meat prices.

Consumers and industrial buyers sought alternative products—rice or maize instead of wheat, grass-fed instead of grain-fed beef—and this additional demand caused a small rise in the price of alternative products and so in the general price level.

In a small, isolated economy with no banks or credit cards, a shock such as a rapid rise in the price or a sudden supply shortage of a commodity will lead to the same amount of money being spent on a smaller quantity of goods. This was institutionalized in many medieval towns, where an annual Assize of Bread (a sitting of the local law court) would examine the grain harvest and set the weight of a loaf of bread; which would then be sold at a fixed, unchanged price. In such an economy, the conditions that triggered the price rise (or unit size reduction) would change and quantities might revert to their trend, or more likely, some other commodity would become scarce or hyperabundant and the total quantity of commodities consumed would change again, while the amount of money changing hands would not. If such a society faced a Malthusian crisis, with the population growing faster than the supply of arable land, there could be a sustained increase in unit prices and a sustained depression of consumption per person.

Normal Inflation

The economics of small, isolated communities is no doubt interesting to their inhabitants. In such communities some commodity is used as a medium of exchange, and prices cannot rise faster than supplies of the designated commodity do. This does not apply to the economies of developed and developing countries.

In developed and most developing countries, there are banks, and this redefines the nature of money. Consumers do not let a sharp rise in the price of one commodity and small rises in the price of many others reduce their consumption: they borrow or reduce their savings by enough to keep their overall consumption constant, although they may rearrange their spending patterns. Total consumption spending now increases, as does the gross margin on commodity sales. Some part of this increase will flow through to profits and some part of it to an increase in nominal wages. When the price of the commodity initially in short supply falls as new supplies become available, nominal wages are not reduced to reflect lower commodity prices, and so the new, higher wages and the new, higher general level of commodity prices becomes established. There may be some reduction in the overall price level from its peak, but it will not return to the level prevailing before the initial supply shock.

Since, in a real economy, various commodities will enter periods of short supply from time to time, an economy with consumer banking services and a constant set of commodities available will experience more or less continuous inflation, albeit at a fairly low rate.

Real entrepreneurial economies are not, however, restricted to a constant set of commodities, and the labor content of any given commodity tends to fall rather than remaining constant:

- Product innovations divide the market, spreading a given level of demand over a larger number of products, and so tending to prevent overall demand increases becoming increases in the demand for individual products; and this reduces the impact of overall demand increases on the general price level.
- Cost innovations reduce the labor content of currently available commodities, and the rational business response to such cost decreases is to pass part of the reduction through to prices, profiting from the increased quantities as well as increased margins, and so tending to reduce the general price level and offset the effect of supply shocks.
- Quality innovations reduce the real price of particular products even if the nominal price stays the same. Those economists who look at the effects of such innovations tend to assume that the supplier of them will raise the nominal price to the point that the real price remains at its original level; but this is not a good business strategy. In practice firms will share the benefits of quality innovations by taking part of the increased value into their earned margins and passing part of it on to their customers in reduced real prices.

Quality innovations cause the statistician considerable trouble; personal computers are a good example. Compared to an original IBM PC of 1983, the personal computer available thirty years later cost about a quarter as much (including software) in nominal terms, was ten thousand times faster, had ten thousand times more main memory and had a hundred thousand times more hard disc capacity.

How much, if anything, should the statistician adjust the nominal price of a more modern PC to work out its contribution to inflation over the thirty years to 2013?

Measurement issues aside, it is clear that there will be a low but continuing rate of inflation in any developed or developing country with an effective banking sector serving consumers.

Hyperinflation

Governments necessarily employ people in administration, law enforcement, and defense, and in many countries, education and public health. These employees must consume to live, but the result of their labors is not, in general, readily tradable. Governments also undertake capital projects, either directly or by engaging contractors, and workers on these projects must also consume to survive, even though their work also does not lead to directly tradable products.

The money needed to pay the workers in government service and on government projects can be raised by taxation, reducing the consumption of those engaged in commercial activities and so maintaining a level of demand consistent with the level of supply. Alternatively, the required money can be raised by borrowing from the public. Again, the money that might have been spent by the lenders and presumptively earned by their commercial operations cannot be spent on their consumption, and so again, government operations financed in this way do not create demand in excess of supply.

During World War II the Allied governments spent vastly more on the supply and maintenance of their military forces than they raised in taxation, ending the war with national debts two or more times the annual value of their gross national product; but on Keynes's advice, they raised the bulk of this money by the sale of war bonds to the public, and over the war period there was very little inflation.

Money can be created by banks on behalf of the bank's customers, and a government can instruct its national reserve bank to buy its bonds, effectively creating money. This newly created money has no direct relationship to any productive process and so can increase demand without any associated increase in supply. Governments that create money by selling bonds to their own reserve bank (or in less sophisticated times and places, simply printing it) will generally do so because they are unwilling or unable to raise sufficient money by taxation or by borrowing from their citizens to meet what they regard as unavoidable expenses. If they do so at a time of substantial unemployment and idle productive capacity, the effect will be to reduce unemployment and bring the idle capacity back into service. The resulting economic buoyancy may generate increased taxation revenue, as well as raise the ability and willingness of investors to make employment-generating investments and purchase government securities. In such cases the reserve bank can sell its excess bond holdings, thus "soaking up" the excess liquidity created by the earlier money creation.

If a government should create and spend money at a time when there are no idle productive resources, the supply quantity is essentially fixed and the immediate result will be an increase in prices. This may increase the amount of money that the government feels obliged to spend, driving prices up further. Quite soon, the citizens of countries in which governments behave in this way may observe that prices rise to multiples of their former level and continue rising. Historic examples of this process include the rebel states in the American Civil War, where the Confederacy printed money to pay its soldiers and suppliers; and the German Weimar Republic, which suffered a critical blow to its revenue when French soldiers occupied the Ruhr in 1923.

Late medieval Spain suffered serious inflation without anyone printing money: the conquest and looting of Central and South America delivered a huge supply of gold to the Spanish crown. Instead of hoarding it or turning it into golden statues, the Crown dissipated it—partly in the form of pensions to various courtiers and favorites and partly on wars in Italy and the Netherlands. Although the Spanish real contained the traditional amount of gold, there were so many of them put into circulation that prices soared; and the ability to live off loot for over a hundred years prevented Spain from developing either modern agriculture or modern industry. One of the great ambitions of the quasi-pirates like Sir Francis Drake who constituted the Royal Navy under Elizabeth I during the late sixteenth century was to capture a Spanish treasure fleet: they never succeeded—a fact that may have been critical in forcing the development of modern Britain.

Asset Price Inflation

When, from the early 1980s, central banks adopted inflation targeting as the basis for their monetary policy, they abandoned both Keynes's and Friedman's concerns about the aggregate money supply. At the same time, neoliberally influenced governments pursued labor market deregulation, or to describe their policies more accurately, deunionization. In Britain following the elimination of the last of the wages boards under

Prime Minister John Major in 1993, until the passage of the National Minimum Wage Law in 1998 under the Blair Labour government, there was no minimum wage at all, while in the United States the minimum wage was raised by less than inflation. These policies led to overall wage rises that barely matched inflation and did not reward workers for increased productivity. Low-wage workers were hit particularly hard, with their wages adjusted for inflation falling.

At the same time as ordinary workers were stripped of their collective bargaining rights, neoliberal orthodoxy redefined corporate managers as agents of their shareholders with a brief to maximize profits. Those managers who succeeded in increasing profits by suppressing wages and retrenching workers were rewarded with massive bonuses. With wage growth depressed but productivity continuing to rise, the profit share of the gross economic surplus rose; but, as Keynes noted, the rich have a lower propensity to consume than the poor and middle classes. The demand for consumption goods, and therefore for investment in consumption goods production, also rose slowly. When the rich did spend their money on consumption, it tended to be on personal services and artisanal goods such as jewelry, couture clothing, and overpriced food and wine. None of these activities require much investment, and although they may involve considerable employment, most of it is at low wages, for reasons explained in Chapter 8.

Reduced production by the investment-goods industries and more intensive exploitation across the rest of the economy caused a substantial increase in the share of national incomes going to the top few percent of the income distribution. On top of this, governments following neoliberal advice reduced the top rates of income tax. The combined effects doubled the real, after-inflation, income of the richest families in less than a decade. Since their consumption needs had been satisfied very handsomely before their income doubled and bank interest rates were low, much of this money found its way into asset purchases, mainly real estate and company shares. Relatively little went into productive investments, because with consumption growth subdued, there wasn't much call for new production capacity.[3]

What did happen is that asset prices rose and kept rising as the share of national income going to the richest families in the neoliberally managed countries continued to rise. Some affluent families were content to invest their surplus income in assets that seemed to be rising in value inexorably; others wished to do even better and borrowed money to gear their position in these rising markets. When private banks create money for their private clients, it will nearly always be secured on some asset; and the faster the banks create money the faster the price of the asset classes upon which the banks' advances are secured will rise. Banks were happy to make loans against assets with prices that seemed to be on a permanent growth trajectory, so new loans led to more purchases, which led to higher prices, which justified more new loans.

Such increases in asset prices are not counted as inflation by the statistician, since economic orthodoxy dictates that all asset purchase prices reflect real underlying value, and the purchase of an asset is an investment for which the expected return will be the revenue stream that asset is believed capable of generating. Speculative asset purchases where the presumptive returns will follow an increase in price cannot be explained using standard microeconomic assumptions and so are ignored.

The 1970s and After

In 1964 the Johnson administration in the United States claimed (falsely and with malice aforethought) that the North Vietnamese had made two unprovoked attacks on the USS *Maddox* in international waters, and successfully persuaded the Congress to support a virtual declaration of war in Vietnam. American efforts to assist their puppet regime in South Vietnam were not ultimately successful, in spite of an "escalation" of US efforts that eventually had 550,000 US servicemen in that country. Pursuing the war caused the death of almost 60,000 American soldiers, over a million Vietnamese soldiers, and perhaps two million Vietnamese civilians.

President L. B. Johnson saw himself as a social reformer in the tradition of President F. D. Roosevelt, and his vision of a "Great Society" was not compatible with running a major war, particularly if he did not raise taxes. The combination caused an increase in US budget deficits and a rise in its external debt. For inscrutable Gallic reasons, French president Charles de Gaulle chose this period to attack the US dollar by converting part of his country's foreign exchange reserves to gold.

The Johnson administration, and the Nixon administration that succeeded it in 1969, ran deficits on a modest scale compared to the Confederacy in the US Civil War or the Weimar Republic in the 1920s, but even so, both fiscal and monetary policies were stimulatory at a time of full employment. One effect was gradually increasing consumer price inflation, while much of the excess money was diverted into speculative investment in property and shares, inflating bubbles in both. Inflation rose to uncomfortable levels, prompting President Nixon to impose temporary price controls on the United States in 1972.

America's exit from Vietnam and tighter monetary policy prevented inflation from accelerating after Nixon's price controls were lifted, but it remained higher than it had been until the "oil shock" of 1973, when the Arab oil producers launched a boycott of the US (and Holland!) to support Egypt's attempt to evict the Israelis from the Sinai desert. The boycott and the conversion of the Organization of Petroleum Exporting Countries (OPEC) from an impotent debating society to an effective manager of output levels led to crude oil prices rising threefold with knock-on effects on general price levels in most developed countries.

In turn, this created massive trade imbalances: most of the world's productive capacity remained in the United States, Japan, and Western Europe, but a substantial slice of global spending power now moved to Iraq, Iran, and Saudi Arabia. None of these countries had a middle class with the income and inclination to buy the consumer goods and services that the developed economies were set up to produce, and most of the increased wealth found its way into the hands of corrupt dictators and royal families. Some of it was spent on racehorses, gambling, and military purchases, but a lot of it was simply hoarded.

In quantity terms, demand for consumer goods and services ceased growing, and so the companies making consumer goods and delivering consumer services cut back on their investment plans. As Keynes had predicted, this led to unemployment in the investment goods industries, and if anything, a slight contraction of demand for consumer products. The United States and Western Europe experienced rising unemployment that, nevertheless, remained far lower than the levels regarded as "full employment" today. This increase in unemployment, coming after twenty years of full employment, was fiercely resented, and the mildly left-wing governments of Callaghan in Britain and Carter in the United States lost elections to Thatcher and Reagan respectively.

The 1980s

The Thatcher and Reagan governments acted on the belief that inflation was a major problem and that it was caused by excessive wage rises. In this they were continuing the policies originally adopted by the Carter and Callaghan governments on the advice of Friedman. Friedman argued that inflation was a consequence of the failure of the governments of the developed countries to control their money supplies. He further argued that lax governments had brought on the crisis by permitting unemployment to fall below the Non Accelerating Inflation Rate of Unemployment (NAIRU); and while most Western governments had had a commitment to full employment from the end of World War II, they now redefined "full" as any level of employment where unemployment rates were above NAIRU, which was variously estimated at levels between 5 and 10 percent.

The Thatcher and Reagan governments adopted Friedman's ideas with considerably more enthusiasm than their predecessors and took no action as unemployment rose toward 10 percent. They took no steps to correct the trade imbalances triggered by the first oil shock and accelerated by the second oil shock in 1979; rather, their aggressive monetary policies raised the relative price of the US dollar and British pound to levels that devastated the exporting and import-competing industries in their countries. Both Thatcher and Reagan persisted with Friedman's policies for almost three years before quietly relaxing the monetary constraints they had imposed at his suggestion. Their labor market policies continued to reflect his view that high unemployment was needed to control inflation.

Relaxing the monetary constraints increased the amount of money available, but most of the additional money flowed into asset purchases, triggering a massive stock-market bubble that burst in 1987. Too little found its way into productive investment; the residue supported ongoing price inflation at a modest level, but still higher than that experienced during the 1960s or in most countries in the period since 1992.

Both Reagan and Thatcher promoted savagely anti-trade-union policies, stating that this was necessary to preserve the modest reduction in the level of inflation that their flirtation with monetarism had achieved. Reagan destroyed the air traffic controllers' union PATCO after it started a strike, sacking all its members and replacing them initially with military air traffic controllers and eventually with new hires. Thatcher fought a year-long battle with the National Union of Miners, in the end utterly crushing the union and commencing the dismantling of the UK coal industry.

In 1990 the United States led a UN-authorized force to evict the Iraqis from Kuwait, in the process forcing up the price of crude oil; and since the increase in military spending was not offset by increased taxation or by borrowing from the public, inflation began to rise toward unacceptable levels. Alan Greenspan, then chairman of the US Federal Reserve, forced interest rates up to the point that investment fell and a global recession commenced, and since the recovery from that recession, inflation in the developed countries has remained low.

Neither Thatcher nor Reagan nor their successors, John Major and then Tony Blair in the United Kingdom and President G. H. W. Bush and then Bill Clinton in the United States, took any steps to encourage manufacturing investment in their countries, ostensibly to free resources for the development of service industries but with a subtext of discouraging the growth of workplaces favorable to trade unionism. Both the United States and the United Kingdom began running substantial trade deficits as their run-down domestic manufacturing sectors could no longer meet their domestic demand for manufactured products.

Initially the lost production moved to Japan and Western Europe; but when Deng Xiaoping became China's supreme leader and opened China to foreign investment, a steadily increasing fraction of US and British demand was met from China, and those of the displaced British and American manufacturing workers who found new employment did so in insecure and low-paid service jobs.

The Great Moderation

The period from the end of the Greenspan recession in 1993 to the onset of the Great Recession in 2007 was described by neoliberal economists as the Great Moderation: consumer price inflation in the developed countries remained low while unemployment did not become unacceptably high. Underneath the calm surface, a huge bubble of debt was slowly inflating, and its bursting in 2007 triggered the Great Recession.

The theories that had dominated economics and driven economic policy over this period were mercilessly skewered by John Quiggin in his book *Zombie Economics*[4] but like the zombies of popular fiction, these discredited theories were still used to set policy in the United Kingdom and the European Union as late as 2015. The effect, as economists as disparate as John Quiggin, Paul Krugman, Joseph Stiglitz, and Steve Keen pointed out, was to turn the Great Recession into a new Great Depression in the countries affected.

During the Great Moderation, central bankers in the developed countries generally followed the example of Alan Greenspan. They kept a fierce eye on consumer price inflation while they totally ignored asset price inflation. As huge bubbles developed in dot-com shares in the late 1990s and in real estate through the whole period, they benignly assumed that these unheard-of prices reflected real values.

Worse, when the dot-com bubble burst in 2000 and stock prices began to fall toward reasonable levels, Greenspan and other central bankers propped up the overexposed banks with bond purchases and accommodating interest rate cuts. Cynics in Wall Street christened this policy "The Greenspan Put": banks couldn't lose money because no matter how wild their speculations, the central bank would bail them out.

America's major banks cast all discretion aside during the period 2000–2007, creating a dazzling array of new financial instruments to keep the real estate boom going. Since at least some of these instruments involved mortgages to buyers who had little hope of paying the interest and none of repaying the principal, their value depended entirely on no one examining them too closely. When these frauds could no longer be concealed, average housing prices in the United States fell by over 30 percent, wiping several trillion dollars off the aggregate value of US housing and leaving up to half of all mortgagee households "under water" with their houses worth less than their outstanding mortgage balances. The associated collapse in the value of the securitized mortgages sent the merchant bank Lehmann Brothers bankrupt and forced several other major banks to the edge of insolvency. A total collapse of the US banking system was averted with $700 billion of taxpayers' money and over $2 trillion of cheap funds from the US Federal Reserve.

The Great Moderation turned into the Great Recession, an outcome that had been inevitable from the day that governments and banks were persuaded to abandon financial regulation and to "trust the market" to regulate itself. The invisible hand proved to be ineffable as well.

The Politics of Inflation

Inflation at rates of up to around 10 percent per year does little harm to wage earners and primary producers as long as the economy concerned is at or near full employment, since their nominal wages and prices will rise sufficiently to keep their real income at least steady and generally rising as well. The owners of productive assets are also unaffected by moderate inflation, since the value of their assets depends on the value of the income stream that they generate; and the nominal value of such income streams will generally increase at least as fast as the inflation rate, protecting them from real losses.

Holders of debt *are* adversely affected by inflation, since the real value of both their principal and their interest declines over time. Sympathy for the plight of debt holders is muted: both the Bible and the Quran state that accepting interest without accepting the risks associated with earning an income is usury, and displeasing to God and man. While the terms rentier and coupon-clipper[5] are less common today, they survived well into the twentieth century. Keynes, in the conclusion to his *General Theory*, proposed the "euthanasia of the rentier" as part of his program for maintaining capitalism without periodic crises. He thought that allowing a class of people to live without working and invest without accepting the associated risks was not simply unethical: it was economically unnecessary.

Overcoming the ethical, and after Keynes, the social and economic, objections to usury has required considerable political effort. Such efforts often focus on the real hardship inflation inflicts on people living off a fixed nominal income, such as the elderly maiden aunts scattered through Victorian literature. State pensions and other social security provisions, regularly adjusted for inflation, greatly reduced the incidence of such hardship as the welfare state evolved over the first three quarters of the twentieth century.

It is a measure of the success of the neoliberal counterrevolution that many developed countries' state pension schemes have been partly or wholly privatized, making increasing numbers of people dependent on investment income, much of which is based on interest-bearing securities. This has created a constituency for measures that prioritize controlling inflation over limiting unemployment and has boosted opposition to measures restoring the Keynesian consensus.

Neoliberalism displaced Keynes's (or more properly Hicks's) scheme of economic management as applied from 1945 to 1972 and replaced it with the Friedman-Hayek model. Both the Keynes and the Friedman-Hayek models are intended to control inflation, and in both cases this requires explicit or implicit management of both demand and of the money supply. The techniques applied were radically different.

Keynes prioritized full employment after inflation control; Friedman and Hayek prioritized economic freedom, endorsing Anatole France: "The law, in its majestic equality, forbids the rich as well as the poor to sleep under bridges, to beg in the streets, and to steal bread."[6]

The major policy levers prescribed by Keynes included progressive income taxes, supporting a generous social wage; effective quantitative controls over money creation by banks and other financial institutions; and substantial government infrastructure investment, ramped up as needed to limit unemployment. When demand exceeded potential supply, as in wartime, Keynes recommended forced saving, releasing the money as productive capacity rose. Keynesian policies were adopted through most of the developed world over the years from 1946 to 1972, and as far as most people were concerned, these policies were wildly successful.

Most economists had predicted a recession following the end of World War II, because every major conflict since the Napoleonic Wars had been followed by a recession as demobilized soldiers entered the labor market and orders for munitions and military equipment dried up. Following Keynes's advice most Allied governments had largely funded the war by the sale of war bonds, and in the late 1940s, consumers spent these savings while factories converted or reconverted to civilian use and churned out consumer products. Demobilization caused barely a blip in the unemployment rate, which rapidly sank to between 2 and 2.5 percent in Britain, and slightly higher in the United States, and stayed there until the 1970s.

There was a brief burst of inflation in the early 1950s when the US government led a United Nations mission to defend South Korea: the Truman administration was unwilling to admit that it had entered a long and costly war[7] and so delayed adopting the policies needed to limit demand.

From the end of active hostilities in Korea in 1953 to the inflation induced by the United States' involvement in the Vietnam War in the mid- to late 1960s, the developed world enjoyed an unparalleled period of prosperity, with low inflation, rapidly rising living standards, reducing inequality, and negligible unemployment. Youth unemployment now plagues most developed countries; during the 1950s and 1960s firms sent recruiters to schools to sign up leavers, so desperate were they for staff.

The same period saw the completion of the US Interstate Highway Network, the national electricity grid in the United Kingdom, and many other major infrastructure projects in all the countries of the developed world. Huge strides were made towards equalizing opportunity, with free higher education in the United Kingdom and Pell grants in the United States greatly increasing the number of people enjoying the benefits of higher education.

The US intervention in Vietnam from 1964 to 1973 led to a huge demand overhang in the United States where President Johnson attempted the impossible task of fighting a major war, introducing major social reforms, and not raising taxes or taking any of the other measures that could have kept overall demand within the productive capacity of the US economy. The gap between demand and US productive capacity led to a sharply increased inflation rate.

Inflation remained stubbornly high throughout the 1980s, in spite of the adoption of Friedman's recommended policies to control it, tipping Britain and the United States into a recession in 1981–83. The economies of the English-speaking countries proved much less sensitive to the short-term interest rate than Friedman had predicted, and inflation was finally eliminated when Alan Greenspan, then chairman of the US Federal Reserve, raised the short-term interest rate as high as 18 percent. This triggered a major recession in 1991–92, one of the effects of which was the election of Bill Clinton as president of the United States at the expense of George H. W. Bush; but consumer price inflation fell toward 2 percent and did not return to its previous levels when the economies recovered.

Notes

1. Iacocca & Novak (1984). This is a relatively old example, but using a more current one without breaching someone's commercial confidence could be difficult.
2. Blas (2012).
3. Wisman (2014) discusses the role inequality played among the causes of the Great Depression, developing a similar argument.
4. Quiggin (2010).
5. Rentier: from the French, meaning someone living off fixed interest investments. Until relatively recently many bonds were issued with a set of dated coupons attached: the holder could present each coupon on its due date but could also sell some or all of them at a discount to meet a cash requirement.
6. France (1894).
7. Hostilities commenced in June 1950 and an armistice was agreed in July 1953. At the time of writing, no final agreement to end the war has been concluded.

7

The Great Recession and the Eurozone Crisis

Stock prices have reached what looks like a permanently high plateau. I do not feel there will be soon if ever a 50 or 60 point break from present levels, such as [various bears] have predicted. I expect to see the stock market a good deal higher within a few months.
—Irving Fisher (October 17, 1929)

How the Scene Was Set

At the time that this book was written, much of the developed world had been in a state of crisis or near crisis since 2007. Tens of thousands of small and medium businesses in Europe and North America had been bankrupted while tens of millions of people had been thrown out of work. By the end of 2014, it was clear that the United States and Britain had emerged from the Global Financial Crisis, but much of Europe was still mired in it.

The deep roots of the current crises can be traced back to the Protestant Reformation of the sixteenth century and the early liberals of the seventeenth: crises are contemporaneous and intrinsic to what we perceive as modern civilization.

The Reformation started a transition in the relationship between individuals and authority from positive to negative. In a feudal society custom, the law and the church determined what people must do, given their station in life. A peasant's son must become a peasant; a gentleman's son would be a gentleman. In a modern society, the church is no longer a monolithic source of authority, while custom and the law prohibit various acts and forms of behavior, leaving men and women free to do as they please as long as they do not contravene those prohibitions; "must" became "must not."

121

From the late seventeenth to the early nineteenth centuries, commercial practice was also transformed, starting in Britain but rapidly followed in North America. The guilds were reduced to charitable and ceremonial organizations, the Statute of Apprentices was first weakened and then repealed, and contract law became the major and in some case the sole legal basis of commercial relationships.[1]

Liberalization proceeded through the nineteenth and into the twentieth centuries: slavery was abolished; trade unions were legalized; married women were allowed to retain their property; the franchise was extended to all adults; and the principle, if not always the practice, of equal pay for equal work became generally accepted.

At every stage of the liberalization process, Jeremiahs predicted social and economic disaster, but such disasters were slow to appear. The basic appeal of the liberal model is simple: if two people agree on a bargain, and no force or fraud is involved, why should the state interfere? Social liberalism takes the same line: what consenting adults do in private is no matter for the law.

Limitations on Liberalism

A little thought backed up by history reveals that private bargains can certainly have public consequences warranting interference by the state.

The first and most obvious is when the parties to a private bargain intend some activity contrary to law, like burglary or fraud. The evolving law attacked such contracts from two directions: a contract to commit a crime or to outrage public policy was void in civil law, and purporting to enter such a contract was the crime of criminal conspiracy.

A second arises from imbalances of power: when masters bargain with servants over wages, the masters seldom get the worst of the bargain. Adam Smith wrote:

> What are the common wages of labor, depends everywhere upon the contract usually made between those two parties, whose interests are by no means the same. The workmen desire to get as much, the masters to give as little as possible. The former are disposed to combine in order to raise, the latter in order to lower the wages of labor.
>
> It is not, however, difficult to foresee which of the two parties must, upon all ordinary occasions, have the advantage in the dispute, and force the other into a compliance with their terms. The masters, being fewer in number, can combine much more easily; and the law, besides, authorizes, or at least does not prohibit their combinations, while it prohibits those of the workmen. We have no acts of parliament against combining to lower the price of work; but many against combining

to raise it. In all such disputes the masters can hold out much longer. A landlord, a farmer, a master manufacturer, a merchant, though they did not employ a single workman, could generally live a year or two upon the stocks which they have already acquired. Many workmen could not subsist a week, few could subsist a month, and scarce any a year without employment. In the long run the workman may be as necessary to his master as his master is to him; but the necessity is not so immediate.

We rarely hear, it has been said, of the combinations of masters, though frequently of those of workmen. But whoever imagines, upon this account, that masters rarely combine, is as ignorant of the world as of the subject.[2]

The Combination Laws to which Smith refers were repealed in the later nineteenth century, and unionized workers continued to acquire rights for collective bargaining, backed up by strike action, until the 1970s. Then politicians influenced by neoliberalism began passing increasingly restrictive laws to limit the effectiveness of trade unions and discourage union membership. Extreme neoliberal polemicists justified such policies on the basis that masters and servants, now renamed employers and employees, had equal bargaining power since job seekers who could not agree on terms of employment with one employer would have plenty of others to choose from. The contempt with which Smith dismissed such arguments is no less justified today.

A third possibility that worried Smith was the joint stock company, familiar to us as limited liability companies and by far the most common form of business structure in the developed world today. Smith was concerned that separating ownership from control would lead to poor decision making:

Joint stock companies, established by Royal Charter or by Act of Parliament, differ in several respects, not only from regulated companies, but from private copartneries.

First, in a private copartnery, no partner, without the consent of the company, can transfer his share to another person, or introduce a new member into the company. Each member, however, may, upon proper warning, withdraw from the copartnery, and demand payment from them of his share of the common stock. In a joint stock company, on the contrary, no member can demand payment of his share from the company; but each member can, without their consent, transfer his share to another person, and thereby introduce a new member. The value of a share in a joint stock is always the price which it will bring in the market; and this may be either greater or less, in any proportion, than the sum which its owner stands credited for in the stock of the company.

Secondly, in a private copartnery, each partner is bound for the debts contracted by the company to the whole extent of his fortune. In a joint stock company, on the contrary, each partner is bound only to the extent of his share.

The trade of a joint stock company is always managed by a court of directors. This court, indeed, is frequently subject, in many respects, to the control of a general court of proprietors. But the greater part of those proprietors seldom pretend to understand anything of the business of the company, and when the spirit of faction happens not to prevail among them, give themselves no trouble about it, but receive contentedly such half-yearly or yearly dividend as the directors think proper to make to them. This total exemption from trouble and from risk, beyond a limited sum, encourages many people to become adventurers in joint stock companies, who would, upon no account, hazard their fortunes in any private copartnery. Such companies, therefore, commonly draw to themselves much greater stocks than any private copartnery can boast of. . . . The directors of such companies, however, being the managers rather of other people's money than of their own, it cannot well be expected that they should watch over it with the same anxious vigilance with which the partners in a private copartnery frequently watch over their own. Like the stewards of a rich man, they are apt to consider attention to small matters as not for their master's honor, and very easily give themselves a dispensation from having it. Negligence and profusion, therefore, must always prevail, more or less, in the management of the affairs of such a company.[3]

At the time Smith wrote, new joint stock companies required an Act of Parliament to exempt them from the Bubble Act, but by the mid-nineteenth century this requirement had been abandoned in most countries, and the formation of a new company only required the payment of a modest fee to the appropriate registry. Smith was concerned about "negligence and profusion," terms that could be used to describe the wildly excessive salaries claimed by the senior executives of many large companies today; but experience has shown that outright fraud is far from uncommon in corporate management. The temptation arising from access to large amounts of other people's money with few constraints on what may be done with it has proved irresistible to many corporate executives.

Attempts to prevent corporate fraud are often resisted strenuously. It will be argued that the behavior of a few "bad apples" does not justify prescriptive regulations that all the companies in a particular industry, or all companies, will have to obey. If people really were selfish and rational, then their decision to obey or disobey the rules of proper conduct would depend on the chance of getting caught and the cost of the punishment. A selfish, rational individual will break the rules when the gain from doing so exceeds the cost of the expected punishment. Studies purporting to determine an "ideal" level of regulation and enforcement are commonplace in the economics literature.

The argument against effective regulation generally takes the form that regulations impose costs on those who would have done "the right thing" in their absence, and the gain from sanctioning the bad apples is less than the cost inflicted on the good ones when added to the cost of operating the regulatory apparatus.

In the wake of the Great Recession in the United States (2008–2010), it became obvious that nearly all the major financial institutions had participated in, or at least knowingly benefited from, major frauds. The Dodd-Frank Act, passed in 2010, sought to outlaw the most egregious of these frauds; but at the end of 2010, control of the US House of Representatives passed to the conservative Republican Party, and every attempt to implement the Dodd-Frank Act, whether by appointing directors of the administering agencies or passing regulations, was bitterly opposed. While several billions of dollars have been paid by major US banks to avoid prosecution for offences, not a single individual has even been charged with instigating or tolerating fraudulent behavior, much less convicted, at the time of writing.

Enter Chaos and Complexity

Let us assume for a moment that we could painlessly and at no cost ensure that no bargains involved force, fraud, or asymmetric power, and that all employees of all corporations were diligent and honest. Everyone would be pursuing their self-interest, but would simultaneously be observing "the rules of the game."[4] Surely, von Mises and subsequently Hayek and Friedman argued, this would lead to an optimal equilibrium, where everyone was as well-off as possible without making someone else worse off.

Unfortunately, mathematicians have proved that any system of more than two interacting components will have multiple equilibria, or more properly, multiple attractors. Death is the only stable equilibrium point; while a system lives and entropy increases, it will pass through an infinity of states, never repeating itself, much less coming to a stable optimum.

An economy has more than two interacting agents (a lot more) and is therefore a complex system that will be changing all the time. The

125

overall state of an economy is described by figures such as GDP, average wages, hours worked, unemployment, inflation, and many more. During the nineteenth century, the developed economies of Western Europe and North America went through crises where GDP fell and unemployment rose, sometimes quite dramatically.

Some of these crises appeared to be caused by events outside the productive economy: the first of them, immediately following the end of the Napoleonic Wars, was clearly triggered by the rapid demobilization of the armies and navies that had been involved in the conflict and the drying up of orders for munitions and military supplies. Some, like the 1840s and 1890s, had no obvious external cause.

Much of the popularity of Marxism during the nineteenth and early twentieth centuries was based on Marx's explanation of economic crises as being intrinsic to the operation of a capitalist economy, and Marx's claim to have proposed an effective solution.

A devoted minority of economists still uphold Marx's claim that crises were the result of overproduction, or at least, overinvestment in productive capacity. "Austrian" economists, who generally regard themselves as the complete opposite of Marxists, see overinvestment as the proximal cause of crises. The majority of economists, or at least all the economists whose papers appear in the leading economics journals, follow the neoclassical paradigm and describe an imaginary world in which endogenous crises, those arising out of the normal operation of an economy, are impossible.

The Great Depression

The events that followed the Wall Street Crash in 1929 and the failure of the Austrian bank Kreditanstalt in 1930 presented a mortal challenge to orthodox economic opinion. The orthodox knew that shocks, such as a major crop failure or demobilization at the end of a war could trigger a crisis, but they believed that such crises would rapidly end and prosperity would return. Among the many people ruined by the Great Crash and the ensuing depression was the economist Irving Fisher (1867–1947), who initially believed that the Great Crash was just a minor correction, and instead of selling his investments, he borrowed money to buy even more stocks.

In the event, Fisher did not live long enough to see stock prices return to their 1929 highs: it didn't happen until the 1950s. He did formulate his debt-deflation hypothesis, which many consider one of the major reasons for the depth of the Great Depression and the slow recovery from it. Fisher observed that most businesses carried substantial debt and that this was defined in nominal, not real terms. If prices were to fall, businesses would earn less revenue and probably make lower profits, even if they sold the same volume of goods and services; but their debts and interest payments would become more onerous, discouraging investment and, in severe cases, bankrupting vulnerable businesses.

Some authors seem to consider that Fisher's debt-deflation hypothesis provides an alternative to Keynes's explanation of depressions in terms of deficient demand; but there is no inherent contradiction. In Keynes's view, demand insufficiency was caused by investment insufficiency, itself caused by an insufficiency of animal spirits. The spirits of the owners and managers of businesses trapped by debt-deflation and desperately struggling to generate enough cash to stay solvent will be more glacial than animal.

Crises, depressions, and recessions are all manifestations of deficiencies of demand; but when accompanied by deflation as in the Great Depression, they are likely to be both more severe and more intractable. The end of the Great Depression was an even more dramatic confirmation of Keynes's theory: governments that had been panicked over tiny budget deficits let defense spending rise until taxation only recovered 40 percent of outgoings. Governments that had made largely ineffectual gestures at relieving unemployment had to address the problem of labor shortages.

The Keynesian Revolution

Keynes's explanation of the Great Depression was so persuasive that even rivals such as Lionel Robbins pronounced themselves convinced. Robbins had set up the London School of Economics (LSE) as a rival to Cambridge generally and Keynes particularly, and even engaged Frederick Hayek to exert a countervailing influence; so with Robbins's defection to the Keynesian camp, there was no credible opposition in the English-speaking universe to Keynes's ideas.[5] The *Ordo* movement in Germany and the Austrian school consisting of Hayek, von Mises, and von Mises's small coterie of devoted followers remained opposed to Keynesian ideas but had almost no influence on the US or British governments over the period 1940–1970. Keynes's advice to the US and British governments during World War II and his role in negotiating the postwar settlement was so valued that he was created a baron with a seat in the House of Lords.

Governments generally accepted Keynes's advice that economies could enter an "unemployment equilibrium,"[6] a state in which large-scale unemployment might persist indefinitely. Governments influenced by Keynes recognized the need for fiscal stimulus—government spending—if demand was weak. They also accepted Keynes's analysis of the effect of interest rates, and so recognized the need to regulate them to prevent an economy overheating and igniting inflation. The Great Depression had been exacerbated, and possibly even caused, by the reckless behavior of banks, and so governments instituted banking regulation with, among other aims, the intention of preventing banks taking risks with their depositors' money.

In Britain the government limited itself to closely regulating banking, both to control the money supply and to limit the risks that banks took. Banking became a secure but boring form of employment, with an established career path, a generous pension on retirement, and access to cheap credit and other fringe benefits to compensate for relatively low wages. Promotion was almost entirely from within (and almost entirely male), and most chief executives of banks had started their first job in a junior position at the same bank.

In the United States, distant echoes of the bimetallism[7] controversy lingered, and while some of the New York banks were very large and prosperous, they were barred from taking over smaller banks and from setting up branches in competition with the many surviving small-town banks. Regulation of the banking system in the United States was largely entrusted to the Federal Deposit Insurance Corporation (FDIC), which had the power to take over insolvent small banks and compensate their depositors up to a fairly generous limit.

Keynes had been relaxed about trade unions, believing that employers would not agree to unreasonable wage claims unless control of the interest rate had become so slack as to permit inflation: he was aware that employers who saw no difficulty in raising their prices would not resist ambitious wage claims strenuously. Partly in consequence the legal restrictions of trade unions were relaxed and explicit antiunion activity by employers suppressed. In Britain a system of wages boards set minimum rates in most industries.

In the United States, a federal minimum wage was established in 1938 after a number of previous attempts had been invalidated by a furiously conservative Supreme Court, and it was raised a number of times in real terms. According to the Bureau of Labor Statistics, it reached its highest real value in 1968, as the long boom was reaching its end. A number of states have set higher minimum wage rates, some indexed to inflation to maintain their real value.

The combination of regulation, protected union activity, and stable interest rates backed up by active demand management policies ensured that the wage share of national income in the developed countries was maintained—in President Kennedy's words, the rising tide lifted all boats—and income inequality fell. Between 1946 and 1973, adherence to the Keynesian system saw a period of unprecedented general prosperity in the developed democracies in Europe, North America, and Australasia.

Turbulence

The Keynesian long boom started to unravel in the 1970s. The proximate causes varied across countries.

In the United States, the Johnson, and then the Nixon, administrations pursued a war in Vietnam at enormous expense without raising taxes or taking other measures to limit the excess demand caused by deficit-financed military spending. The result, as Keynes would have predicted and Friedman did predict, was steadily increasing inflation. The Nixon administration's initial response was a price freeze, which was abandoned once Nixon had won the 1972 elections. The US Federal Reserve raised interest rates, which discouraged investment, but the US government continued to run deficits. The low level of investment led to rising unemployment, but this was not nearly sufficient to offset the effect of government deficits, so inflation and unemployment rose in parallel. This became known as "stagflation," and since Friedman was alive and Keynes wasn't, "Keynesian" policies took the blame.

In Britain the postwar Labour government had nationalized several industries, including the railways, the electricity supply industry, and the coal mining industry. All these industries were heavily unionized. The railways and the coal mines had particular problems. The railway network had been shrunk drastically after the Beeching Report[8] was implemented but still had many routes where the fares barely covered direct operating costs and the freight operations had been drastically affected by the reduction in the reach of the network. As a result, the railways required government subsidies to continue operations.

British demand for coal was dramatically reduced by the Clean Air Act of 1956, which effectively banned domestic coal fires, a response to the great smog of 1952. The discovery of North Sea Gas and its exploitation in the late 1960s and early 1970s eliminated the use of coal for gas making and the progressive adoption of gas central heating eroded the demand for "smokeless" coal for domestic heating. The British coal industry was operated by the Coal Board, an enthusiast for research and innovation and a pioneer of long wall mining. These innovations dramatically raised productivity, but the Coal Board, pressured by the government of the day, was reluctant to authorize redundancies on the scale required to bring the workforce into line with the reduced demand for coal and the new levels of productivity. The coal industry also required government subsidies.

By general British standards, neither the coal miners nor the railway workers were particularly well paid; and whereas a private employer would have insisted on reorganization and retrenchment to raise productivity before conceding wage claims, British governments of both persuasions preferred to increase subsidies than risk extremely damaging strike action. When the British Conservative government of Sir Edward Heath (1916–2005, prime minister 1970–1974) refused to accede to demands from the mine workers, the mining union launched a crippling strike, forcing the government to ration electricity. This limited most firms to three days' electricity supply per week. The Conservatives lost the ensuing election.

A combination of deficit spending—as British governments subsidized the railways and coal industry—and rising interest rates—as the government attempted to maintain the value of the pound sterling—suppressed investment and caused unemployment to rise: Britain, like the United States, entered a stagflationary period.

The Carter Democratic administration in the United States and the Callaghan Labour government in Britain faced elections in 1980 and 1979, respectively, and the combination of inflation and rising unemployment threatened their reelection prospects. Both were persuaded by Friedman and his advocates in the *Wall Street Journal* and the *Economist* magazine and elsewhere that governments could not control unemployment but they could, by limiting government expenditure and deregulating regulated industries, control inflation.

Neoliberalism Ascendant

Carter and Callaghan may have had reservations about adopting the neoliberal agenda; but their successors, Reagan and Thatcher, did not. Carter had deregulated the US airline industry; under Reagan, the regulated monopoly AT&T, which had run the US telephone system almost since Bell invented the telephone, was broken up.

In the 1980 election campaign, Reagan pointed to the rising unemployment and interest rates of the previous three years and assured voters that his program of tax cuts and deregulation would provide a painless solution to all their problems. If "government was the problem," then cutting it would be an easy solution. Carter was not helped by the Iranian hostage crisis, with a number of Americans held by Iranian revolutionaries in spite of an attempt to rescue them. Reagan won forty-four states, leaving Carter with six plus DC.

The Conservative election slogan in Britain leading up to the 1979 election was "Labour isn't working," alluding to the one million unemployed at the time: under Thatcher unemployment rapidly rose to three million and did not drop below that figure during her time in office. As a grudging concession to traditional concerns about unemployment, Mrs. Thatcher's government redefined the reported unemployment for statistical purposes several times; but no manipulation ever got the figure below three million.

Reagan and Thatcher appeared to recognize that neoliberal policies were not going to be popular and moved quite cautiously. They made modest cuts to the top rate of income tax, and in Britain compensated by raising the VAT sales tax from 7 percent to 15 percent. They each destroyed one union: PATCO, the air traffic controllers' union, in Reagan's case; and the NUM, the miner's union in Britain. Thatcher waited until her second term before making a major privatization, that of British Telecom.

Thatcher's and Reagan's immediate successors, G. H. W. Bush (b. 1924, president 1989–1993) in the United States and John Major (b. 1943, prime minister 1990–1997) in Britain plodded rather than galloped down the neoliberal path. The speed of neoliberal "reform" picked up under the Democratic administration of Bill Clinton in the United States and the Labour government under Tony Blair in the United Kingdom. Between them they set the scene for the Global Financial Crisis starting in 2007, Clinton signing the repeal of the Glass-Steagall Act and Blair instituting "light touch" (i.e., no) regulation of the London financial markets. The locks were removed from the doors of the tiger cages.

The Southeast Asian Crisis

The crisis of 1997 should have warned the world that neoliberal policies and reality were not closely related. The Asian economic crisis of 1997 was not caused by trade imbalances; rather, the countries affected were running trade surpluses. The affected countries had, under the tutelage of the IMF, deregulated their foreign exchange markets; but they had also attempted to fix their currencies' value against the US dollar, also at the instigation of the IMF. This created a speculators' paradise, and when speculation threatened to force the Thais to devalue the Baht, the IMF vigorously inflamed the crisis, enabling it to take control of the economies of Thailand, Indonesia, and South Korea. Malaysia defied the IMF and reintroduced exchange controls, and in spite of dire predictions survived the crisis largely unscathed.

The IMF, having dictated the policies that provoked the crisis then used it to inflict further neoliberal "reform" on the unfortunate countries Thailand, South Korea, and Indonesia. The IMF forced fierce retrenchment policies on Thailand and Indonesia and blackmailed South Korea into raising dollar loans at usurious rates.

Japan toyed with the idea of an Asian Monetary Fund that would stabilize the Baht, Rupiah, and Won, but gave up on the idea after a furious reaction from the United States. Klein[9] suggests that the whole crisis was arranged to force South Korea to open its capital markets to US speculators and to enable predatory US firms to buy productive assets throughout the region at distress prices. Well before Klein's book *Shock Doctrine* appeared, such theories had considerable currency in Southeast Asia.

In the aftermath of the crisis, the Southeast Asian countries, and China, appear to have decided to build up currency reserves so vast that they could shrug off any speculative attack. A small fraction of these balances has found its way into "sovereign wealth funds," which make both speculative and productive investments in other countries, but most of the money seems to have been kept in highly liquid securities and so has financed consumption spending in the United States and Britain.

Joseph Stiglitz (b. 1943) was chief economist at the World Bank from 1997 to 2000 and offered some pungent criticisms of the behavior of the IMF during the Southeast Asian crisis, leading to the termination of his appointment. If this was intended to intimidate him, it failed, and as mentioned below, he has continued to criticize both the theory and practice of neoliberalism.

The economists of the IMF, already stung by Stiglitz's criticism, could hardly ignore the fact that Malaysia defied the IMF and prospered while Thailand and Indonesia obeyed the IMF and were forced into recessions—in the case of Indonesia, destroying the Suharto government. (The Suharto government had been corrupt and brutal, but it was not the IMF's job to replace it, or to humiliate Suharto and by implication all Indonesians with a photo showing the IMF managing director Michel Camdessus standing over Suharto like a headmaster reprimanding an unruly schoolboy.) The IMF economists proved incapable of reconsidering their theories and devoted considerable effort to explaining why Malaysia was a special case. Their arguments would have been more convincing if any of them had identified Malaysia as a special case before the crisis.

Crisis Phase 1: Subprime[10]

The repeal of the Glass-Steagall Act liberated America's bankers to pursue their self-interest free from any regulatory constraints. Most central bankers adhered to neoliberal orthodoxy, which held that regulations were an unnecessary cost impost on business. Alan Greenspan, chairman of the US Federal Reserve System (1987–2006), practiced "light touch" regulation. After the crisis he said:

> One of the things that I had been almost taking as a given was that corporate executives, specifically bank executives, knew enough about their organizations and cared enough to act in the support of the solvency of their institutions. I was wrong. They did not.[11]

The best account of the subprime crisis is in Stiglitz's book *Freefall*.[12] When banks make loans they create money; and America's major bankers discovered that even when borrowers could not pay interest, a bank could make a new loan, create the money required, and pay the outstanding interest to itself from the proceeds. Interest paid this way was treated like any other payment and recorded as income, increasing the reported profit. US housing prices had been rising since the early 1990s, and so, free from any effective supervision, the banks could claim that they were not taking undue risks, but rather making huge profits that justified multimillion-dollar bonuses for their executives.

The banks were still obliged to observe the prudential standards set by the Bank of International Settlements, Basel II, and this appeared to limit their ability to lend; but with the constraints imposed by Glass-Steagall lifted, they discovered that they could package loans into marketable securities known as Collateralized Debt Obligations (CDOs), selling some of them to investors and others into "special purpose vehicles," which did not appear on their balance sheets except as obscure footnotes.

With their loan book reduced by the value of these CDO sales and after 1999, with Glass-Steagall repealed, the banks could resume lending, earn even higher profits, and pay even bigger bonuses.

By the early 2000s, bankers in the United States ran into another problem: a shortage of creditworthy applicants for loans. The solution to this problem was to subcontract the writing of mortgages to agents who earned commissions based on the aggregate value of the mortgages that they wrote, and to hint rather than to directly advise the agents that the banks did not expect credit standards to be observed too closely.

Many agents understood this to mean that they should get a loan applicant to sign a blank mortgage application leaving the agent to apply his or her imagination to the completion of messy details such as income and the list of other debts. Mortgage agents sold these "liar loans" so effectively that they acquired an acronym "NINJA" (no income, no job or assets) loans; in polite circles, they were described as "subprime," valuable only as long as real estate prices kept rising.

Meanwhile, London's "light touch" regulation appealed to the world's largest insurance company, AIG, and it set up a subsidiary to sell "credit default swaps"—insurance policies against the risk that a security might fall in value. The New York bankers packaged their NINJA loans into CDOs and added a credit default swap bought from AIG's London office. The ratings agencies obligingly gave these compound CDOs AAA—as safe as government—ratings, meaning that they could be sold to investors such as local governments and pension funds that were legally barred from taking risks.

Nobody bothered to notice that AIG had not reinsured or otherwise hedged these credit default swaps and that its own reserves were hopelessly inadequate to the cover the risks.

Reality began to reassert itself when on August 9, 2007, the major French bank BNP Paribas suspended payment on three of its funds because of doubts about the value of the subprime mortgages underpinning the CDOs held by them. BNP Paribas was not the only affected bank: many banks in the United States and elsewhere had included subprime CDOs as part of their capital base, and had these securities been "marked to market" and their actual (very low) value acknowledged, the banks concerned would have been in public breach of the most basic BIS rules.

As mentioned in Chapter 4 above, money lent by one bank may be deposited in another, and so banks participate in an overnight "repo" market, making loans to each other to keep every bank's loans and deposits in balance. BNP Paribas's announcement caused every bank to study the securities in its capital base and the assets against which it had made advances, most of them discovering at least some subprime rubbish and some of them finding lots of it. Every bank suddenly looked at the overnight market as a trap, where other banks might pledge worthless securities and make their own position worse. Almost immediately the overnight interest rates on the repo (interbank) market shot up, and some banks found it impossible to find a counterparty at any rate.

The global banking system staggered on until in March 2008 the New York merchant bank Bear Stearns was on the point of failure; another bank was persuaded to take it over with a $28 billion advance from the US Federal Reserve. In the following months, the two American mortgage refinancing firms Fannie Mae and Freddie Mac were rendered technically insolvent and were effectively nationalized; and on September 15, the merchant bank Lehman Brothers collapsed, triggering a global financial crisis.

It turned out that the British and American governments had not forgotten the lessons of 1930 and set out to rescue their banking system energetically. The British government nationalized Northern Rock and Royal Bank of Scotland and paid Lloyds-TSB to take over HBOS, the former Halifax Building Society. The Bush administration in the United States set up a $700 billion troubled assets relief program (TARP) to restore liquidity to the major US banks while the US Federal Reserve advanced several trillion dollars to the banking system against dubious security.

As in 1930 the banking crisis spread rapidly to the rest of the economy; but unlike 1930 the governments in the major countries launched stimulus programs to create new job opportunities. Only China and Australia launched programs sufficiently powerful to prevent a sharp rise in unemployment, but even so, unemployment in Britain and the United States never approached the levels seen in the Great Depression.

The United States and Britain successfully stabilized their banking systems. Although large numbers of pounds and dollars were involved, the sums were only a fraction of each nation's GDP and did not send government debt levels uncomfortably high, a fact masked by much political rhetoric. As sovereign states with their own currency, both the United States and Britain could, *in extremis*, have printed sufficient money to recapitalize their banks. The banking bailouts were unpopular: countries that officially lauded private enterprise as the risk-taking part of the economy found themselves in the awkward position of having to use public money to rescue bankrupt private companies. Those who supported the banking bailouts argued that the banks were "too big to fail"—that the regrettable decision to bail them out was preferable to letting them crash and burn the economy with them.

By mid-2010 the US and British economies had stabilized and begun to grow, with unemployment slowly falling, but the US recovery was not fast enough to save the Obama administration from a "shellacking" in the 2010 midterm elections, with a new Republican majority in the House of Representatives determined to reduce debt and shrink the size of government, irrespective of the effect on unemployment and economic growth. The administration resisted these efforts but could not avoid some cuts, and US growth remained tepid until it began to accelerate at the end of 2013.

In May 2010 the British Conservative Party under David Cameron won more seats than Labour in the General Election and, in coalition with the Liberal-Democrats, formed a government. The new government abandoned the stimulus policies it had inherited on the specious grounds that government spending would "crowd out" private investment and that government debt damaged "confidence." The American economist and liberal commentator Paul Krugman derided these policies as based on a belief in the "confidence fairy," but the British government plowed on with cuts and privatizations. Krugman predicted that these policies would send Britain into recession, which they did; but the government ignored such criticism. In 2013 the British economy showed some slight signs of life, and the government claimed vindication. Neither debt nor the deficit had actually been reduced, and Britain's recovery was far weaker than the weak American one, but neoliberal ideologues are immune to evidence, and the Conservatives promised that, if reelected in 2015, they would implement even more austerity.

What is truly depressing is that the opposition Labour Party endorsed austerity and refused to commit to repealing egregiously unfair and economically ineffective policies such as the bedroom tax levied on public authority tenants. Not surprisingly, the Conservatives under Cameron won the election.

Crisis Phase 2: The Eurozone[13]

The link between the subprime crisis, a US phenomenon, and the Eurozone crisis, may have been indirect.

The seventeen members of the common currency block, the "Eurozone," had given up the right to print their own money or set their own interest rates. The ECB set a single interest rate for the Eurozone, which might have worked in theory but in practice it was too low to prevent huge real estate bubbles from developing in Ireland and Spain. All bubbles in a capitalist system are financed by credit and they are, to a point, self-sustaining. Recent price rises are held to justify the expectation of future price rises and new loans to finance new purchases.

In Ireland and Spain, the local banks had made generous loans to developers who had used the proceeds to buy land and build houses; but the terms of these loans were often so generous that the covering assets would not actually match the loans in value until the houses were built and were selling at the forecast prices. When BNP Paribus's actions triggered a freeze in the repo (overnight) market, banks across Europe became reluctant to write new loans; consequently the potential buyers for houses on the newly developed estates in Ireland and Spain could not obtain mortgages and so could not complete purchases.

The developers, unable to meet their repayment schedules, defaulted and the banks affected seized assets that were almost worthless: some had completed houses that could only be sold for a fraction of the anticipated value; some had houses that had been completed but then severely damaged by tradespeople removing copper pipes and wiring and sometimes architectural features such as staircases to satisfy their unpaid accounts; and some that had never been completed.

Every loan is an asset of a bank, and to satisfy the basic balance sheet equation, the assets of a bank must be equal to the sum of its liabilities and its equity, including its reserves. If an asset must be written off, the bank's equity is reduced by the same amount; and if sufficient loans are deemed unrecoverable, a bank can only pay out any depositors who ask for their money by using the balances owed to other depositors, a criminal act in most jurisdictions.

When the housing bubbles burst, first in Ireland, then in Spain, the major banks in those countries were forced to write off around 30 percent of their outstanding loans; and since their equity before the crash had been around 5 percent of the size of their loan book, their governments had the choice of recapitalizing them or telling the depositors that they had lost a third of their money. The amounts required were of the order of half of Spain's GDP and the whole of Ireland's. Nonetheless, the fear of a financial meltdown and pressure from the ECB forced Spain and Ireland to recapitalize their banks, but since they had given up the right to print their own money when they joined the Eurozone, they had to borrow the required money from German,

Dutch, and French banks. This forced total government borrowing in Ireland and Spain from a comfortable faction of GDP to a level in breach of the Maastricht Treaty, and the ECB and the European Commission demanded that they started paying down this debt by increasing taxation, reducing pensions, and cutting government services.

Many Eurozone countries (not including Spain) had run budget deficits in the years before 2009. These deficits should have been financed by sales of bonds to the public with a national reserve bank buying and selling these bonds in order to maintain appropriate levels of liquidity; but under the Eurozone treaty, the zone members had surrendered the right to operate reserve banks in this way, and the European Central Bank was prohibited from doing so. It was simpler to borrow from banks, not necessarily their national ones; but the various banks created the money required.

A further complication was trade imbalances: in theory, if not always in practice, countries with trade surpluses will see their currencies appreciate, which will eventually restore balance. In the Eurozone such currency adjustments were impossible, and trade surpluses, mainly those of Germany, the Netherlands, and France, were balanced by loans from banks in these countries to banks in those with a trade deficit. If a Greek family bought a new Volkswagen or Mercedes, their dealer paid for the car with a loan drawn on a Greek bank; the Greek bank would then pledge this loan (its new asset) to a German bank in return for the cash needed to pay the German manufacturer.

Experienced macroeconomists such as Krugman and Stiglitz argued that the austerity measures demanded by the ECB and EU would force the countries concerned into recession, cutting net government revenue faster than the tax increases and program cuts increased it, and the net effect would be higher, not lower debt and deficits. EU economists, headed by Olli Rehn, the European Commissioner for Economic and Monetary Affairs and the Euro and a vice president of the European Commission, ignored this advice. Instead they relied on the work of Alesina and Ardagna and Reinhart and Rogoff. Alesina and Ardagna claimed that cutting government spending in a recession led to rising output, and purported to prove it by citing a number of cases where they claimed that this had happened. Reinhart and Rogoff claimed that if a country let its debt-to-GDP ratio exceed 90 percent, economic growth would cease.

Economists reviewing the work of Alesina and Ardagna discovered that only one of the cases that they cited did not directly contradict their conclusions, while the rest actually supported Krugman and Stiglitz. Several economists tried to reproduce Reinhart and Rogoff's results without success, and eventually a graduate student obtained access to their Excel database and showed that their conclusion depended on a programming error—a bug.

The total destruction of their theoretical platform seems to have had no effect on the advice given by Rehn and like-minded economists, suggesting that their agenda has nothing to do with fostering economic growth and a great deal to do with their detestation of the welfare state. This was confirmed when France implemented budget-balancing measures by raising taxes while preserving social benefits. This earned France's president Hollande an extraordinary spray from Rehn. Rehn's half-hearted retraction a few days later changed nothing.

Mark Blyth, in his book *Austerity: The History of a Dangerous Idea*,[14] suggests an additional reason behind the brutal austerity currently being inflicted on Greece, Spain, and Portugal: it is that German, French, and Dutch banks hold so much of these countries' debt as well as Italy's as a result of financing trade deficits and bank bailouts that a default by these countries would create a banking crisis too great for even the German government, much less the French or Dutch governments, to handle while remaining within the Eurozone.

The rhetoric, particularly in Germany, is all about austerity being an appropriate punishment for past profligacy; but the reality is that the German and to some extent the Dutch and French governments have enlisted the elites of the so-called PIIGS (Portugal, Ireland, Italy, Greece, and Spain) to subject their population to brutal and ultimately self-defeating austerity in a desperate attempt to keep the Euro project alive.

The austerity program has been a total failure in terms of reducing debt and deficits, but it has caused extreme distress, with unemployment levels over 20 percent and youth unemployment over 50 percent, in Spain, Greece, and Portugal. It is hard to see democracy surviving under such stresses, and antiausterity parties are gaining ground across Europe. Some share attributes such as xenophobia with the historic far right; others have reverted to left policies as understood before the mid-1970s, and are described as "far left" in consequence.

Syriza, a left-oriented antiausterity party, won the largest vote in the Greek elections of January 2015 and formed a government. Its leadership immediately came under pressure from the German government and the EU Directorate to repudiate their election promises and continue to enforce austerity. Ominously, the neofascist Golden

Dawn party came third in the Greek election and stands to be the main beneficiary of any backsliding by Syriza.

Blyth reminds us that in the 1928 German elections, the Nazi Party had won just 8 percent of the popular vote; but as the Depression bit, the Socialists failed to oppose Chancellor Brüning's austerity program of tax increases and program cuts while bankruptcies and unemployment soared; by 1933 the Nazi vote had risen to 33 percent, and Hitler had become chancellor.[15] In Germany the myth that Hitler's rise was a consequence of the great inflation, which ended with the currency reforms of 1923, is used to justify enforcing austerity on the Eurozone. Myths have great persuasive power, even when, as in this case, they are clearly disproved by the historic record.

To paraphrase George Santayana, those who don't learn from history are condemned to repeat it.

Perhaps we should hope for the more cheerful outcome attributed to Marx: "History always repeats itself, the first time as tragedy, the second time as farce." A party led by the comedian Beppo Grillo won over a quarter of the votes in the 2013 Italian election, offering some hope that Marx, on this occasion at least, was the better prophet.

Notes

1. Atiyah (1979).
2. Smith (1776 Bk I Ch. 8).
3. Smith (1776 Bk V Ch I Pt 3).
4. Friedman's term.
5. Wapshott (2011).
6. Complexity theorists would say that the economy could be in the basin of an involuntary unemployment attractor. Economies, even those in deep depression, are not in an equilibrium state.
7. See page 75.
8. Beeching (1963): Sir Richard (later Lord) Beeching recommended a drastic shrinking of the British railway network, closing many branch lines and links between second-tier towns. His recommendations were substantially, but not completely, implemented and have been partially reversed in later years.
9. Klein (2007).
10. Substantial parts of the following section initially appeared in *Dissent* Magazine (43, Summer 2013–2014).
11. Rose (2011).
12. Stiglitz (2010).
13. Substantial parts of the following section initially appeared in *Dissent* Magazine (43, Summer 2013–2014). Podkaminern (2015) offers a post-Keynesian perspective on the crisis illustrated by several statistical charts.
14. Blyth (2013).
15. Blyth (2013: pp. 193–197).

8

The Labor Market

What profit hath a man of all his labor which he taketh under the sun?
—Ecclesiastes 1:3

Classical Theory

Smith noted that there was an effective minimum wage set by childhood mortality. Only one child in two was expected to reach adulthood at the time that he was writing, so if wages were less than that needed to keep a family of husband, wife, and four children alive, the laboring classes could not reproduce themselves.[1] Smith noted that particularly arduous or disgusting work could command a premium; and at a time when "ordinary" laborers had to survive on one shilling a day (twenty cents in America at eighteenth-century exchange rates), coal heavers, who unloaded colliers with shovels and buckets on London's wharves, earned three shillings and sixpence a day (seventy American cents).

Smith observed that some people earned far more than coal heavers because of circumstances, education, or talent, but he was shocked by the incomes of stage performers. Smith explained the high incomes of actors, singers, and dancers not by their skill, but by the disgusting and immoral nature of their work:[2]

> There are some very agreeable and beautiful talents, of which the possession commands a certain sort of admiration, but of which the exercise, for the sake of gain, is considered, whether from reason or prejudice, as a sort of public prostitution. The pecuniary recompense, therefore, of those who exercise them in this manner, must be sufficient, not only to pay for the time, labor and expense of acquiring the talents, but for the discredit which attends the employment of them as a means of subsistence. The exorbitant rewards of players, opera-singers, opera-dancers &c. are founded on these two principles: the rarity and beauty of the talents; and the discredit of employing them in this manner. It seems absurd at first sight, that we should

despise their persons, and yet reward their talents with the most profuse liberality. While we do the one, however, we must of necessity do the other. Should the public opinion or prejudice ever alter with regard to such occupations, their pecuniary recompense would quickly diminish.

In this, at least, Smith appears to have been seriously mistaken.

Malthus is famous as the man who turned economics into the dismal science. He argued that laborers, like rabbits, would breed as long as there was sufficient food. Eventually their rising numbers would outrun the supply of food: this would ensure that there was always a surplus of common laborers and their wages would never rise above subsistence levels. He inserted a proviso relating to "vice," a term which he would certainly have applied to contraception and abortion.

Most countries experience a demographic transition as general living standards rise and infant and childhood mortality declines. Families respond to the rising affluence by limiting the number of children they conceive, and so the falling rates of infant and childhood mortality do not lead to a population explosion. The development of the railway and the consequential opening of the American prairie and the Russian steppes to agriculture, coupled with advances in agricultural technique, has prevented a general Malthusian crisis from occurring so far. While there have been major famines since Malthus wrote, most have either been the result of local crop failure or political interference in the food markets. People may still starve, but it is because they cannot afford to buy food, not because there is none available.

Ricardo, and after him Marx, accepted Smith's arguments in general and agreed that the laborer's wage would never rise significantly above the minimum needed for subsistence and reproduction.

Neoclassical Theory: Outline and Critique

The world that Smith, Malthus, Ricardo, and Marx described was a dynamic, changing one. Smith observed the close link between economic growth and laboring wages by comparing wages in British North America (the United States before the Revolution) with those in England. Later economists did not object to this observation. The neoclassical model is, however, built around the concept of equilibrium when all changes lie in the distant past.

In the neoclassical model, wages represent the marginal product of labor: in equilibrium employers will, according to the theory, have engaged labor until the production capability of the first laborer not to be engaged would fail to cover that laborer's wage; and by the efficient operation of the labor market, the wage of the last person employed is expected to become the wages for all the laborers in that enterprise. Because, in the neoclassical model, all products are interchangeable and all production processes perfectly known, the wage of the last laborer to be engaged by the last firm to engage labor will (or should) become the general wage level.

Among the other assumptions underlying the theory of perfect competition is the assumption that the price the firm receives for its product is fixed, no matter how much or how little it produces; and unspecified diseconomies of scale mean that its output is limited by rising marginal costs. If the general wage level fell, so would each firm's costs, and so unless there were artificial barriers to wage reduction, employment would rise until there was no one left wishing to work and unemployed. The inconvenient fact (see Chapters 3 and 5) that firm output is limited by demand, and the total demand in an economy is determined by a combination of employment and wage levels, is generally ignored.

Moseley argues that marginal productivity theory is incoherent because physical production involves the transformation of raw materials into finished goods: you can't subtract "quantity of steel" from "number of motor cars" and expect a meaningful result.[3] Moseley has surveyed a number of recent introductory and intermediate economics textbooks and has concluded that many, but not all, textbook authors have removed marginal productivity theory from the syllabus.[4]

Those economists who cling to marginal productivity theory need to account for the fact of large differences in the wages paid to different workers. They account for this by asserting that productivity differs between workers, and so every worker will create a different marginal product; and this difference is reflected in the wage offered. When Jim the laborer earns $12 per hour while John the boss earns $1,000 per hour, this is because Jim, or the last person employed performing similar duties, adds $12 per hour to the value of his employer's output while John adds $1,000 in the same hour. The inconvenient fact that if there were no "Jims" then "John" would add no value whatsoever is generally ignored, as is the incoherence that this exception introduces to the basic neoclassical model. A theory that starts from the assumption that all real workers can be replaced, for analysis purposes, by the same number of identical "representative" workers is rescued by adding the assumption that the representative workers aren't actually representative.

The idea that wages are determined entirely by an individual's inherent productivity is obviously false: the same laborer will shift more dirt in an hour with a shovel than with a teaspoon, or a Bobcat instead of a wheelbarrow. At the other end of the scale, major American banks paid out billions of dollars in bonuses in 2007 to employees who, as events in 2008 revealed, had dissipated even greater sums by a combination of greed, recklessness, and incompetence.

In early 2013 the board of the mining giant Rio Tinto sacked its chief executive for making bad decisions on acquisitions. These decisions had cost the company's shareholders at least $14 billion; during the four years that he had held the position, he had been paid $13.5 million.

The Inside/Outside Disparity

A fact about wages that concerns orthodox economists is the "inside/outside" disparity: many workers are paid more than the minimum wage, even though there are unemployed workers surviving on much less and presumably willing to take a minimum-wage job. If the labor market was properly and perfectly competitive, they argue, such disparities should be competed away.

Ultraorthodox economists and members of the conservative network argue that the inside/outside disparity is a sign of imperfections in the labor market, such as the existence of unions, minimum wages, and labor-market regulations. Since they believe, or pretend to believe, that competition is perfect and that perfect competition is perfect in every way, they argue for the removal of such imperfections. Their policy prescriptions are for labor-market deregulation, insofar as regulations limit the freedom of employers to determine working conditions and pay rates; increased labor-market regulation, wherever such regulations can limit or proscribe the activities of unions; and reduction or abolition of the minimum wage.

Labor Market Structure: The Galbraith Analysis

The American economist James Galbraith (son of the iconic John Kenneth Galbraith and brother to the acerbic diplomat Peter Galbraith) used advanced statistical techniques to analyze a large database of US payroll information. Traditional econometric cross-industry studies are based on the Standard Industry Classification (SIC) codes and often agglomerated such that all firms where the first two digits of their SIC code are the same are treated as having common characteristics.

144

Galbraith used three-digit codes and looked for common characteristics using a technique called cluster analysis. Industries where the
magnitude and trend in wages are similar will be part of a single cluster,
clearly distinguished from those with different trends (which may be
part of different clusters).[5]

Some of Galbraith's clusters are pretty obvious: 201 (Meat products)
is in the same cluster as 202 (Dairy products) for example. A different
cluster includes both 234 (Women's and children's outerwear) and 285
(Paints and allied products), which is far less obvious, at least at first
glance. Galbraith wrote:

> The results may look surprising at first, less so on reflection. For
> instance, girls' and children's outerwear seems oddly assorted with
> printing . . . . But what are girls' and children's outerwear if not—
> prints? Too, the similarity of aircraft and communications equipment
> manufacture is at least suggestive: both these industries are highly
> concentrated, and both supply advanced goods to operators of
> networks.[6]

Galbraith also identified three "super-clusters" or sectors that he
distinguished as K-, C-, or S- by plotting annual changes in average
wages paid against annual changes in industry performance.

The K-sector could be considered as either the capital goods or
the knowledge sector, delivering defense equipment and intermediate goods and services to firms that supply consumers. The C-sector
consists of firms that buy services and equipment from the K-sector
and use them to produce goods and services for consumers; while the
S- (or service) sector provides consumer and other services that do not
require a substantial prior investment.

The S-sector is by no means limited to firms in traditional service
industries, and there are traditional service industries found in the
other sectors. The delivery of health care is part of the C-sector while
the production of pharmaceuticals and surgical equipment lies in the
K-sector.

The K-sector embraces more than capital goods and medicine:
software development firms are generally found in the K-sector.
Employees in the K-sector industries received relatively substantial
year-on-year wage and salary increases, irrespective of the performance
of the individual firms. At one extreme there was the "medical" cluster,
where industry performance grew at a little over 7 percent per year
and incomes rose at just under 7 percent per year; while the other end

of the sector held the "computers" cluster, with industry performance rising at over 12 percent per year and incomes rising at a little under 7.5 percent per year.

Not all K-sector workers benefited equally from these patterns: for example, in the "computers" cluster, hourly paid workers saw little of the rapid income growth, and the difference went to salaried workers in that cluster. Anticipating the discussion of Michael Manove's work below, the professional staff of a silicon chip manufacturer develop expensive intellectual property and specify expensive fabrication systems, while the production workers deal with single chips of little intrinsic value. If a chip design is faulty, the expense of correcting the flaws can be very high; but if a single chip is spoiled during the production process, the loss is negligible.

Incomes in the S-sector essentially track the minimum wage, or in some instances over the period Galbraith studied, fell back towards it. C-sector industries bridge the gap between the S- and the K- sectors. Although all the C-sector industries exhibited similar performance growth rates, income growth rates varied from a low of about 4.5 percent for the "apparel-women's" cluster to almost 7 percent for the cluster "construction."

Galbraith used his extensive database to perform a series of statistical tests covering the usual explanations for growing income inequality in the United States. The only explanation that leads to a statistically significant correlation is that between levels of investment and incomes: industries where capital investment is rising strongly have strongly rising incomes.

Michael Manove's work (see below) provides a direct explanation of this effect.

How It Really Works

In the real economy, there are a number of reasons for variations in wages, including the inside/outside disparity. The single most obvious one is that engaging a new employee is far from costless. A job must be advertised, applicants interviewed, and an offer negotiated; the new employee must be instructed in his or her duties and his or her early mistakes corrected; and people who might otherwise have been engaged in profitable activities must supervise and instruct the new employee. The total cost of recruiting and inducting a new employee, including training, supervision, and reworking mistakes, even in an entry level clerical/administrative role, will typically exceed a year's wages. An employer who sacks an established employee in order to take on a replacement at the minimum wage will lose the investment made in recruiting and inducting the original employee and must still make a similar investment in the new one.

Since no worker will stay with the same employer for an infinite length of time, even the simplest of competitive models will predict that the inside wage will be significantly higher than the minimum wage, even when there are unemployed potential workers willing to accept the minimum.

Another important source of wage differentials was identified by Michael Manove, who showed that a rational employer would pay higher wages to employees who were responsible for more expensive capital assets or larger unit production values in order to encourage diligence.[7] Manove pointed out that a minimum-wage employee in a society not racked by serious unemployment would not be seriously disadvantaged by losing one job since others at the same low wage would be easy to find; but an employee paid well above the minimum wage would dread the possibility of losing his or her current job and being forced to accept a minimum-wage one. It is futile to expect diligence and attention to detail from a minimum-wage employee, and so their tasks must be kept simple and repetitive and their work closely supervised. By contrast, an airline pilot cannot be closely supervised, and his or her attention to detail and diligence in task performance is all that stands between the airline and an expensive disaster.

The airlines provide a particularly good example of Manove's principle at work. There is very little difference, technically, between flying an intercontinental B747, B777 or B787 twin-aisle aircraft and an intercity B737 aircraft; the Boeing Company prides itself on its standardization of cockpit layouts and flying procedures across its range. Nevertheless, a B777 pilot with a major airline can expect to earn twice as much as a B737 pilot with the same airline; the most notable difference between their tasks is that a B777 costs four to five times more than a B737. The B737 pilot earns substantially more than a suburban train driver; a B737 costs three times as much as a suburban train but is also more fragile and so more likely to be totally destroyed in an accident; but even the suburban train driver is paid over twice the minimum wage.

Unions are a factor, but not a major one, in maintaining the inside/outside differential. While the stagnation of US median wages has accompanied a huge shrinkage in the number of unionized private sector workers, this has been an effect of the restructuring of the US economy away from manufacturing, with its high capital intensity and high value added per employee to services, and from larger establishments to smaller.

Real competition is not perfect, and apart from those heading rapidly to bankruptcy, all trading enterprises make "excess" profits or "monopoly rents" (to use the terms favored by orthodox economists in private). The sources of these excess profits are a combination of goodwill, brand equity, and intellectual property, all of which enable firms to command prices that exceed their average unit costs. The division of these rents between dividends to shareholders, wage premiums for ordinary employees, and senior executive rewards is largely a matter of relative power.

Comparisons between unionized and nonunion firms in similar industries suggest that a union is able to raise wages about 10 percent over the nonunion level; international comparisons suggest that the gains made by ordinary workers through union membership largely come at the expense of senior executives. International capital mobility tends to harmonize dividend yields across the global economy; but the crony networks that select senior corporate executives and pamper them with wildly excessive pay tend to be much more local in scope.

Unemployment

The orthodox economic explanation for unemployment is that it represents "leisure preference": the unemployed are choosing not to work, possibly by demanding a wage that exceeds their potential marginal product. In this view, anyone who is currently unemployed could find a job if they were prepared to accept a sufficiently low wage. The clear implication is that employers view labor like children look at ice cream: if it were cheaper, they would consume more of it.

Until the mid-twentieth century, there were many employers who did in fact consume labor: the middle classes employed servants and the upper classes employed retainers as well. An early nineteenth-century nobleman might set out in his carriage with a coachman and three liveried footmen on the outside and four or six running footmen clearing a path through the crowds. One coachman would have sufficed to get the carriage and His Lordship to his destination; the rest were simply conspicuous consumption.

Servants at the bottom of the hierarchy in a nobleman's house were paid little or nothing in money, but they were permitted to eat the scraps left over from the higher servants' meals and wear clothes that first the master or mistress, and then the upper servants, had worn and discarded. Even the higher servants' emoluments were mainly in kind: they received food, accommodation, and second-hand clothing, and these were supplemented by a small cash allowance.

Marx and Engels[8] argued that household servants were not actually employed at all: they were part of their master's extended household—a walking washing machine. Since most or all of their remuneration was in kind, they were not really actors in the money economy, where payment in kind ("truck") had been illegal in Britain since the early nineteenth century—but domestic service lay outside the law.

When the Second Reform Act of 1867 extended the British suffrage to all male householders, servants were specifically excluded. The members of the House of Commons knew that servants would be compelled to obey their masters' orders if permitted to vote and did not wish to amplify the influence of the great magnates any further.

The eighteenth and nineteenth centuries saw huge rises in both agricultural and industrial productivity while the railway and the opening of the American West increased the amount of arable land available to supply the markets of the industrialized countries just as dramatically. Working-class families responded to higher incomes and falling mortality by limiting their families; and while the population grew, the growth never threatened to approach the limits of agricultural production (and hasn't yet, in spite of a six-fold increase in global population).

From the mid-nineteenth century, unemployment appeared in the great industrial towns, rising at times of crisis and falling when growth resumed. Although trade unions had been legalized and there were some strikes, by and large employers set the wage rates; this did not prevent the economic rationalists of the day from blaming worker greed for unemployment.

One of the major problems of democracy from the plutocratic point of view is that every adult is eligible to vote, and it becomes impossible for an elected government to ignore the wishes of a substantial fraction of the voting population entirely. One of the strongly expressed wishes of the part of the population qualified only for hourly paid work is employment; and high levels of unemployment are widely viewed as a sign that the incumbent government is incompetent and should be evicted at the next electoral opportunity.

Keynes on Unemployment

Keynes made the decisive break with the economic tradition, combining two obvious facts. Firstly, employers employed additional labor when they foresaw it as being profitable to do so, and refrained from adding employees, or even retrenched some of those that they had, when it was difficult or impossible to sell their output profitably. Secondly, a deficit in demand could appear if household savings exceeded entrepreneurs' demand for capital, and such a deficit would lead to employers retrenching labor.

Keynes accepted, at least for the sake of argument, that the labor market was "perfect" in the sense that an employer who wished to offer a certain number of jobs and was prepared to pay the going wage could instantly and costlessly hire the workers that he or she needed. This was almost true for laboring and some semiskilled jobs at the height of the Great Depression: a firm that took down its "No Vacancies" sign would be besieged by desperate job seekers.

The perfect labor market assumption is untenable when considering skilled and professional jobs, and even for laboring and semiskilled jobs with significant responsibilities. Hiring for these types of positions is far from costless. The general wage level will not have much effect on employers' hiring decisions, since a high general wage level leads to a high level of demand. Henry Ford set the daily wage at his plants to five dollars, well aware of the knock-on effect that this would have on other employers, because he needed well-paid customers for his cars.

Regulated conditions of employment, including layoffs, may have a marginal effect on overall employment but are more likely to bias employers against full-time employment in favor of casual, labor hire and outsourcing arrangements.

The conservative network has created a political tool called supply-side economics, based on blowing the small effect of the cost of wages and employment protection out of all proportion. Careful US studies have found that small changes in the minimum wage have no effect on unemployment levels;[9] further studies have shown a statistically significant but absolutely small correlation between employment protection laws and unemployment. Keynes's solution for persistent unemployment was to stimulate demand by government programs; some might involve the direct employment of the formerly unemployed but most would take the form of contracts let to private firms to fulfill some social or public purpose. Keynes favored rebuilding slum housing and reequipping the British armed forces, both obviously urgent tasks in 1936 when Keynes published his *General Theory*.

The conservative network has little objection to governments awarding contracts for the supply of military equipment, but strenuously opposes government expenditure for social purposes. By and large the conservative network offers a five-point program for reducing unemployment:

- A government can grant monopolies over some useful item of infrastructure and permit private-sector firms to exploit this under the rubric of "private finance initiative" or "public private partnership," encouraging investment in line with Keynes's recommendations but not, perhaps, the way Keynes would have gone about it.
- A government can cut taxes in order to stimulate demand, on the assumption that the recipients will spend the extra income rather than save it or pay down debt; unfortunately the conservative network generally recommends that the bulk of the benefit of tax cuts go those with high incomes who, many studies have suggested, are the least likely to spend it on consumption goods and services; and with no increase in the demand for goods and services, the rich beneficiaries of the tax cuts won't put the money into productive investments either.
- A government (or the monetary authorities) can lower interest rates, reducing the cost of capital for entrepreneurs (and making consumer credit cheaper, also stimulating demand).
- The government can reach back to the world of Charles Dickens and Oliver Twist and punish the unemployed for not trying hard enough to find a job; by implicitly blaming the unemployed for their own plight, the government can evade or attempt to evade the political consequences of previous poor economic management.

NAIRU and Full Employment

In 1960s the US economy had been bubbling along with strong growth, low inflation (apart from a brief burst during the Korean War), and full employment for over twenty years. In the United States, unemployment hovered around 3 percent; in Britain the level was closer to 2 percent. Firms still went broke and people still lost their jobs, but anyone not suffering from physical or intellectual disabilities had little trouble finding another one. Rather than potential workers complaining about unemployment, employers complained about labor shortages.

At 2 or 3 percent unemployment, an economy can fairly be described as being in a state of full employment with the remaining unemployment "frictional." Some of the unemployed will be people on the margins of the labor market, by reason of disability or poor education, who rely

151

on seasonal and casual work, and some will be workers between jobs. If a typical worker stays with an employer for four years, and then takes four weeks to find another job, unemployment will be measured at 2 percent. In the United States in the 1950s and 1960s, unemployment hovered between 3 and 4 percent, which may reflect a shorter average tenure than that found in Britain and Europe at the time. In particular, firms in the United States then and now offer blue-collar workers very short paid vacations, and when American economists describe unemployment as an expression of "leisure preference," they may be reflecting on reality fifty years ago.

Milton Friedman became president of the American Economic Association in 1968 and used his presidential address to assert that there was a "natural" rate of unemployment, and if unemployment was allowed to fall below this figure, there would be indefinitely accelerating inflation: the natural rate of unemployment was renamed NAIRU, or the Non-Accelerating Inflation Rate of Unemployment.

Since US unemployment was, at the time, well below any conceivable measure of NAIRU and inflation had been low for fifteen years at the time of Friedman's address, the economists at the meeting were not unduly impressed, but history turned out to be on Friedman's side. As described in Chapter 5, the United States and much of the developed world began to experience rising inflation in the late 1960s as the United States ran budget and trade deficits to finance its escalation of the conflict in Vietnam. Following the "oil shock" of 1973, unemployment began to rise as well, but from the very low levels experienced over the years 1946–1972. The combination became known as "stagflation." Governments whose policy advisers relied on bastard Keynesianism attempted to reduce unemployment by public expenditure, but this had little effect on unemployment and led to a considerable increase in inflation.

Friedman's proposed solution was to attack inflation by controlling the money supply and to take no account of the rising unemployment that this caused. Unemployment, he argued, should be allowed to reach its "natural" or NAIRU level. There proved to be a couple of problems with this approach: first, that Friedman's approach to controlling the money supply proved to be almost completely ineffective; and second, no one knew how much unemployment corresponded to NAIRU: estimates ranged between 5 and 10 percent.

Savagely contractionary monetary policies, leading to recessions in 1981 and 1991, brought inflation in the United States and Britain to less than 3 percent, and there it has stayed. These actions also forced unemployment toward 10 percent, and "full employment" became redefined as "less than 6 percent." These levels became politically tolerable, at least among politicians and their economic advisors, as necessary to avoid renewed inflation.

Education and Training

Equity Considerations

Even at times of rising demand, companies can be remarkably unwilling to invest in increasing productive capacity. Even when required to pay a substantially higher hourly rate for overtime, a firm will be aware that it is far easier to offer more or less overtime than to hire and train new workers with the possible need to retrench them shortly afterward.

When such firms are asked in surveys why they are not hiring to meet the increased demand, their spokespeople are almost certainly unaware of real options theory (even the financial heart of many firms, the CFO's department, may have only a passing acquaintance with newfangled concepts that have only been around for twenty or so years) and the easiest explanation can be drawn directly from the conservative network's hymn book: the unemployed are inadequately trained and lack a proper work ethic. It is not the firm's or the government's fault.

Differences in qualifications and experience clearly account for part of the difference between the wages earned by different individuals. A skilled tradesperson generally earns more than a common laborer in any given business; a medical specialist is usually better paid than a general practitioner in any given country. These differences raise the obvious question of how certain individuals acquire particular skills and experience while others do not.

Institutions of various kinds provide education and training, some of it free to the student, some of it subsidized, and some where the enrolled students are expected to pay the fully allocated cost, possibly including a substantial profit. In addition, many employers provide training, either through an in-house training department or by a contracted training provider. Some of this training is relatively formal, as with apprenticeship schemes or sponsored higher-education courses; some is more ad hoc. Experience comes with employment and is pretty well inseparable from it.

Matching Skills to Need

It is obvious that people receive education and training in different fields, when they receive any at all, which raises the question of how particular people are matched with particular education and training opportunities. Some people are not offered, or do not accept, any post-school education or training at all. There is a related but separate issue of how some people gain experience in particular fields while others, including people who are educationally qualified for such experience, do not.

People differ in their aptitude for different tasks and their motivation to attempt them: there may be a rough correlation between motivation and aptitude; but many people find themselves in uncongenial occupations in which they may perform their assigned tasks well or badly. There are also limits to the number of desirable positions available in any given trade or profession, set by economic and other considerations. Given that education and training are costly activities, it must constitute a waste of resources, financial and human, to equip more people for a given trade or profession than there are remunerative opportunities available; it is also a waste to prepare someone for a trade or profession in which they will be unhappy, if there had been an alternative.

Most modern economics is steeped in Ricardian vice: its conclusions are embedded in its assumptions. This enables many economists to ignore the problem of unhappiness: under the assumption of perfect foresight, nobody would prepare themselves for a trade, profession, or occupation in which they will be unhappy. If anyone is unhappy in reality, the assumption of perfect foresight suggests that they would be unhappier still in any other occupation. The logic is impeccable; unfortunately it is the underlying assumptions that are false.

The assumption that a real population of humans with different aptitudes, capabilities, and aspirations may be replaced by a number of identical "representative" persons eliminates the possibility of an excessive supply of people educated and trained for any given occupation. By assumption, an excess supply of trained people will cause individual incomes to fall, and these price signals will deter preparation for entry into that occupation until the supply of appropriately educated and trained people matches the demand for them. Unfortunately, in a real employment market, the price signals are far from clear.

Winner Takes All?

Markets where the personal attention of a provider is an essential part of the service are generally "winner takes all"—or at least, "winners are grinners." Any given individual can only perform a limited number of tasks in an hour, or day, or week, and in most circumstances there will be a demand for more tasks to be completed than any single individual can address within the relevant time constraints. Those responsible for commissioning the completion of any task will seek the best possible outcome and, in the absence of any constraints, will seek to engage the task provider with the highest reputation for successful work. Only where the expected service quality does not differ between potential providers, or the difference is not considered significant by the commissioning person, will that person consider price in coming to a decision.

When delivered quality is important to the person commissioning a service and the participation of an identified person in the service delivery is essential, the providers with the best reputations will be asked to address more tasks than they can possibly handle, and some form of rationing will be required. In an unregulated or lightly regulated market, rationing will be by price: the service providers with the highest reputation will raise their prices until the number of tasks commissioned is within their capacity. There may be a second, third, and even more tiers of suppliers, each succeeding tier charging less but still loaded with work to their capacity or at least to their inclination to perform it. Only at the lowest end of the hierarchy will there be an excess of potential providers and potential price competition between them.

Personal service markets differ from more general service markets because of the impossibility of simple replication. Airline travelers do not specify a specific aircraft, pilot, or cabin staff member when they make a booking: they trust the airline company to have been diligent in its maintenance and personnel selection and training procedures such that the identity of the actual staff involved does not affect the delivered service quality. By contrast, someone requiring life-saving surgery will be very interested in the qualifications and reputation of the surgeon in charge of the procedure.

The global professional golf industry is a good example of a market where the value of the delivered service is closely related to the identity of the individual delivering it. At the top of the hierarchy of golf professionals is a small group of stars who can demand and receive substantial payments for simply entering a tournament: the prize money comes on top of their appearance fee. There is a broader group who must pay their own expenses on the various professional circuits, relying on prize money to stay solvent while they hope that a big win will catapult them into the star category. At the bottom of the heap is a horde of professionals running golf shops and offering tuition to weekend hackers at private and public golf courses across the world. Many of these people struggle to earn a subsistence income.

When a young person with an aptitude for golf considers making it a career, what price signal do they rely on? Is it the meager earnings of the professional at their local suburban course or Tiger Woods and his multimillion-dollar appearance fees?

Education and Experience

Aptitude and education only go so far. As the proverb has it, "practice makes perfect." Education and training can only carry someone part of the way to expertise in any field: the rest is the result of experience gained from repeated practice. In many professions and trades, the first stages of gaining experience will be supervised before the entrants become principals in their own right. Such supervision is costly, as is the need to correct the mistakes a trainee may make. The people supervising the trainee are diverted from the direct performance of value-adding activities, while the cost of supporting the trainee will, at least initially, exceed the value that they can add.

The medieval apprenticeship system put a value on experience by requiring apprentices to work for their master for seven years for little or no pay beyond board and lodging. Well into the twentieth century, apprentice wages were kept low even when, in the final years of an apprenticeship, the apprentice was performing tradesman's work. This underpaid work at the end of an apprenticeship compensated the tradesman (or employer in the case of a company apprenticeship scheme) for the effort of supervision and the payment of early stage apprenticeship wages well before the apprentice could perform work at a speed and standard that would justify them.

In the third quarter of the twentieth century, a system similar to apprenticeship applied to professional and clerical employment in the English-speaking countries. Firms took on management and techni- cally qualified trainees and rotated them through a series of positions, supplementing this experience with in-service training. Such employees were encouraged to stay with their employer after their training period was complete by generous superannuation schemes and a substantial seniority element in the pay calculations.

Such schemes continue in Germany and in a slightly different form in Japan.

Few if any of these schemes survived the ascent of neoliberalism in the English-speaking countries. Publicly listed companies discovered that sacking staff ensured an immediate boost to the stock price because of an immediate boost to profits. Overall the loss of experience and "corporate knowledge" meant slower average growth and weaker long-term prospects; but this was of little concern to managers focused on the daily stock price. Generous "golden parachutes" ensured that the managers whose myopic decision making led to poor medium-term performance did not suffer financially.

The jobs that were once handled by loyal staff on long-term employment arrangements must still be done, but an increasing fraction of them are now outsourced to low-wage countries such as India or the Philippines, while many of the remaining tasks are performed by casually employed staff or by contractors. Experience is still accumulated, though less effectively; but corporations no longer have the benefit of loyal and experienced managerial and technical staff.

Policies and Results

Publicly funded training for workers in the skills needed by particular firms or industries is a subsidy, transferring public expenditure on training into the private profits of various firms. Firms and industry associations that argue for publicly funded but industry-specific training are at least partly motivated by simple greed: anything that reduces their costs goes straight to the bottom line; but they also have a legitimate concern about free riding.

Workers, even in authoritarian countries such as China, are not serfs, and there is nothing to stop them accepting training from one employer and then moving to another one. If all the employers in an industry provide training in proportion to the size of their workforce, then such movement of workers involves no net loss or gain; but if some employers offer no training and rely on recruiting staff that others have trained, there is a clear transfer of value.

No rational employer expects its staff to remain with it forever, and taught skills are progressively made obsolete by developing technology anyway; so there is a level of turnover at which a rationally managed employer would provide training even if other employers in its industry did not. In practical terms this corresponds to an average stay with one employer of five to seven or more years. When turnover is significantly more rapid than this, employers will not provide anything more than employer-specific and task-specific training, and will be reluctant to provide even that.

In the post–World War II period, workers did expect to stay with an employer until retirement, and employers encouraged this with defined benefit pension schemes and other rewards for loyalty. Manufacturing and construction firms offered apprenticeships to trainee tradespeople, with a very low wage in the first three or four years offsetting the cost of training; but even in this "golden age," a major proportion of trade training in Britain took place in the publicly owned railways and tramways and the state-owned gas, electricity, telephone, and water utilities. The United States had fewer state-owned industries, but in the post–World War II period, the telephone system, the railways, and most of the electricity and water utilities were closely regulated.

As state-owned or closely regulated monopolies, these employers were less concerned with cost control than other companies may have been. They could also justify training apprentices who would not stay long with them as tradesmen, both for public good and commercial reasons: by playing a large role in the training of electricians and gas-fitters, for example, the electricity and gas utilities could be confident that their customers' installations were carried out efficiently and safely. In this period most large firms offered education and training programs to staff recruited with university degrees into professional and administrative positions, enhancing their learning from their paid work experience.

Graduate recruitment programs became something of a corporate status symbol, initially in the United States but rapidly adopted across much of the developed world. Firms introduced them as a demonstration of their long-term commitment to the markets that they served and the staff responsible for serving them.

The adoption of the neoliberal agenda at the instigation of the conservative network from the late 1970s onwards destroyed these training systems and put nothing in their place. Deregulation, corporatization, and privatization of the transport and utility enterprises introduced managers who saw the extensive apprenticeship schemes as an unnecessary cost and wound them back or closed them altogether.

The arrival of shareholder sovereignty and the pressure for short-term profits saw major companies abandon employment for life and, in particular, abandon the defined benefit pension schemes for accumulation schemes or no schemes at all; private-sector firms became much more ready to retrench employees; and employees responded by looking for opportunities to jump before they were pushed. Large private sector firms also cut back or abolished their management and professional education and training facilities.

Firms were rewarded on the share markets for retrenching employees, and many did so without regard to the impact on their long-term viability. This inclination increased worker turnover and further reduced the economic viability of industry-specific training.

By the early twenty-first century, there was a serious shortage of tradespeople in the English-speaking countries, and the average age of those tradespeople still active was rising almost year for year. During the mineral resources boom of 2010–13, billions of dollars of construction projects were delayed or postponed because of a shortage of skilled workers; and increasing numbers of workers from developing countries were admitted to the developed English-speaking countries to fill the gaps.

In the United States, employers in the construction and related industries filled the skills gap by employing tradespeople and semi-skilled workers of Hispanic origin[10] without looking too carefully at their immigration status. Immigration became, in the twenty-first century, a subject of heated debate in the United States, and the economic damage from overzealous enforcement of the immigration laws may be considerable.

In Britain Enoch Powell, later to become famous for his speeches attacking nonwhite immigration, was minister for health between 1960 and 1963 in the Macmillan government (1957–63). His department actively recruited West Indian nurses to migrate to Britain and fill vacancies in the National Health Service.

Responding to the Skills Crisis

The Hayekians and the orthodox neoclassical economists argued for user charges for public education, the abolition of in-house education and training by corporations, and the deregulation or privatization of the great public utilities and consequent elimination of their vast apprenticeship schemes. They argued that these changes would make the economy more efficient; they certainly did not predict a burgeoning skills crisis. Having started from the premises that education and training conferred a private benefit and that credit markets were perfect, the Hayekians and the orthodox neoclassical economists expected that workers would invest in their own training, having used their perfect foresight to make a rational estimate of the returns in the form of higher wages that they would enjoy when the training was completed. Paying fees would not be a problem, since workers could access the perfect credit markets, where bankers would use their perfect foresight to advance the fees only to students who would earn enough after graduation to repay their loans.

Workers, the Hayekians and the orthodox neoclassical economists argued, would recognize that experience was valuable, and so they would offer to work for low or no wages in order to gain it. In the United States in particular, this led to an explosion in the number of unpaid internships; some interns at least found themselves practicing rather different skills than the advertised position had promised.

Overall the outcome has not been the one that the Hayekians and the orthodox neoclassical economists predicted, with a skills crisis developing at every level of the economies of the English-speaking countries.

Bringing skilled workers from developing countries into the English-speaking developed ones may provide short-term amelioration but not a long-term one. First-world countries can only plunder the skilled workforce of developing ones for a limited time: for one thing, offshore competition will drive up the wages earned by professionals, paraprofessionals, and tradespeople in developing countries; and for another, this rise will sooner or later discourage the training providers in those countries. Already the ordinary experience of someone with a health problem in an English-speaking country will include Indian doctors and Philippine nurses.

At an individual level, a plumber or welder trained in a developing country may find the rewards of even a temporary assignment in a first-world one surpassing his or her wildest hopes: at the peak of the mining boom, contractors building mining infrastructure in the Pilbara region of Australia offered welders thirty times the average income in China, and if more money would have created more welders, the contractors would have happily offered it.

Examining the past may help determine a path to the future, but a conscious reversion to the past, even should it be attempted, would be unlikely to reproduce the benefits without greater offsetting costs. The past does, however, allow theories to be tested painlessly: if they can explain the past, they are not automatically disqualified from suggesting measures to secure the future.

The apprenticeship system in the United States and Britain is wrecked, probably beyond the possibility of repair. Even if young people were prepared to spend three to five years on a low income in the hope of obtaining a trade qualification, the public utilities and major manufacturers that used to run apprenticeship schemes are changed beyond recognition; and most of the middle-aged tradesmen running their own contracting businesses are not interested in picking up the training task.

What we can do is examine some successful economies where education is regarded as a proper subject for public policy—"intervention," as orthodox economists describe it.

Proven Labor-Market Alternatives

France

The French have never accepted neoliberal theory, which they refer to as "Anglo-Saxon economics," as a basis for public policy. They see it as proper that the state should guide the economy, a practice referred to as *dirigisme*. Their policies include extensive labor-market regulation and a system of levies to support vocational training.

> The French system has made extensive use of an employer training levy since 1971, which compels all firms employing 10 or more workers to contribute an amount of at least 1.5 percent of payroll to training (and firms with under 10 employees to contribute a smaller percentage). Firms that undertake approved training can offset their costs against the levy, whereas non-training firms either pay into mutual funds for training jointly administered by employers and unions, or pay a tax to the central exchequer. Alongside the joint funding of workforce training by all employers, there is also considerable government subsidy to training, including since 1989 a marginal tax credit designed to reward firms that increase their level of training expenditure. In the first two decades of the levy, expenditure on training more than doubled as a share of wages and greatly exceeded the legal minimum in many firms. Although the major share of the training expenditure is dedicated to adult worker training, a substantial share is also reserved for the initial training of new entrants via alternating school and work programmes. There is also a small share of funds reserved for training initiated by individual employees to further their careers.[11]

The French system of levies effectively punishes free riding: employers cannot rely purely on recruiting other employers' trained staff to supply their skill needs. Studies cited by Greenhalgh suggest that the levy on its own is not enough to prevent free riding and reward firms with training programs, but there are additional benefits to those employers who provide training: these studies "demonstrate that vocational training activity is associated with increased net output by firms, a higher rate of return on assets, payment of higher wages and a greater propensity to innovate."[12]

The primary motivation for the French government in raising the skill levels of the French workforce has been to match, or at least stay in touch with, the Germans. Enjoying higher median living standards, higher productivity, and a vastly better level of public amenity than the English is considered an additional benefit.

Germany[13]

The medium-size engineering firm or *Mittelstand* is frequently referred to as the "engine room" of the German economy. Most of these firms are too small to have formal training departments, but nearly all German employers participate in the apprenticeship system. Apart from those heading to university to obtain professional qualifications, practically all school leavers enter the labor market through an apprenticeship. Approximately two-thirds of all German school leavers enter an apprenticeship involving a combination of on-the-job training and classroom education.

There is necessarily tension between the interests of employers (who want their apprentices trained in the specific tasks relevant to their businesses) and the state (which seeks a reasonably flexible labor force so that economic changes do not strand groups of workers with obsolete skills). These tensions have been managed reasonably successfully, although the scheme has been subject to a number of reviews and modifications.

Those who complete an apprenticeship receive a certificate, without which obtaining a job in Germany is very difficult. Many small and medium firms do not offer continuing employment to all those completing apprenticeships with them, considering access to their skills less valuable than the low training wages that they can offer new apprenticeships. Most large firms do retain their apprentices, often rotating them through a number of roles to enhance their skills.

The German system suffers to some extent from a "free rider" problem, with a few employers refusing to participate in the apprenticeship system and relying on workers trained by other employers. Levies have been proposed at various times to spread the training load but have been stalled by political opposition, and so free riding is deterred by moral suasion and the free riders' fear that they may not be able to recruit adequately trained staff.

The success of the German system is demonstrated by the fact that its workers earn the highest median incomes in the developed world, yet its firms are profitable and the country consistently runs a trade surplus.

Japan

Japan, prior to the Meiji Restoration in 1868, was not an underdeveloped country: it had an effective and relatively uncorrupted government, a highly educated population, and a strong craft tradition. The

American Commodore Perry[14] exposed Japan's military inferiority when compared to developed Western countries, and a primary aim of the Restoration government was to develop a modern military machine and build the industries needed to build and supply a modern army and navy.

It became apparent to some enlightened Japanese people quite early in the process that building a modern economy had national benefits going well beyond military strength: in 1894 the education minister wrote: "It is clear that competition in the world is essentially industrial, rather than military. Our science has advanced satisfactorily, but not our technical training at the lower levels."[15] The minister was justifying his policy innovations, aimed to overcome the tendency, far from unique to Japan or to the late nineteenth century, to see academic education leading to a professional career as more prestigious and desirable than vocational education.

The Japanese military retained enough pre-Restoration attitudes to overcome rational objections based on economic arguments and launched a war against the United States in December 1941. The consequence was a total military defeat and unprecedented levels of devastation. At a physical level, by the end of 1945 Japan's industrial system had been returned to the pre-Meiji era and a second restoration was necessary. Fortunately for Japan and the wider world, the *Bushido* spirit that started and sustained the war was reduced to the province of an eccentric minority (such as the author Yukio Mishima). In the post–World War II era, Japan's chosen path was one of industrial rather than military conquest.

The education and vocational training systems were remodeled to meet the new demands on them, incorporating elements of both the American and German systems. The school and undergraduate university systems were reorganized on notionally American lines with grade schools and two stages of high school. Japan did not devolve administrative and curriculum authority in line with US practice, and the central Ministry of Education asserts total control over the curriculum.

From 1945 to the mid-1950s, Japanese industrial relations followed an American model, with basically adversarial relations between unions and management: strikes were frequent, often involving violence and sometimes fatalities. In response, Japanese managers at Toyota and elsewhere developed a unique Japanese system, involving a compromise between Japan's feudal traditions and the American-mandated doctrines of equality. Two crucial ingredients of this system were seniority-based wages and a management commitment to a minimum-layoff policy (not employment for life, but the best approximation that management can achieve).

The expectation of long-term employment subdued workers' militancy, since the longer they were employed, the greater the loss of wages and benefits if they left. Management responded to the situation by extensive job rotation and training, most famously by the adoption of statistical process control as taught by the American engineer, mathematician, and consultant W. Edwards Deming (1900–1993). The cultural symbols of feudalism, or even American management, were abandoned: managers on the shop floor could only be distinguished from line workers by discrete badges on their overalls. Management dining rooms were closed, and managers ate in the common cafeteria.

Japanese workers, at least in the exporting and import-competing industries, develop considerable task-related skills but also make decisions on matters that in other countries and traditions might require a separate layer of managers and clerks. With the fear of inventing themselves out of a job removed, Japanese workers make frequent suggestions for improving operations and raising quality, a practice known as *kai-zen*, or "the way of improvement."

Japanese workers are well paid, and Japanese companies are internationally competitive, as shown by Japan's persistent trade surpluses.

Notes

1. Smith (1776 Bk I Ch VIII).
2. Ibid Bk I Ch X.
3. Moseley (2012a).
4. Moseley (2012b).
5. Galbraith (1998); see also http://utip.gov.utexas.edu/ for working papers and current research.
6. Galbraith (1998: p. 103).
7. Manove (1997).
8. Marx & Engels (1848).
9. Card & Krueger (1997).
10. Newkirk (2011).
11. Greenhalgh (2002).
12. Greenhalgh (2002).
13. Tremblay & Le Bot (2003); Soskice (1991).
14. See http://www.history.navy.mil/library/online/perry_exp.htm for the official US Navy account of Perry's expeditions.
15. Passin (1982).

9

The Engine of Growth

Add as many mail-coaches as you please, you will
never get a railroad by so doing.
—J. A. Schumpeter

Growth in Theory

Mainstream economists treat economic growth as the result of two causes: population growth, and saving leading to investment in income-generating assets.

Robert Solow won a Nobel Prize in Economics for demonstrating, among his other contributions, that saving and population increase accounted for no more than 20 percent of historically observed growth in per capita income in the United States over a fifty-year period. He explained the difference as the result of "technological change" but offered no economic explanation as to why such changes would occur. Technology, in the Solow model, "dropped like manna from Heaven."[1]

Solow's difficulty in providing an economic explanation for economic growth came from preserving the assumption of perfect (or almost perfect) competition, including the internal assumption of instantaneous and costless transmission of knowledge. Under such assumptions there can be no economic reward for innovation, since every valuable innovation would be instantly copied and the "excess" profits competed away as quickly.

Economists eager to preserve the pure neoclassical model have argued at length that innovations are, indeed, exogenous: innovators, they assert, work for the pure intellectual pleasure of invention. Why a rational, egotistical, selfish econ[2] would work for the general benefit of mankind with no expectation of personal reward is not explained.

Smith had observed that there were economies of scale in manufacturing arising from the specialization that larger-scale operations permitted. Marx built on this to explain the mechanism of capitalist growth in the mid-nineteenth century by pointing out that larger firms could both organize production more efficiently and buy or develop improved machinery to reduce their costs further. The smaller and less efficient producers would be forced into bankruptcy or taken over ("One capitalist eats many"), and industries would tend to monopoly; although during this process output and productivity would rise.

Adam Smith had not anticipated the tendency to monopolization caused by scale economies, and while he claimed that following his advice would lead to increased prosperity, he was unable to quantify this statistically: systems of national accounts would have to wait for Keynes.

Marx's account only included what is now called process and organizational innovation (although some authors consider that in work published posthumously he mentioned product and quality innovation). Schumpeter completed Marx's picture during the first half of the twentieth century by demonstrating that new products, higher-quality products, and organizational change at the industry level could also form the basis of economically significant innovations.

Marx prophesied that the combination of ever-more-efficient production and finite demand would lead to pressure on wages and the progressive immiserization of the proletariat. By the early twentieth century, it was obvious that the British and German working classes were enjoying rising rather than falling living standards. Lenin attempted to defend Marx's assertion by postulating that the domestic working classes in England and Germany were being bought off with the proceeds of the more intensive exploitation of the workers in the periphery, notably in India but also in Eastern Europe (including Western Russia). Contemporary evidence gave some support to Lenin's view; even now some Indian commentators adhere to the Leninist view that the British Industrial Revolution was financed by the exploitation of India.

More realistic analysis of the Industrial Revolution suggests that, while exploitation of India made a number of otherwise ordinary British families very rich, the money needed to drive the Industrial Revolution was created by the English banking system as it was needed (see Chapter 4 for an account of the method) and Indian gold was largely irrelevant. A number of factors, including explicit British policy, prevented an Indian industrial revolution in the first part of the nineteenth century, but the depredations of the British East India Company were only part of the story.

Schumpeter's Spiral Staircase

Schumpeter believed that any tendency to immiserization associated with process innovation would be overcome by the effects of product and product quality innovation. He demonstrated how the "circular flow" of wages purchasing commodities and so providing the finance for more wages and the production of more commodities could become an ascending spiral though the activities of innovating entrepreneurs.

The archetypal Schumpeterian entrepreneur plans to introduce a new product to the market: to do so, she will need labor and materials. Since there is no reason to expect that the required labor and materials will be idle, waiting for the entrepreneur, she must bid them away from their current use, offering in particular higher wages than had been customary. Existing firms will be forced to raise the wages that they pay in order to retain their workforce and replace the key employees enticed away from them by the entrepreneur, and at the margin some of the least efficient employers will not be able to afford higher wages and will cease trading.

Because the entrepreneur's product is of higher value than the products of the inefficient firms forced out of business by the rise in wage levels, the total value of all production is higher than before, and equal to the higher wages now generally paid plus the increased profits earned. Real wages have therefore risen, as has real production; there has been economic growth accompanied by rising living standards.

Heinz Kurz and Neri Salvadori applied techniques developed by Piero Sraffa[3] to Schumpeter's model of innovation disrupting the circular flow of an economy previously in equilibrium and demonstrated that process innovation also led to a permanent increase in wages.[4] Their approach by no means demonstrates that the increase in wages will be evenly or fairly distributed, just that there will be more to distribute. Immiserization, if it occurs, will reflect an unfair division of the benefits of economic growth: rising productivity is consistent with rising inequality.

Neoclassical Growth Theory[5]

There have been two recent attempts to inject growth into the essentially static models used by orthodox neoclassical economists. One is associated with Grossman and Helpman; the other with Romer. Their work, and that of other economists who have extended their research, is generally referred to as "endogenous growth theory" or "new growth theory." The first version carries the implication that innovation and therefore growth is the result of purposive profit-seeking activity taking place within the economy (hence "endogenous"), not the "manna from heaven" associated with the Solow residual being filled by exogenous (i.e., external to the economy) technological change.

Grossman and Helpman[6] postulated an innovative cream floating on the stagnant pond of perfect competition, in which entrepreneurial firms race to complete valuable innovations with the winner of each race seizing the entire market segment. Grossman and Helpman introduced two classes of knowledge: manufacturers' knowledge of production processes, gained through costly R&D and at least partly protected by patents and secrecy; and buyers' (both industrial and final consumption) knowledge of the attributes of all available products, which is instantaneously transmitted and costlessly acquired.

Romer is associated with a macroeconomic approach to growth. He starts with a two-dimensional division of intermediate goods (i.e., goods such as machines and partly processed materials used to produce consumer goods). Such goods can be rival or nonrival, and excludable or nonexcludable. A rival good—for example, a pizza oven—can only be used by one firm at a time; while a nonrival good, such as the complete instructions for manufacturing pizza ovens, can be used simultaneously by as many firms that have the required capital, skilled labor force, and desire to produce pizza ovens.

An excludable good is one whose owner can prevent others making use of it: returning to the pizza oven, it is clearly excludable as long as it is behind the counter of its owner's shop; but a good such as a parking spot may be nonexcludable, although rivalrous, because the cost and difficulty of preventing others using it may exceed the value of the benefit its exclusive use would confer. A nonexcludable good is clearly one that no one can prevent others using: for example, a set of designs posted on the Internet.

In Romer's view innovative firms necessarily generated nonrival goods in the form of the knowledge of how to reproduce their inno-vation, and these "spilled over" to their competitors, not necessarily promptly.

Romer's major conclusions include the importance of economies of scale and the possibility that a national economy may be so deprived of skilled workers that it is unable to commence technologically driven economic growth. As mentioned above, he rejected the assumption of perfect competition among price-taking firms as incompatible with innovation or the evidence.[7]

Paul Geroski pointed out that direct spillovers were a relatively minor contributor to economic growth;[8] he was echoing, possibly inadvertently, Schumpeter's assertion that innovation did not, in general, depend on scientific novelty but an innovation was rather a "new combination," none of the components of which were necessarily scientifically new. Geroski's main point was that modern industrial processes and products are so complex that simply stealing the "recipe" conveys no useful information unless the recipients have technical skills comparable to those of the original inventors. Successful industrial espionage may save those who deploy it some money, but they will still face major costs if they want to turn the stolen secrets into a marketable product.

During World War II the British decided to contract American firms to build the Rolls Royce Merlin aircraft engine, which was used in the Spitfire fighter and the Lancaster bomber. A Foreign Office courier was instructed to collect the blueprints and deliver them to the US manufacturer. He took a train to Crewe and a local taxi to the Rolls Royce factory, where he was expected. "How are you going to carry them?" asked the Rolls Royce engineer in charge of the transfer project. The courier tapped his trusty briefcase, duly chained to his waist. The engineer silently led the courier to the loading dock, where the blueprints had been prepared for shipment—in four large crates, weighing approximately a ton each.

Product Differentiation: Consumer Fraud or Valuable Innovation?

One of the preconditions for perfect competition is that there is only one product, or at least, all the available products are perfectly interchangeable. Under these and certain further relatively improbable circumstances, all consumers will choose the lowest-price product, and competition will ensure that this becomes the ruling market price. When obvious counterexamples to these assumptions are raised, economists may point out that, subject to the existence of perfect capital markets, product interchangeability will hold "in the long term": if chalk is cheap and cheese expensive, over a sufficient time resources will move from chalk to cheese production and so eliminate the difference.

Grossman and Helpman, in their most widely cited models of endogenous growth, focus almost exclusively on quality differentiation over a fixed set of products, where each successful innovator is able to determine a profitable price at a level that permits its rivals no profits, and no sales, at all. Despite it being unrealistic in at least two

169

dimensions, the Grossman and Helpman models do demonstrate the possibility of endogenous growth under highly restrictive assumptions and have been used successfully to explain observed growth differentials between countries.

In modern markets even things like chalk and cheese are available in many different styles and with many different properties. The suppliers of such products rely on the variation in consumer tastes to force consumers to make their choices on grounds that may include price but are not solely determined by it. One consumer may lust for Stilton cheese while another prefers brie: there is no such thing as the "cheese" price since the Stilton lover would not take the brie if it was free, and vice versa.

As discussed in Chapter 3, there are some products for which the assumption of perfect competition involves only modest distortion of the facts; but there are many products where different suppliers are highly differentiated and the various suppliers are not subject to price competition in any meaningful sense. To those economists who have been taught and continue to believe that only perfect competition can produce a perfect economy, every attempt to avoid price competition is a distortion of the market taking the economy further away from perfection.[9] One variation on this position is the investigation of "adequate" product variety: theoretical investigations of the benefit gained by consumers from the availability of products more closely tailored to their personal tastes, as against the general disbenefit of the higher prices that are assumed to follow the further division of the market into taste segments.[10]

In reality, as against theory, there are both negative and positive arguments to refute both the assertion that "excess" variety raises consumer prices and the belief that departures from perfect competition harm consumers.

In a market dominated by monopolistic competition and oligopoly with product differentiation, firms set their prices with primary reference to the behavior of their own customers. Firms that raise their prices beyond the pure monopoly point actually lose money; so firms that set their prices slightly below the monopoly point, as the evidence, such as it is, suggests that they do, are behaving rationally. The entry of a firm offering a new, differentiated product into an established firm's market will attract some of the existing firm's customers if its value proposition suits them better; but there is no reason to believe that those customers who don't switch will suddenly become more tolerant of price rises. A firm that raises its prices when faced with a shrinking market will rapidly if not immediately reach the point that the shrinkage accelerates. The argument that product differentiation raises prices does not hold under monopolistic competition or oligopoly with product differentiation.

The second argument against the possibility of excess product differentiation comes from Schumpeter and has two prongs. The first is simply that the normal competitive situation is dynamic, not static: direct price competition occurs, but is relatively rare and economically marginal. New products, organizational forms, and production processes are the major competitive weapons in a modern market economy: in Schumpeter's words competition through innovation when compared to competition through price is like "a bombardment compared to the forcing of a door." The second point made by Schumpeter is that human progress is marked by innovation, not lower prices relative to incomes. New products are not, in general, a manifestation of excessive variety, but rather steps in economic progress generally. If a new product does not offer net value to its prospective customers, it will fail in the market.

Innovation in the Real Economy

Schumpeter's fivefold definition is generally regarded as complete:

> [Innovation is one of] (1) The introduction of a new good—that is one with which consumers are not yet familiar—or a new quality of good. (2) The introduction of a new method of production, that is one not yet tested by experience in the branch of manufacture concerned, which need by no means be founded upon a discovery scientifically new, and can also exist in a new way of handling a commodity commercially. (3) The opening of a new market, that is a market into which the particular branch of manufacture of the country in question has not previously entered, whether or not this market has existed before. (4) The conquest of a new source of supply of raw materials or half-manufactured goods, again irrespective of whether this source already exists or whether it first has to be created. (5) The carrying out of the new organization of any industry, like the creation of a monopoly position (for example through trustification) or the breaking up of a monopoly position.[11]

Schumpeter's alternate definition is less well known and is reproduced here as a demonstration that Schumpeter understood marginalist theory and was quite capable of making fun of it:

> It stands to reason, finally, that outside factors and growth factors do not exhaust the list of the influences which produce and shape

economic change. Obviously the face of the earth would look very different if people, besides having their economic life changed by natural events and changing it themselves by extra-economic action, had done nothing else except multiply and save. If it looks as it does, this is just as obviously due to the unremitting efforts of people to improve according to their lights upon their productive and commercial methods, i.e., to the changes in technique of production, the conquest of new markets, the insertion of new commodities, and so on. This historic and irreversible change in the way of doing things we call "innovation" and we define: innovations are changes in production functions which cannot be decomposed into infinitesimal steps. Add as many mail-coaches as you please, you will never get a railroad by so doing.[12]

Innovation starts with someone observing an opportunity to improve upon the familiar productive and commercial methods and the creation of a new combination of materials, components, and processes that will achieve that improvement. There are very few historical instances of an innovation arising directly out of basic scientific research and relatively few out of applied scientific research. Scientific discoveries may make certain innovations possible; but such discoveries are not, in Schumpeter's sense, innovations.

Schumpeter's insistence on the essential discontinuity created by an innovation means that single incremental changes are not innovations under his definition, even when the cumulative effect of a series of such improvements does constitute a discontinuity. The Japanese "way of improvement," *kaizen*, was an organizational innovation with enormous productivity implications, even though most of the changes in production methods occurring in the firms that adopted *kaizen* were incremental changes with a barely measurable impact on productivity.

Part of the justification for distinguishing incremental change from major or *Bahnbrechen*[13] innovation is that such major innovations will generally require an investment that will exceed the resources available to an individual innovator or small, innovative firm.

Schumpeter described two innovation pathways. "Schumpeter I" conflates the innovator with an entrepreneur seeking to break into the upper middle classes; the entrepreneur secures the finance needed to turn his or her concept into a marketable product or service from a merchant bank. In "Schumpeter II" the innovator is an employee, or even a team of employees, of a corporation in a department with a general charge to devise profitable product and process improvements, and the necessary finance will be drawn from the corporation's cash flow.

There is no point in Schumpeter's writing where II replaced I: II appeared and I remained. Klepper explained that there is a practical reason both for the distinction and for both modes of entrepreneurship continuing.[14] A large corporation will necessarily have a substantial market share and so can obtain a prompt return on cost and quality innovations that is inaccessible to the individual entrepreneur or small- or medium-scale enterprise.

The record of corporations in introducing genuinely new products, as distinct from product line extensions or facelifts, is patchy. A corporation will be able to deploy far greater resources for both development and initial marketing than a small or new enterprise, but this is not always an advantage. The major corporation Xerox developed the first computers with a graphical user interface and even sold a few; but it was the far smaller Apple that incorporated a graphical user interface into an affordable computer, the Macintosh, and marketed it successfully. The former Xerox staff who joined Apple are believed to have complained that they were frustrated by Xerox's corporate bureaucracy while Apple, at least in its early days, believed itself part of the counterculture.[15]

A corporation considering introducing a new product or service may proceed cautiously for fear of cannibalizing its existing product range or diverting sales and marketing effort from its established product lines. Cost and quality innovations emerging from a corporate R&D division can generally be put into profitable service immediately, but new products cannot be profitable before they have built a sufficient market share, which will have cost quite a lot to build.

Market Introduction Cost

Marketing is dealt with at greater length below; but it is worth anticipating the material to point out the very high marketing costs associated with a genuinely new product. There are well-verified cases[16] where the expenditure on marketing a new product after its launch has been a multiple of the total cost of development to the point at which it was ready for the market. The major pharmaceutical companies, probably the most research-intensive of all industries, spend more on sales and marketing than they do on product research and development.

Naïve models of innovation (and naïve would-be innovators) often fail to take these market introduction costs into proper account; certainly, economists used to the assumption of the instantaneous and costless transmission of knowledge, as well as many critics of corporate capitalism, tend to see something wasteful or even sinister in sales and marketing expenditure. If a product offers the best value on the market, they ask, why do companies need to spend millions of dollars telling us about it? Surely, they argue, the facts should speak for themselves.

Few economic assumptions represent such a serious departure from reality as the assumption that knowledge is instantaneously and costlessly transmitted. Even learning to talk about the instantaneous and costless transmission of knowledge takes three or four years' study toward an undergraduate degree in economics. Edith Penrose understood, and her recent popularizers such as Gary Hamel understand, that a company is a learning organization; and part of what it must learn is how to identify likely customers for its products and convert them into actual ones at a bearable expense.

Major corporations can sustain their marketing efforts out of their operating cash flow; and by accounting convention, they report it as a current expense; but entrepreneurs and small companies seeking to exploit large opportunities have inadequate or no cash flows and must seek finance elsewhere. Such firms are unattractive to major lenders, since they lack sufficient assets to provide security for loans of the scale required.

Venture Capital

An extensive venture capital industry emerged in America in the 1950s and a smaller but still significant one in the other English-speaking countries in the following decades to advance the money required by entrepreneurs and new enterprises attempting to introduce new products; and the returns expected by venture capitalists are closer to Shylock than ordinary banking practice. A venture-capital firm will suggest that its investors should expect an 18 percent per year or better return after all fees; the gross return on a properly managed venture fund is of the order of 25 percent.

A simplified model venture-capital firm invests equally in six enterprises, harvesting each of them in five years: one yields nothing, four return their original investment with a modest increment, and one returns eleven times its venture investment for a 25 percent per year overall return.[17] In practice the distribution of returns will not be quite so rectilinear; but still, a VC firm must expect some bad years as well as some particularly good ones. To make an uncertain return averaging 18 percent attractive to major investors, VC firms set up "closed-end" funds that are wound up after a defined period, returning their investment plus accrued returns to the fund's investors; by accumulating a number of years' operations, the VC firm bends the statistics in its favor.

A VC firm has a second point of leverage: the people and companies coming to a normal VC firm seeking investment will have exhausted all other possibilities for getting the funding necessary to continue. The VC firm, when preparing an offer, will set its cash contribution as low as possible and its corresponding equity share as high as possible, undervaluing the contribution of the founding entrepreneurial team to the extent that they can get away with it. This ensures that even when the investee firm is only moderately successful, the VC will emerge with a handsome profit.

The model described above looks too easy, but the skill required to ensure that the companies chosen for investment meet the profile should not be underrated. A successful VC must win, effectively, one out of six "bets"; and the winner, assuming an average portfolio return for the remaining five, must be a stunning success. A real VC firm will make more than six investments; but it still relies on extraordinary returns from at least a sixth of them to achieve its target and satisfy its investors. Plenty of VCs have chosen a portfolio with a few modest winners and too many losers that only their mother could have loved, leaving their investors lamenting and the VCs themselves looking for another profession.

Harvest and Exit

Many venture-capital firms operate by raising closed-end investment funds on which they pay nominal or no interest or dividends, but they are committed to returning the capital and accumulated earnings less their fees on a designated date. This means that when a venture-capital firm takes a position in an enterprise, it is definitely not a long-term position.

There are two broad routes for a venture-capital firm to exit a successful investment: the trade sale and the Initial Public Offering. In a trade sale, all the assets of the firm are sold to a larger firm and the original firm is then wound up. The new owner may offer to employ the entrepreneurs or may not, but either way they will no longer have a financial interest in the business that they founded.

An Initial Public Offering of shares to the public followed by a listing on a stock exchange is a less common but more lucrative form of exit, and the entrepreneurs may choose to sell their interest into

175

the flotation, or they may choose to retain what will usually now be a minority interest. Flotation is relatively rare for at least two reasons: one is that only a few new ventures achieve growth rates high enough to make them attractive to stock-market investors inside the time horizon allowed by venture capitalists; and the other is that stock-market investors may be reluctant to subscribe to the float of a company in an unfashionable industry.

There are clear structural consequences to this system of relying on venture capital to drive product innovation. One of the most obvious is the separation of the growth-driven innovators from their products very early in their life cycle: it has to be possible that this premature maturity is also associated with early senility, but in the absence of contemporary comparators, this is little more than a guess supported by a few anecdotes.

Another structural consequence may be that potential product innovations that cannot be turned from bench-top concept to commercial success inside five or so years may be neglected, at least by companies in countries that follow the Anglo-American model of capitalism. Major innovations such as Pilkington's float glass process, Toyota's lean production system, or Rio Tinto's HIsmelt don't fit either the venture-capital or the corporate stock-price maximizing models.

Alternative Forms of Venture Capital

From Bismarck's time in Germany and those other developing economies that followed its example, notably Japan and Korea, industry-focused banks adopted the role of venture capital supplier, usually taking a small equity stake in the ventures that they supported and following this with very large interest-bearing loans. One result of this is that firms in countries following the German development model run far higher debt-to-equity ratios than are acceptable in English-speaking countries; another is that writers familiar with the Anglo-American model denounce the close relationship between banks and their business clients in countries using the development model as "crony capitalism."

Crony or not, Chalmers Johnson[18] among others has pointed out that without the use of loans from closely associated banks, the East Asian miracle would have been stillborn.

Capitalist development needs money, and there are only two ways for a developing country to get a sufficient quantity of it. One is to create it using a home-grown banking system, as described in Chapter 4; the other is to welcome foreign direct investment. Foreign direct investment can be a quicker path to development, bringing proven technical and marketing expertise to a country; but the concessions that make a country attractive to foreign investors can prove expensive in the long run, and if a country is unwilling to maintain the concessions, the industry can leave as rapidly as it arrived.

Using local banks to provide most of the capital needed for industrial development means that the new industries stay under local control: there may be some waste and inefficiency as they get established but they are less likely to abandon operations in their parent country than a subsidiary owned and controlled from overseas. Germany in the nineteenth century, and Japan also in the nineteenth century after the Meiji Restoration, used local banking networks, as did the countries of the East Asian miracle: Korea, Taiwan, and China.

Marketing and Innovation

Most economists seem to have a major blind spot when it comes to the role of retailing and distribution in a modern economy, even though these sectors account for more than a fifth of a typical developed country's GDP.

The scale of the retail and distribution industries in developed countries is a highly visible rebuttal of the assumption of perfect competition. Under perfect competition all an economy can produce is a single product, or a number of perfectly interchangeable products. Under perfect competition all these products must be sold at a single, market-determined price to consumers who have perfect knowledge of the available products and perfect foresight of their own requirements. At the same time, the market forces operating under perfect competition must eliminate all forms of wasteful investment.

In the United States, recent statistics[19] showed that production (mining, agriculture, manufacturing, construction, and utilities) accounted for 14.5 percent of employment while retail and wholesale accounted for 14.1 percent, plus some fraction of those employed in transport and storage. Other services, including government and defense and in particular business services such as advertising, accounted for the rest.

Before considering business services, the real American economy was so far from "efficient" that for every person employed in production another was employed in retail and wholesale. The numbers speak for themselves: this employment distribution could not arise in an economy

177

based on perfect or even nearly perfect markets. When the advertising component of the business services classification (11.2 percent) is added to the retail and wholesale total, it is clear that marketing and selling products requires, in the modern American economy, more labor power than producing all the goods and services on sale.

Since real competition is obviously not even nearly perfect, there is no need to continue with its many ungrounded assumptions, such as the assumption of a single universal product, when they are so obviously contradicted by everyday reality. Real markets involve multiple products, none of which are perfect substitutes for any other. Each of the many products on the market are each only partial substitutes for a tiny fraction of the products available and not a substitute at all for the rest.

Perfect competition also requires the assumption that consumers are identical in everything except their purchasing power; that is, given the same amount of money to spend, any two consumers would make exactly the same purchasing decisions. This assumption is strictly redundant under the assumption of a single universal product, but it can nevertheless be found in the economic literature.[20] Marketing bridges the gap between the standard economic assumptions of a single, unchanging product and representative consumers, and the reality of diverse consumers and a rapidly changing array of diverse products. It also bridges the gap between the standard economic assumption that knowledge is instantly disseminated and costlessly acquired and the reality of the slow and incomplete diffusion of information and the even slower conversion of information to actionable knowledge.

In the real world, marketing and sales effort is applied to assist consumers to become customers of a particular set of suppliers and consumers of a particular set of products; and competition is not about offering a version of the universal product at the lowest feasible price but rather in making a superior value-for-money offer to those consumers who have the means and inclination to respond to it.

As an obvious fact, most products are complex and all consumers are complex, and so the effect when an arbitrarily selected consumer interacts with a previously unfamiliar product is simply unpredictable. As far as the marketer is concerned, the interaction is a success if the consumer makes the new product his or her favored choice for addressing the needs and wants for which that product is suited and a failure otherwise; but the product is equally a failure if the consumer never tries it, even though, had that consumer tried it, he would have become a regular user. Such outcomes are impossible in most economic models, but all too frequent in the real world of retailing and marketing.

Some product innovation attempts fail because, although the trial users like the product and wish to continue using it, it is priced at a level that eliminates any net benefit from owning and using it. The Xerox Star was the first workstation with a graphical user interface,[21] but it was so expensive that very few of its potential users could justify the cost. By contrast the Bic disposable ballpoint pen was launched at a wholesale price below its initial cost of production; the high sales and the rapid volume build-up enabled the Bic company to bring costs down rapidly, and the product soon became extremely profitable. Price can deter potential users from buying an otherwise attractive product; but an unattractive product won't succeed at any price.

The innovation-driven growth that characterizes a modern economy would not occur at anything like its present rate without active marketing by producers and distributors of goods and services. The first truly modern entrepreneur was Josiah Wedgwood, properly famous as the innovator of the factory system of manufacture. What may be less well known is that he was the innovator of modern marketing practice in order to sell the many novel products and designs that his factory produced.[22]

Buyer Behavior

Consumers

Consumers are mostly reasonable: the hyperrationality assumed by neoclassical economics is generally seen as a symptom of mental illness; but asserting that consumers are not hyperrational does not mean asserting that consumers are generally stupid or reckless. The reasonable consumer is aware that he or she has only a finite time to live and a finite time to act in any day; and time spent on one activity cannot be spent on another.

When it comes to actual consumer choices, very little is known with certainty. In the early nineteenth century, when most of the tablets of stone that define economics were chiseled, the majority of consumers were at most a few days from starvation, and so their motivation in the market was pretty clear. Even in the early nineteenth century, there were middle- and upper-class households for whom starvation was no threat, and their purchasing behavior was much more capricious than that of the lower classes.

In a modern developed economy and even in most developing economies, incomes for the majority of consumers are significantly higher
in real terms than those enjoyed by the British lower middle classes
in the early nineteenth century; and so their purchasing decisions are
much more complicated than choosing between buying unprocessed
or partly processed food or starving. Pleasure, vanity, and love can all
influence consumer behavior in a modern market. Economists may talk
about "utility" but go on to state that utility is incommensurable and
personal—a word with no meaning. (If utility was measurable and the
same goods or services delivered the same utility to every consumer
of them, there would be an irresistible case for redistribution from the
rich to the poor; it is only by asserting that interpersonal comparisons
of utility are meaningless that orthodox economists can avoid advocating extreme egalitarianism.)

In a market supplied with many products, each of which has some
partial substitutes among those on offer, a consumer must make a
conscious choice and make it before he or she starves to death like the
fabled Balaam's ass. Consumers who enter a modern supermarket with a
shopping list containing twenty items will be offered a choice of at least
ten thousand items and as many as twenty-five thousand. Consumers
whose shopping list is generic rather than brand- or product-specific
(e.g., "two portions of high-protein food" rather than "two frozen
chicken breasts with a particular brand") will have to consider at least
a hundred and as many as a thousand alternatives for each item on
their list: if they take five seconds over each decision, they will be in
the supermarket for at least four hours—and that is if none of their
choices are contingent on others.

It becomes a simple matter of saving time for a consumer to create
a subset of the available products and limit his or her purchases to that
subset.[23] Depending on the category, a consumer may have a favored
supplier or a favored brand. Both choices may be applicable, as when
a consumer visits a favored supermarket and then selects a favored
brand; for other product categories, the brand or the supplier may
dominate the consumer's choice.

Experimenting with an unfamiliar product is never costless: even a
consumer offered a free sample must consider the possibility that she
won't like the consequences of using or owning the product in question. For example, a hairdresser opening a new salon may offer free or
deeply discounted haircutting and styling to attract customers; there
is no guarantee that those who accept the offer will like the result; but

180

unless they want to shave their head, they have to put up with it until their hair has regrown.

For these reasons consumers do not, without an incentive or other form of encouragement, give an unfamiliar product a trial. The cost of providing the encouragement, information, and incentives required to induce a statistically significant number of consumers to try a product with which they were previously unfamiliar generally exceeds the gross profit on the sales so achieved. For common supermarket product categories, the cost of providing incentives, information, and encouragement may exceed the gross revenue from prompt sales of the new product.

Industrial Buyers

Industrial buyers, or buyers in B2B markets to use the alternative term, have a much more straightforward motivation than consumers. Practically all B2B purchasing is carried out on behalf of incorporated firms; and the dominant motive for expenditure by a firm is the belief that the purchased goods and services can be resold profitably or put to profitable use. Reality is a little more complicated: vanity and personal relationships can also play a role in B2B choice; but rather than a search for ineffable utility, the B2B buyer expects to gain more money than he or she spends. It is an easy but misleading leap to the assumption that the value of a B2B offer can be assessed precisely, and so the conscientious B2B buyer will always select the deal with the greatest value. Anyone who hasn't shaken off the various economists' assumptions about perfect knowledge and foresight will underestimate the actual complexity of a B2B buyer's decision.

Time generates uncertainty in even the most mundane purchasing decisions: there is generally a delay between placing an order and accepting delivery; a further delay before the received goods or services are incorporated into a deliverable product of some sort; yet another delay before the product is sold; and in general another delay before payment is received. If downstream market conditions change, a purchasing decision that looked appropriate at the time can seem ruinous in hindsight.

Major purchasing decisions, such as premises or plant, are based around assumptions that are inevitably going to be proved more or less wrong. Viewed in hindsight, some decisions will be seen to have led to outcomes better than expected while some will have turned out worse. The effect of changes in the downstream market will be compounded by changes in technology: equipment that was state of the art when purchased may become hopelessly obsolete long before it wears out or is fully depreciated in the accounts.

Much of the economics literature treats purchasing decisions as an essentially simple matter of picking the right point on the production function to optimize the use of capital and labor. The production function itself only makes sense if capital is fungible—that is to say, all capital items are interchangeable. If I own a blast furnace and the price of beer rises, I can, under the assumption of fungible capital, turn my blast furnace into a brewery without expense. If only.

When considering the purchase of equipment of a type that a firm has no previous experience of, uncertainty takes on yet another dimension. The new equipment may function as promised or it may not; and the workers who must operate it may prove competent to do so or they may not. Under either or both contingencies, the costs of remedial action can easily exceed the expected benefits of taking on the unfamiliar technology—and that is if it works at all.

Decisions that economists model as a simple matter of picking a point on a well-known production function informed by perfect foresight and complete knowledge are far more complicated in the real world. The real B2B purchaser acts under considerable uncertainty, and while the choice may be narrower than that facing a typical consumer in a supermarket, the consequences of an error can be much worse. The consumer who tries an unfamiliar brand of biscuits and doesn't like them has lost a few dollars; a B2B buyer who makes a sufficiently serious mistake may lose his or her job and possibly even destroy the firm that he or she works for.

Because the risks are so much greater for B2B buyers, the incentives needed to persuade them to try an unfamiliar product are also much greater than they are for consumers. These incentives may include deep discounts, detailed guarantees, and free staff training on top of a great deal of personal attention to the buying firm's managers. These incentives may well consume the entire gross margin on a sale—or more.

The Three Rs

An established firm with an established customer base, whether of final consumers or other businesses, would appear to be in an impregnable position, since its potential rivals can only hope to get a start in its markets by selling at a loss. An aspiring entrant may advertise and deploy sales staff in the hope that the effect will be cumulative and eventually the sheer weight of advertising and selling will lead to profitable sales; but such hopes are vain. Research has established that the stimulus effect of promotion and advertising decays quite rapidly such that there is little residual effect a week after the promotion and/or advertising ceases. The apparent economic impossibility of successful new product introduction cannot be overcome by the accumulating influence of advertising and other forms of promotion.

On the face of it, every attempt to introduce a new product would appear doomed, with the cost of sales staff, advertising, and other promotion exceeding any possible profit. The "three Rs" of recommendation, replenishment, and repurchase turn the situation around, at least when the product creates sufficient satisfaction in its trial users to trigger them.

Replenishment has the potential to drive supermarket products and most other consumables into profit without a contribution from the other two. If a sufficient fraction of those consumers who were induced to try a product by promotion and advertising are sufficiently satisfied by their experience to buy that product again for use when their first purchase has been consumed, and this habit is sufficiently persistent, the product may become profitable through repeat purchases.

Andrew Ehrenberg was one of the earliest marketing academics to build and verify statistical models of consumer behavior in frequently purchased consumer-good markets. He confirmed the tendency of customers to stick with a familiar brand, and he developed a predictive model for the rate at which this behavior would erode. His model has been verified over many product categories in many countries. His model implies and detailed research has verified that consumers are not, in general, "loyal" to a brand; rather, they establish a purchasing habit. He also established that consumers spend very little time, on average, making purchase decisions in branded product categories, implying that the expected benefit of a switch is typically less than the cost of the time and uncertainty involved in making it.[24]

Further work by Ehrenberg and his associates examined the relative significance of price and advertising in prompting consumers to try unfamiliar products or to persist with the use of familiar ones. Their results emphasized the importance of securing a trial of a product by a consumer previously unfamiliar with it; and the equal importance of the trial outcome being satisfactory in that a reasonable fraction of the users added the trialed product to their mental set of acceptable purchases.

Recommendation ("word of mouth" promotion) is almost certainly the key engine of profitability for both consumer and industrial durables. The time between purchases by any one user in such categories is typically a matter of years, and to sustain a cash flow drain to support advertising and promotion over a period of years without any return from profitable sales would be financially suicidal. If, however, the early purchasers of a product are sufficiently satisfied with it to demonstrate their ownership by ostentatious use and to recommend it to other possible purchasers explicitly, sales to these referred purchasers may be profitable. This can generate the cash flow necessary to maintain both production and advertising and promotion.

Frank Bass extended Ehrenberg's work to the product life cycle for consumer durables, proposing a relatively simple differential equation, the solution of which generated an extraordinarily close fit to the actual pattern of adoption of a large number of consumer durable products.[25] Bass and those who followed him established that the recommendation effect was about 50 percent per fully satisfied customer per year; that is, if you start the year with two completely satisfied customers, their recommendations will give you one more. Achieving such high levels of satisfaction is difficult, and in the absence of powerful network effects, a prudent planner won't assume a recommendation rate much over 30 percent per year.

Bass was able to define the adoption cycle with only two parameters, which he termed the coefficients of innovation and imitation, respectively; Mahajan and others preferred to refer to the parameters as the coefficients of external and internal influence.[26] The addition of parameters for churn and repurchase interval enable the model to be extended to cover the full product life cycle, while it can be confidently argued that the coefficient of external influence is positively correlated with promotional effort.

In a relatively mature market, a substantial number of durable product owners may find their product worn out or lacking the most advanced features. Such owners may seek to replace their product with a newer equivalent; and if their initial satisfaction has been maintained, they may patronize the original vendor without "testing the market." Such replacement sales are a key to profitability for durable goods suppliers servicing relatively mature markets, and relatively small differences in the persistence of customer satisfaction after the first purchase can have a significant impact on a supplier's profitability.

Frederick Reichheld was a principal consultant with Bain & Co, where he observed a significant correlation between customer retention rates and profitability. Reichheld was not an academic, and so his studies tended to be anecdotal rather than coming decorated with P-statistics; but the depth of his experience, and his many accounts of the success of clients for whom he developed customer retention enhancement programs, make his conclusions as convincing as those in any academic paper.

Extended Bass models, as discussed above, can be used to simulate the operations of companies with high and low retention rates, and when suitable parameter values are used, the simulated companies reproduce Reichheld's results. In particular, Reichheld's claim that a modest improvement in retention rates of the order of 5 percent could lead to a profitability improvement of 50 percent[27] appears entirely reasonable in the light of model studies.

Both repurchase and recommendation may apply to a retailer or dealer rather than to a specific product; and even in the case of products, the brand often guides recommendation and repurchase rather than a more specific product specification. A satisfied owner of a Ford motor car may recommend "Ford" cars to his friends or may recommend a particular dealer; when that person decides to trade in his current car, he may himself go to the nominated dealer or seek a Ford-branded car; but he would not be amused if, after a lapse of years, he was offered a replica of his original purchase.

The effects of recommendation and repurchase may include "lock-in," where a technically inferior product may come to dominate a market. One of the best documented examples is how Matsushita's[28] VHS came to dominate Sony's technically superior Betamax in the market for home video recording systems. The trigger was a moment of inspired *chutzpah* on the part of Matsushita's CEO that made VHS the "first mover" in the US market through a distribution agreement with RCA.[29] Recommendations both from early users and trial purchases by those who trusted the RCA brand then maintained this lead long enough for video stores to stock VHS titles preferentially, and the limited selection of titles available on Betamax restricted its sales to the point that Sony eventually switched its own production to VHS.[30]

Increasing and Decreasing Returns

First-year economics students are taught a great deal about decreasing returns, known to engineers and scientists as negative feedback. I mentioned in Chapter 3 the way economists inferred decreasing returns from studying English agriculture in the nineteenth century: the best land was worked first, and getting a crop became progressively harder as farmers tried to increase output.

I also mentioned the fact that most real firms do not experience decreasing returns to output. At least some economists find this hard to believe because in their models, if the negative feedback is removed, output rises towards infinity. As Sraffa[31] pointed out in 1926, the limit on most firms' output is not rising costs of production, but the cost of gaining new customers.

Marketing involves both increasing and decreasing returns. It is expensive to gain a customer, but once gained that expense is returned for as long as that customer remains a customer and can be invested in marketing to build the customer base further. In many, by no means all, markets a customer's recommendations gain suppliers yet more customers. These increasing returns explain how a company like Apple can come from being an also-ran in the personal computer market to the world's most valuable company in less than a decade.

Decreasing returns never go away entirely. The number of potential customers for any product is finite, and the more of them that are turned into actual customers, the harder it is to find more potential ones to covert. Recommendation worked very well for Apple as early iPhone users told their friends about its many wonders; but as these friends became users themselves, they could continue to enthuse about their iPhone's features and benefits, talking to each other on their iPhones.

Some economists continue to give excessive weight to decreasing returns, ignoring the turbulent present to describe a vision of the distant future. Many business analysts make the opposite mistake, observing growth in a particular market and assuming that it will continue at the observed rate forever. It won't.

Marketing and Economic Growth

There are plenty of economists and economist-influenced writers who persist in explaining economic growth as a function of population growth and household saving in defiance of the evidence of their own everyday experience. Average real income in the developed countries has risen eightfold or more in the last hundred years; but a typical citizen of a developed country on today's average income who was only allowed to buy and use products that were available a hundred years ago would not feel very happy about it.

As explained above innovation is the key driver of economic growth and development, and the successful introduction of new products, new qualities of products, and new methods of production are all examples of innovation. As also explained above, without successful marketing new products and new production methods are stillborn: it is only when a firm can successfully deploy the three Rs of replenishment, recommendation, and replacement that a product can move from an idea to a commercial and economic reality.

Marketing academics, as a body, are remarkably reticent about the economic significance of marketing.[32] This reflects, in part, the way economics has come to dominate the social sciences, causing academics in other disciplines to be reluctant to challenge economic dogma, and in part the degree to which economics PhDs have taken marketing lectureships when no economics positions were available. The necessary fact that marketing is firmly based in the reality universe also drives a wedge between marketing and economics academics: assumptions may be critical to economic theory, but they can be lethal to marketing practice.

Both marketing academics and practitioners necessarily spend much of their time on highly focused activities. A well-executed marketing program can't save a bad product, but a badly executed program can certainly kill a good one. When a professional marketer can enjoy the accolades that follow the successful launch of a new product and its subsequent creation of a substantial customer base, she is more likely to recall the brilliant advertising and perfect sales briefings that she was responsible for than to muse on the step forward in economic and social progress that the innovation whose birth she enabled represents.

Notes

1. Robinson (1962).
2. See page 33.
3. Sraffa (1960).
4. Kurz & Salvadori (2006), Kurz (2008).
5. See Swann (2014) for a realist economist's view of innovation.
6. Grossman & Helpman (1992, 1994).
7. Romer, Paul M (1986, 1990, 1994).
8. Geroski (1995).
9. See, for example, Snell (1971).
10. See, for example, Lancaster (1975).
11. Schumpeter (1934).
12. Schumpeter (1935).
13. Path-breaking or path-changing; *Bahn* can be used for a railway.

14. Klepper (2002).
15. Sculley & Byrne (1987).
16. Including one where the present author was an expert witness in related litigation.
17. "Modest" here would be the 12 percent average return (without any adjustment for inflation or taxes and assuming all dividends reinvested) for a stock-market portfolio.
18. Johnson (1982, 1985).
19. Employment Projections Program, US Department of Labor, US Bureau of Labor Statistics, http://www.bls.gov/emp/ep_table_201.htm accessed 23 January 2015.
20. Gorman (1953) quoted in Keen (2011).
21. See page 173.
22. Freeman & Soete (1997).
23. Ehrenburg (1990, 1998).
24. Ehrenberg, Goodhardt & Barwise (1990), Ehrenberg & Goodhardt (2002).
25. Bass (1969).
26. Mahajan, Muller & Bass (1990).
27. Reichheld (1996).
28. Matsushita changed its name to Panasonic in 2008, well after these events.
29. Yamashita (1989).
30. Cusumano, Mylonadis & Rosenbloom (1992).
31. Sraffa (1926).
32. Hunt (2000) is an exception.

10

Investment

Our doubts are traitors
And make us lose the good we oft might win
By fearing to attempt.
—William Shakespeare, *Measure for Measure* 1:4

Economists of every persuasion agree that investment is important as a source of employment and as a foundation for future growth. In pure neoclassical theory, all decisions regarding investment have already been made. Even the more relaxed discussions of investment generally take place under the assumptions of perfect foresight and perfect capital markets.

Neoliberal/Austrian theorists argue that investment decisions should be left "to the market" on the basis that only a market can generate the price signals that entrepreneurs will use to guide investment. Friedman added a requirement for strict control of the money supply to prevent an economy being cluttered up with bad investments made on overoptimistic grounds.

The person who makes decisions about investments is an entrepreneur: an individual in neoliberal theory and an individual or a corporate investment committee to those influenced by Schumpeter. Until the work of Dixit and Pindyck discussed below, economics in any flavor had little to say about how entrepreneurs made decisions.

Schumpeter described the entrepreneur as an innovator, identifying some "new combination" of components and technology and putting it into profitable service with the support of a bank that will create the money needed; investors are only important insofar as they give comfort to the bank and make good its losses in the event that the entrepreneurial venture fails.[1]

In neoliberal/Austrian theory, the entrepreneur is an arbitrageur, scanning the economy to find a price discrepancy and profiting from it until her activities cause the discrepancy to disappear.[2] In pure neoclassical theory, the entrepreneur is a conceptual source of limited services, whose presence is necessary for companies to function but whose only effect is to limit the size to which they can grow.[3]

Risk and Uncertainty

Any discussion of investment in the real world must acknowledge that some investments fail and some exceed their entrepreneur's expectations: the world is an uncertain place where the only way to be certain about the future is to wait for it to happen. Every investment involves the sacrifice of current consumption in the expectation of receiving future benefits. Money and effort that might have been directed to immediate gratification is instead expended on a project that promises greater, or at least different, benefits in the future. The separation of investment, which occurs now, and the rewards, which are expected in the future, necessarily involves both risk and uncertainty. The investment is certain; the rewards are not.

Uncertainty comes in two flavors: ergodic and nonergodic.

There are various technical definitions of ergodic processes, but essentially an ergodic process produces outcomes that can be analyzed using standard statistical tools. While any specified event may or may not occur in a given time interval, the statistical expectation of such an occurrence doesn't change (or doesn't change by much) if the starting time of the interval changes. The science of statistics began as an analysis of gambling and has become the center of the insurance industry; and from insurance we generally use the term "risk" to describe a situation where an adverse event may occur and the probability of such an event is known.

To take an easy example: an American roulette wheel has thirty-eight numbers: eighteen red, eighteen black, and two green or gray. A winning bet on red or black pays double, and the probability of such a win is 18/38, since a zero (the gray slot) is a win for the house. A casino needs to take precautions against the risk of one gambler getting very lucky and does so by setting house limits; equally the casino doesn't want to discourage bets that present no risk to its solvency, and so the limits should not be set too low. Such risks can be estimated using elementary statistical analysis, and an appropriate policy can be determined.

The actions of an honest roulette wheel are ergodic because of two factors: the odds don't change between spins or from day to day or from place to place; and the odds on any single spin are completely independent of the result of the previous spin. If the ball has just landed on black for the first or the tenth time, the odds of another black are still 18/38.

Life insurance started with an estimate of birth and death rates, and from there it was relatively easy to work out a relationship between a "risk's" regular premium payments and the payout on death. Some of the insured would die young, and their heirs would receive more than the insured had paid in; but most of the "risks" would live long enough to put the insurance company ahead. Statistical analysis was used to set out premium schedules, and the profession of actuary arose to verify the solvency and good practice of life insurance companies.

Nonergodic uncertainty could be broadly defined as "everything else." The small print on most insurance policies summarizes the many events that will not be covered by the policy; and these are principally those events for which no reliable statistics exist and for which history provides no guide to the future. The world is nonergodic—full of surprises. In our everyday lives, we make plans based on predictions about the future; but things seldom turn out exactly as we planned them, and sometimes the outcome is totally unexpected.

To invest requires a plan, and to produce a plan requires assumptions about the future. Most plans start from the assumption that those circumstances and factors that haven't changed recently won't change to the detriment of our objectives, and that where there have been recent changes, either the established trends will continue or they will stabilize. In the unlikely event that all our assumptions prove correct, our plan will lead to a completely successful outcome; but as potential investors, we should be concerned with the robustness of our plan under changing circumstances.

Financial economists have largely adopted the geometric random walk as a tractable type of nonergodic process, for which the mean and standard deviation are not stationary, but they are well behaved over a finite time interval. Informally, they assume that, while we can't predict the future precisely, we can assume that tomorrow will be rather like today, the day after only slightly less so, and so on. These assumptions are consistent with human behavior: if we need to predict the sales of beer for the coming year, taking the sales for the past year as a starting point should not introduce, barring extraordinary and totally unexpected events, unacceptable errors.

Financial economists go further and generally assume that the amount that any variable of interest will vary between today and tomorrow can be estimated by examining its pattern of variation in the recent past, its "volatility." This assumption is consistent with *uncoordinated* human behavior: if individual beer drinkers make individual choices about how much and how frequently to drink, the change in consumption from period to period will be small. The assumption is less true of linked choices, as when people copy other people's behavior. If one fund manager decides to buy a tranche of shares in a particular company, other fund managers may notice this, assume that the first manager has got inside knowledge, and buy shares for their own funds. This will cause the price to rise, and yet more fund managers will see investing in the company as a good idea, causing its price to move far higher than could be explained by a geometric random walk. When one of the fund managers decides that the price is unreasonably high and sells her fund's holding, the price will fall, other fund managers will also sell, and the price will fall far lower than a geometric random walk can explain.

To take an example, given the volatility of shares in Amazon.com, a "six sigma" event, with the stock price moving more than 26 percent in a single day, should occur no more often than once in a billion days of trading under the standard assumptions. In fact, it occurred three times in a fifteen-year period.[4]

The third form of uncertainty comes from the completely unexpected and unpredictable event. From the launch of the IBM PC in 1981 until mid-1985, IBM appeared ready to move into the PC era with the same dominance it had enjoyed over the mainframe computer market; but in August 1985, Don Estridge, the man who had shepherded the PC through the IBM bureaucracy, was one of 131 people killed in the crash of Delta 191 in Dallas; and within two years IBM was an also-ran in the PC market and rapidly losing its dominance over corporate computing.

The risk of Don Estridge, or anyone else, dying in an airplane crash in 1985 was small but well known; but the possibility that the loss of a single executive could derail the strategy of America's most successful and profitable corporation could not, before the event, have been reduced to a statistical risk. It was unexpected and uninsurable.

Economists have been concerned to explain behavior in response to risk for many years, looking for reasons why otherwise similar households adopt different ways of managing risk.[5] Daniel Kahneman spent much of his distinguished academic career examining human responses to risk and uncertainty. One of his major conclusions was that most people will not accept a significant risk unless the rewards for success are disproportionately large. What is significant varies depending on a person's circumstances: a billionaire might regard a $10,000 bet as trivial; but to an ordinary working person the risk of losing $10,000 would be unacceptable unless the rewards were large and the chances of success approached certainty.

Kahneman suggests that the insurance market works because of this differential approach to risk. Most householders take out fire insurance, even though the premiums represent a "bad bet," costing more than the statistical probability of a devastating fire would appear to justify. Fire insurance is acceptable because a small premium eliminates a very large risk. At the other end of the insurance market are the reinsurers, who accept such large risks in return for (relatively) small dividends. "Names" at Lloyds of London agree to cover large but unlikely claims if called upon to do so, but because such Names are wealthy, the possibility of an occasional loss that an ordinary householder would regard as devastating but that, to them, is no more than a potential irritant is outweighed by the certainty of a regular income.

Defining Investment

Human motivation is varied and complex. Economists make hard distinctions between activities where the human performing them may be much less certain. Some people may "work to live" but others "live to work" or at least take pride in their occupation and get pleasure from performing the associated tasks well. The German language distinguishes between "labor" (*Arbeit*) and "rewarding activity" (*Werk*): the distinction survives in English when we refer to an artist's "work."

As far as economists are concerned, business activity can be directed toward current consumption or to facilitate future production; the latter is generally referred to as investment. A farmer grows a crop of wheat: this is clearly production for consumption. She buys a harvesting machine to bring in this and future crops: this is clearly investment.

Sometimes the issues get blurred: if a house is built to be offered for rent, this is clearly an investment, and the rent is the anticipated future product; but if a similar house is built for owner occupation, purchasing it may be seen as a form of consumption. The new harvesting machine may replace a perfectly good older model, with at least part of the buyer's motivation being her wish to show her neighbors how prosperous her farm is.

Further blurring occurs when expenditure is directed toward something than can neither be used for future production nor consumed, now or in the future. Public monuments are seldom economically useful as objects of consumption or as aids to production. Head offices with huge atriums built on choice city center sites do nothing to increase or even sustain production. Both monuments and atriums may, however, act like the tail of a peacock: much as the peacock's glorious tail demonstrates his health to potential mates, the statue or the towering atrium demonstrates the nation's or corporation's financial health to its citizens, investors, and customers.

Planned Private Investment

Much of the economy is in the hands of incorporated businesses, many of the largest of these taking the form of listed public companies. Such companies don't really have juridical owners, and they are managed by directors who may not even own shares in them. The directors are obliged to make decisions "in the interests of the company";[6] they are also bound by statute and case law not to mislead or deceive anyone who deals with them; to maintain a healthy and safe workplace; and to sell products that are both safe and that satisfy the relevant statutory warranties.

The combination of laws, regulations, and marketplace realities make many management decisions "no brainers"—they are purely a response to circumstances. Others, like gold plating the taps in the executive washrooms, escape sanction because there is no one in a position to object. There are two levels of executive decision that are neither routine nor self-indulgent.

One set determines how the company that they manage maintains its market share and profitability, and concern cost and quality issues. The second are the "you bet your company"[7] decisions that lead to the launch of new products or an entry into new markets. When successful, as with the IBM System/360 or the Boeing 707, such decisions lead to many years of profitable growth. When they fail, as did the de Havilland Comet jet aircraft and the NCR Century computer system, they place the long-term viability of their sponsoring company in doubt.

Before the directors of a company agree to a major investment, they must convince themselves that this is "in the interests of the company"—that the company will be better off if it makes the investment than if it doesn't. Every investment faces both risks and uncertainty: relatively quantifiable risks of budget overruns and the various unquantifiable possibilities that may reduce or eliminate the expected returns on the completed project.

A proposal as mundane as replacing a boundary fence might be seen in hindsight as a failed investment if changing economic circumstances lead to the plant that the fence protects being closed.

Various directors and boards of directors may have idiosyncratic ways of evaluating investment proposals, but the most common requires the cash flows associated with a project to be estimated and either the internal rate of return estimated or the net present value computed using a company hurdle rate. In the former case, the estimated internal rate of return will be compared with the hurdle rate.

Proposed investment projects where the net present value estimated using the hurdle rate as a discount rate is positive, or the mathematically equivalent case where the internal rate of return exceeds the hurdle rate, are considered further, while those that fail these tests are rejected without further examination.

Some very experienced directors believe that the necessary calculations can be completed on the back of an envelope; others may look for elaborate spreadsheet models supported by multivolume research reports. The underlying heuristics are the same.

The Economics of Investment Decisions

Economists have two principal reasons to study investment decisions. The first is that public and private investment decisions affect a substantial part of any developed country's GDP and have a profound effect on the future income of individuals and the welfare of society at large. The second is to establish their role as the theoreticians behind business education and so enjoy their share of the income streams generated by postgraduate management education.

The profligacy of capitalism was mentioned in Chapter 1, and clearly many investments fail to produce the desired or any returns. The investments made are still a quasi-infinitesimal subset of the investments that might be made on a purely random basis; and developing this argument strongly suggests that the existence of any successful investments cannot be explained without assuming some selection process. The record of many investment failures proves that the selection processes generally employed are imperfect.

Pure economic theory in either its neoclassical or Hayekian guise has nothing useful to offer to those responsible for making investment decisions. Under the Arrow-Debreu conditions for general equilibrium in the neoclassical model, all the investment decisions that will ever

195

be needed have already been made. In Hayek's model, entrepreneurs respond to "price signals" to guide their investments; but since there can be no price signals pointing the way to new products or new levels of product quality, the most significant investment decisions lie outside that model. Neoclassical economists who relax the Arrow-Debreu conditions sufficiently to discuss purposive investment decisions tend to assume perfect foresight and perfect capital markets, neither of which form part of any real entrepreneur's environment.

Keynes explained that if the rate of investment was too low, an economy could descend into a state of persistent involuntary unemployment, but his explanation for the level of investment, the adequacy or otherwise of entrepreneurs' "animal spirits," does not take the subject of evaluating prospective investments very far. Schumpeter's innovating entrepreneur has a more rational motivation, but Schumpeter himself did not discuss the venture evaluation process in any detail.

Every investment means diverting resources from consumption: someone building a factory or a hotel is clearly not engaged in growing crops or tending livestock. Since consumption is generally preferable to not consuming, there needs to be some incentive or compulsion involved in suppressing consumption to favor investment. Stalin's forced collectivization of Soviet agriculture in the 1930s was intended to free resources for rapid industrialization; the less violent processes of taxation for public works in more civilized countries also divert resources to investment.

The Net Present Value Rule

The economist Marshall explained investment decisions in terms of an exchange of current for future consumption. Deferring consumption requires that an investor accepts a loss of immediate benefits in exchange for a promise, not entirely believable, of future ones. It follows more or less directly that such a decision will only be made willingly when the value of the promised future benefits exceeds the value of the immediate benefits forgone.

Finance students are taught that money has a "time value": current cash is worth more than the most believable promises of future cash. Promises of future cash can be reduced to a "present value," the amount of current cash that is a fair equivalent of a given amount of future cash. If, for example, a government sells bonds that promise to pay the bearer $105 on a particular future date, and buyers of these bonds are prepared to pay $100 in cash, the discount is 5 percent.[8]

Partly for convenience, and partly as a reflection of our ignorance about the future, students are taught that a discount can be specified as a discount rate and a time between the present and when the future value is to be delivered. In the previous example, if the government's promise became due in one year's time, the discount rate would be 5 percent per year.[9] Many investments do not lead to a single future payment, but as long as a discount rate can be set, any schedule of payments and receipts can be given a net present value simply by adding up the contribution of each of the expected future payments and receipts after discounting them at that rate for the time from now until each expected payment or receipt date. Spreadsheet programs such as Microsoft Excel include functions to largely automate this process.

Marshall suggested that rational investors would compute the present value of an opportunity, and if this exceeded the cost of investing, they would proceed. The rule is simple, but applying it successfully requires knowledge of the appropriate rate of return. In the Britain of Marshall's day and in most developed countries, there were and are "safe" opportunities for investment in the form of government securities. It would not make sense for an investor to support a proposal with a lower expected return. This "risk-free" rate becomes a logical floor; but the question of just how much the expected rate of return on a proposed investment in a venture less secure than government bonds should exceed the risk-free rate remained an open question.

Putting a value on a proposed investment is therefore a two-stage process: firstly, the planner must set out a schedule of costs and returns, putting an expected date on each; then the planner must determine an appropriate discount rate. The purely mechanical task of reducing the schedule to a net present value can be safely left to a computer.

The Capital Asset Pricing Model

A breakthrough, of sorts, in the problem of determining an appropriate rate of return came with Sharpe,[10] who proposed that stock prices would reflect the expected return and the volatility of that return to investors who held these shares. Sharpe assumed that there existed a "market" portfolio holding an appropriately weighted fraction of every possible income-generating investment. In such a portfolio, idiosyncratic variations would cancel each other out and the only changes in the value of the portfolio would follow changes in conditions across the whole economy.

Sharpe's Capital Asset Pricing Model (CAPM) assumed that each individual security would have a characteristic parameter "beta" that reflected the extent to which changes in the broad economy would affect the price of that security: a security with a beta value of zero was not affected at all by changes in the wider economy; a security with a beta value of one reacted to the same extent as the "market" portfolio; and a security with a beta value greater than one reacted to a greater extent than the market portfolio.

In broad terms Sharpe's model reflects reality. Firms supplying basic household consumable products are not greatly affected by broader economic pressures: people must eat. Firms supplying household durables, on the other hand, can be seriously affected by economic changes: households can put off replacing their car or television set if they feel the need to limit their expenditure. The onset of the Great Recession barely affected companies like Wal-Mart or Tesco while Ford, General Motors, and Chrysler were forced to the edge of bankruptcy.

In developing the CAPM, Sharpe assumed that "idiosyncratic" variations in a company's stock price, reflecting specific information about that company, would be essentially random, and in a well-balanced portfolio, the idiosyncratic fluctuations in individual company performance would cancel each other out. So the only factor affecting the expected rate of return for a company would be its sensitivity to fluctuations in the general economy.

Sharpe's CAPM, as extended by Sharpe and others, has become a staple of all MBA programs where budding corporate managers are taught to calculate the expected return on equity by reference to the average market return and the beta specific to the firm concerned. This, after adjustment for any debt finance in use, becomes the weighted average cost of capital, the WACC, and this in turn becomes the discount rate to be used in investment planning.[11] Most MBA programs then teach that if a project's projected cash flows, when discounted at the WACC, yield a positive net present value (NPV), the project should proceed. Unfortunately this approach suffers from three critical problems:

- As Fama and French demonstrated in 2004,[12] the theory does not fit the facts.
- Project returns are uncertain, and a project that appeared to promise a small positive NPV when its projected cash flows were discounted at the WACC might in the event prove to have subtracted value from the corporation that undertook it.

- Using a methodology that assumes that firm- and project-specific factors can be ignored when determining an appropriate discount rate for evaluating specific projects lacks coherence.

MBA graduates who rely too heavily on their textbooks discover, when they take proposals to real corporate finance managers, that projects that only promised to earn the WACC are not considered, by most corporate finance managers, as being sufficiently valuable to pursue.

One spectacular exception that proved this rule came when the giant mining company BHP Ltd. commenced a billion-dollar project to make hot briquetted iron (HBI) using a new process in a new plant at Boodarie near Port Hedland on Australia's northwest coast. The financial projections for the project showed that it would meet or exceed BHP Ltd.'s WACC of 12–15 percent. Unfortunately the plant was plagued by cost overruns, eventually costing 70 percent over its original construction budget, and operational problems, only producing 50 percent or so of its planned output. It was permanently closed after a fatal accident. The final cost to BHP exceeded two billion dollars. This fiasco led to the replacement of BHP's managing director[13] and all of his direct reports.

The use of the CAPM to guide a company's internal investment decisions introduces an insidious problem: as mentioned above the development of the CAPM explicitly excludes "idiosyncratic" risk—that is, the risks specific to a single company, under the assumption that such risks are diversifiable. If a fund manager chose to include a biotech start-up in her portfolio, the CAPM derivation assumes that she would then purchase shares in every other biotech start-up: several may fail, but some at least should succeed and generate an investment return. By analogy, the risk involved in betting on a horse can be diversified by betting on every horse in a race: you won't lose much money, but you certainly won't win much.

A company undertaking a specific investment is quite explicitly accepting an idiosyncratic risk; and the risk and uncertainty associated with project "A" won't be changed if a company simultaneously undertakes project "B."

Overcoming the CAPM Problems: Real Options Theory

Although business schools continued to teach the CAPM and NPV rules to MBA students, corporate finance directors generally stuck with heuristically determined hurdle rates, and by the time most MBA graduates were promoted to a senior corporate role, they abandoned the theory and stuck with practice.

Theory has now caught up with practice, although few if any finance textbooks have caught up with theory. The key events were Black and Scholes's demonstration of a systematic way to value financial options[14] in 1973 and the collaboration of Robert Pindyck and Avinash Dixit in the last decades of the twentieth century.

A financial option may be a "call" or a "put"; the first gives the owner the right to buy an underlying "physical" for a fixed price on or by a certain date, while the second gives the holder the right to sell the underlying physical, again at a fixed price and again on or by a certain date. For example, a speculator may have formed the opinion that the shares in a given firm ("XX Ltd.") will shortly rise from their present price (say $10). The speculator could buy some shares in XX hoping to sell them at a higher price: if the speculator invested $100,000 and the price rose by 20 percent, they could sell the shares, making a profit of $20,000 before dealing costs. Alternatively, the speculator could buy call options with an exercise price of $10 for perhaps $0.40 each. If the shares rose by 20 percent, the 250,000 options would be worth at least $2 each and the speculator, for the same outlay as before, would have made a profit of $400,000.

Real option theory followed Myers's and Turnbull's 1977 insight that a plan for a real project was closely analogous to a financial call option.[15] Developing the plan and completing the associated technical and marketing research has a cost to the firm undertaking it, but having completed the work the firm now has the option of proceeding with the project or waiting for more information about the opportunity. Looked at from the opposite perspective, a firm might decide to spend a certain amount on research and planning simply to acquire the option to proceed with the project: at times of low mineral prices, mining companies may be reluctant to open new mines, but it may be well worth their while to maintain exploration programs and to pay ongoing tenement charges so that, should prices rise, the firm would be in a position to benefit promptly.

More subtly, the outcome of a research or exploration program is not known with certainty (if it were, there would be no point in undertaking it). An exploration program might discover an unusually rich or accessible mineral deposit, such that even at low prevailing prices a new mine would be profitable. This possibility adds value to the exploration program, even if the rich deposit was unexpected.

The last drops of theoretical interest were squeezed out of the topic with the publication of Dixit and Pindyck's magisterial work on investment under uncertainty[16] in 1994.

Black and Scholes took as their starting point a market where prices evolve in a geometric random walk. For such a model, the standard deviation is unbounded in time: accurate prediction is impossible, and even approximations become less accurate as time passes. A financial option acquires its value from the possibility that the price of the underlying physical may move in a favorable direction; so even if a call option is currently "under water," with the exercise price above the spot price, the spot price *may* rise above the strike price during the life of the option.

Dixit and Pindyck built on the Myers and Turnbull insight. If a project is valued as a real option, a decision to proceed with the project extinguishes the option value: the true cost of a project is not simply the cost of building and operating it; the loss of the option to proceed (or not) must be added. A corollary enables the required rate of return on a security to be valued, given the expected volatility of its price (which will generally be assumed to equal the historic volatility of that price).

All investment decisions take place under conditions of uncertainty: perfect foresight is not available to real entrepreneurs and managers. The uncertainty is at two levels: the real return to any investment cannot be known in advance; and there is always a finite possibility that all or part of the principal will be lost. As Kahneman demonstrates, real people (as distinct from the agents of economic theory), have an asymmetric attitude to gains and losses. Once more than trivial amounts are involved, real people will decline a gamble involving a possible loss unless the prospective gain is a multiple of the potential loss.[17]

When the investment takes the form of equity shares in a listed company, the price of the shares will reflect the company's expected performance. If at some future time the performance is expected to be poorer than it was expected to be at the time that the shares were purchased, the price will fall and part of the investment will be lost. If the price falls, the holder suffers a loss, even if it is not "crystallized" by a sale at the lower price; even if the price eventually recovers, the holder has suffered a period of reduced relative earnings.

Dixit and Pindyck's account of investment under uncertainty can be treated as an extension of Keynes's concept of liquidity preference. Cash and short-term deposits don't earn much interest; but the capital remains safe and they offer the holder flexibility to make an investment if it appears sufficiently attractive or to look for alternatives if it does not. Once an investment is made this flexibility is lost, and Dixit pointed out that since liquidity has a value, the loss of liquidity must be considered a cost. The prudent investor, therefore, only invests when the prospective returns are sufficient not only to replace the interest income from the previous holding of cash and short-term deposits, but to compensate for the loss of liquidity as well.

Real Options Theory to a large extent reflects theory catching up with practice; but under many circumstances theories that explain current practice can illuminate the path to improved practice in the future.

Revisiting BHP Ltd.'s disastrous HBI investment: a one-tenth scale pilot plant would have revealed the risk of low yield and high construction costs: spending perhaps $200 million on acquiring the real option to proceed with the full-scale plant would have saved BHP $2.5 billion by showing the infeasibility of the original proposal. Real options aren't only ways to lock in a profit: sometimes they can lock out a loss. Some options are better lapsed than exercised.

Caveat

The Black-Scholes and Dixit hurdle rate formulas both incorporate the assumption that share and project values follow a geometric random walk over time, such that the variations in each period are normally distributed. This is only approximately true for shares, and cannot be justified except as a convenience for project valuation. Some factors that affect project values may be normally distributed; some are almost certainly not. No project can be completed in less than zero time; but all too many projects run far beyond their planned completion date. In the case of stock prices, it is known that variations are *not* normally distributed: variations that would be impossibly rare under a normal distribution occur relatively frequently.[18] Even in the absence of such large deviations, daily price movements are not "normal" but somewhat fractal or submartingale, with a tendency for a lot of small rises to be followed by a larger fall. Various alternative assumptions are explored in Dixit and Pindyck's book.

As a practical matter of investment management, real option theory works quite well in avoiding most disasters. Assuming that a company planning many investments used real options theory to select some and reject others, and assuming further that the company used realistic estimates of likely outcome variances, if these variances were normally distributed only one in six of the projects selected would destroy value; the rest would increase it. In practice, since the variances are not normally distributed, there will be more disasters and more triumphs than the real options models predict, and the possibility of successive disasters or triumphs is also greater than that likely under a normal distribution. Nevertheless there is every reason to expect that a clear majority of the projects selected after a rigorous application of real option analysis will add value.

When companies apply sophisticated extensions of Real Options Theory such as stage gate modeling,[19] the proportion of failures does not change, but the losses incurred in the case of a failure can be dramatically reduced by aborting failures before they have absorbed too much money.

MVP—Minimum Viable Product

Many information technology developers have adopted a different risk-control approach: building a product that addresses a known user need but does so in the most basic possible way, with limited features and few options. This is then actively sold to potential users with urgent problems of the appropriate type and potential users known for their willingness to experiment with new software products. If these early users continue to use the product after trialing it and provide useful feedback, the developer will launch a major project to add features and functions and actively market the product to the widest possible class of potential users. If the early users are lukewarm or worse, the product can be quietly dropped.

Creating an MVP can be seen as buying a real option to proceed with the development of a major product. The approach works with software systems because of the low cost of replacing or upgrading them as long as forward compatibility can be assured.

Corporate Investment Decisions

Corporations act under the control of their directors—in effect, their Chief Executive Officer (CEO), who is expected to rely on the advice of his or her Chief Financial Officer (CFO). Neither the CEO nor the CFO has a clear set of legally verified objectives as distinct from constraints.

Friedman's assertion that the duty of a company's managers was "to make as much money as possible" (Chapter 13 below) is facile and unsupported by law. A more sober view would observe that a corporation seeks subscriptions from the public on the basis of its forecast financial performance, and both the original and subsequent investors are entitled to rely on the directors' statements in making their decisions.

Investors are entitled to expect the directors to deliver results consistent with past levels of profit and volatility except as modified by official company statements and reports. Directors are permitted to announce new objectives and new strategic directions, and once such announcements are made, the directors are obliged to use their best efforts to achieve these forecasts; but in the intervals between such strategic statements, shareholders have a right to expect that a firm's past performance as qualified by its directors' statements will be a guide to future performance. Such rights are based on the common-law prohibition of misleading and deceptive conduct.

In the absence of specific guidance by the directors, this means that the expected return on equity for a listed public company should equal its historic return on equity when both figures are properly adjusted for the earnings growth rate and earnings volatility.[20]

Investment committees inside corporations will be aware that, should any project that they support return less than the projected return on equity, this will tend to reduce the overall return on equity, upsetting the company's investors. Historically directors of most companies have avoided such outcomes by demanding that any project they support has prospective returns that exceed a hurdle rate that in turn substantially exceeds their company's investors' expectations for their return on equity. Thanks to the work of Dixit,[21] it is possible to compute hurdle rates; in general a Dixit calculated hurdle rate will be very close to the rate set on heuristic grounds by experienced managers.

The overall effect is that corporate investment decisions are substantially more cautious than one would expect decisions made by individual investors to be. Individual investors considering the purchase of shares require an equity premium to compensate them for accepting the uncertainty of their returns. This then becomes a floor for corporate investment decisions, with a second risk premium added.

Consider a firm with a historic earnings volatility of 20 percent (about the middle of the range for listed companies): investors, if offered a "risk-free" investment choice returning 5 percent, would only support this company if the prospective return on equity was 11.9 percent or better. Inside the company, if offered an investment opportunity with an expected earnings volatility of 20 percent and aware that their shareholders expect a minimum return of 11.9 percent, the directors would test the expected returns against a hurdle rate of up to 21.1 percent.

The economy does not stagger to a halt under the yoke of such high hurdle rates because a lot of the investment decisions made by corporations are relatively low risk. Market shares are relatively stable, and so the returns to investments intended to raise product quality or to reduce unit costs are relatively predictable and suited to hurdle rates close to the WACC. Many large companies in the English-speaking countries also minimize their risks by avoiding new product development, preferring to let small start-up ventures prove such products in the market before making a takeover offer.

Venture capital has been described above;[22] venture capitalists are neither patient nor modest in their ambitions. A successful new venture could be earning as much as 50 percent on its invested capital, but its venture capital sponsors would still wish to harvest their investment and leave; so an offer from a larger company could look very attractive to both the large company and the venture capitalists. To the large company, access to a new market segment with the technical feasibility and the market attraction of the entry product both established will appear a sound, low-risk investment; while the venture capitalists will be eager to cash out their investment to boost the returns on their closed-end funds.

Public Investment

Public investment takes place in at least three separate circumstances: there are publicly owned trading enterprises; there are investments required by national defense or other pressing need; and there are investments with a social purpose but little or no revenue-generating potential.

Publicly owned trading enterprises can adopt the investment valuation methods described by Dixit and Pindyck practically as they are. They face a discount rate issue: should the government, standing in for the community at large, permit its subsidiaries to invest as if they were members of the community, with the rate of return on government bonds as the "risk-free" rate, or should they be required, on competitive neutrality grounds, to assume the higher base cost of funds experienced by listed corporations?

For a typical project where individual investors would regard a 12 percent return as satisfactory, a corporation might require at least 21 percent. If a government-owned trading corporation is allowed to use the "investor" rate of 12 percent, it may have a decisive cost advantage over listed corporations using a much higher rate.

The UK Treasury has suggested that a discount rate of 12 percent is appropriate when making public investment decisions; the number is close to the average returns (without adjusting for inflation) on the stock market. The implication is that governments are simply agents for consumers, and so should secure the same returns from public investment as consumers could achieve by "buying the index".

Treating government as an agent for essentially private investment may not accurately reflect the expectations citizens have of their governments. A major reason for the equity premium is that investors' aversion to losses greatly exceeds their wish for profit. Much government activity is directed precisely at reducing citizens' risk of loss: suggestions that the police should be self-financing from fines and confiscations do not replace the typical citizen's wish that the police should prevent their home being burgled and their persons being assaulted. It is the fear of burglary and mugging that makes taxpayer support of the police force acceptable.

Police corruption may be one consequence of excessive emphasis on the benefits of the market. Neoliberal political leaders deride concepts such as "society" and "duty" and focus on financial incentives to the exclusion of all other motivations. Taking them at their word, a policeperson may be tempted to set the possible rewards for corrupt behavior against the present value of the benefits due to an honest cop.

Some of the most significant and most valuable publicly owned trading corporations were in the electricity supply industry, led in the United States by the Tennessee Valley Authority (TVA) and in the United Kingdom by the Central Electricity Generating Board (CEGB).

The difference in expected rates of return between publicly and investor-owned power stations in the United States has had one highly visible consequence: while publicly owned thermal power stations almost always use the capital-intensive but technically efficient natural draft cooling towers, many (not all) for-private-profit power stations use the much cheaper but less efficient induced draft towers. (Natural draft cooling towers are the huge hyperboloid towers with a wisp of visible steam when operating that most people associate with power stations. Air flows through such towers by natural convection at no additional energy cost. Forced draft towers are far smaller (although for power stations, still very large) and resemble the cooling towers often seen on the top of office buildings. Electric fans replace natural convection and absorb as much as 2 percent of the station's gross output.)

Electricity supply is a natural monopoly: there is simply no consumer or community benefit in having two sets of wires down each street; but it is also, at the price and consumption levels common in the developed world, sold in an extremely inelastic market. A profit-maximizing private-sector supplier would limit supply and allow prices to rise to a multiple of their fully allocated cost: it was exactly this behavior that made the establishment of the great publicly owned electricity-supply enterprises of the twentieth century politically acceptable. The privatization and corporatization of the electricity supply industry must have the medium-term effect of raising prices by as much as 45 percent to cover the higher cost of capital; the peculiarities of national income calculations will ensure that such an increase is recorded as a rise in GDP; but it is not clear that any consumer benefit will have been achieved.

Some government investments are immune from scrutiny on rate-of-return criteria: nobody expects a commercial return on equipment bought for national defense. While the pre-Conquest English kings paid Danegeld rather than pay for an effective national defense force, their example is not regarded as one to follow in modern times.

This leaves a range of government investments that generate no cash return but lack the imperative force of the defense budget. Since governments have limited capital funds available, they attempt to allocate these in the way that delivers the greatest social benefit. (Cynics may substitute "political" for "social" in the preceding sentence.) Governments are faced with a multidimensional problem: they must allocate the available capital funds into various budget areas, and they must rank projects within each area.

Allocating capital funds between categories is far from straightforward: even within budget categories there can be conflict. Road funding, for example, must be divided between eliminating particular danger spots and improving traffic flows. The former will save a statistically predictable number of lives and prevent a statistically predictable number of injuries; the latter will save motorists time and reduce their operating costs per kilometer traveled. Within the final categories there are often specific methodologies used to help the allocation process: road engineers estimate the cost of eliminating a particular danger spot and the number of lives such an improvement will save and postpone or abandon proposals where the cost per life saved exceeds some threshold.

Advisers to governments find it tempting to try to adapt the investment rules developed for profit-seeking businesses to the budgetary allocation problem. This requires putting a monetary value on the social benefits each program is expected to deliver and computing a net present value for each of them. Projects with a negative NPV are discarded and those with the highest NPV are considered the highest priority.

This raises two new problems: the quantification of the benefits a program may deliver, and selecting an appropriate discount rate. Businesses have a relatively easy way to find out the value of the goods and services that they sell: they can stand in the market and offer them at various prices until they hit on a satisfactorily profitable price. When each deal is concluded, the purchaser has received value equal to or in excess of the price, and the supplier has the money.

Social benefits can be much harder to quantify: consider the famous example of the British Treasury official arguing against antismoking campaigns, on the grounds that smokers paid huge sums into the exchequer as excise during their lives and then died before they drew much if any of their old-age pension or made use of other services for the elderly. In the United States, tort law reform has meant that in some states there is no civil penalty for killing a child or an adult without dependents, since the only value of the deceased was the present value of their potential income and no living person has a legal interest in it.

Applying the same logic to public policy generally suggests that only a minimum of public resources should be devoted to preserving the lives of children and adults without dependents. If presented in this way, perhaps tort law reform would lose some of its political appeal.

Discount rates in a business environment start with the "risk-free" rate available on short-term deposits and then add a premium to reflect the uncertain returns to investors in the corporation's shares and a further premium to reflect the uncertain returns to each separate project that the corporation undertakes. One key risk that corporations do not, in general, face is that of being locked into a project even in the face of unsatisfactory returns: Dixit and Pindyck showed that a substantial part of the value of many private-sector investments comes from the option to abandon them rather than finance endless losses.[23]

Public investments are much harder to abandon; those who have come to rely on them will be vociferous in their defense, while those who might, in theory, share the benefits of the savings to be made from such an abandonment may doubt whether there will be any savings and whether they will get any benefit from such savings as are achieved.

Anthropogenic Climate Change

The Stern Report into the financial impact of global warming triggered a number of economic debates, and in one of them the choice of discount rate became a critical issue. For the purposes of economic debate, Stern was deemed to have predicted that humanity could enjoy thirty years of ignoring anthropogenic climate change, at the end of which global GDP would be suddenly reduced by 30 percent; alternatively, 1 percent of global GDP could be allocated to climate change amelioration starting immediately and there would be no adverse impact in thirty years' time. Using a discount rate of 12 percent and ignoring growth and inflation suggests that it is not worth doing anything for at least twenty years; but under the assumptions used by Stern and endorsed by Quiggin, the present value of the benefits of commencing climate change amelioration immediately exceeds the present value of the cost fiftyfold.

The conventional explanation for discount rates is that they reflect consumers' preference for "birds in the hand": cash today rather than some future benefit. We introduced Kahneman's demonstration of people's asymmetric response to gains and losses above. Gains are one thing: losing what one currently has is something quite different. Consider a person with a net worth of $5 million who is offered a "double or nothing" bet by a billionaire. They are comfortable now; if they win the bet, they will become more so; but if they lose they will be destitute. Pathological gamblers may accept such bets, but nobody else would.

According to Avinash Dixit,[24]

> Climate change is especially interesting because it involves a two-sided irreversibility. If we invest in clean technology, that may prove to be a waste if later research shows that climate change is not a big problem. But if we don't, and climate change proves to be important, we will have caused irreversible damage to the environment. This was nicely analyzed in a real options framework by Charles Kolstad.[25]

As Quiggin pointed out, using a high discount rate to value the cost of averting future dangers implies that people value their children's lives and well-being at a dramatically lower value than they value their own. This does not reflect normal human behavior: parents who will go to any lengths to save the life of a baby threatened by neonatal diseases are hardly likely to be indifferent to the possibility of the same child being killed, injured, or rendered destitute shortly before their twenty-first birthday.

Quiggin and Stern's view is by no means unique, but it is also not uncontested. A significant group of US economists have argued that measures to ameliorate the future impact of climate change should be tested against a significantly positive discount rate: valuing our children's and grandchildren's lives at the same level as we value our own is, they argue, an ethical matter; and following Hayek, they consider that ethics are personal choices that have no place in economics—or public policy.

Notes

1.   Schumpeter (1934).
2.   Kirzner (1982).
3.   Baumol (1968).
4.   Legge (2012).
5.   For example, Pratt (1964) and other authors contributing to the literature concerned with risk aversion coefficients.
6.   Kay & Silberston (1995).
7.   In 1964 IBM announced that it was replacing both its existing computer ranges with the new System/360. A spokesman was asked, "Is this an important decision for IBM?" The reply: "You bet your company it is."
8. FV is future value, PV is present value, d is discount then $PV = \dfrac{FV}{1+d}$.
9.   If t is the time to maturity and r is the discount rate, then $1+d = (1+r)^t$.
10.   Sharpe (1964).
11.   Expected return is R_E, risk-free rate is R_F, market average rate is R_M, $R_E = R_F + \beta(R_M - R_F)$.
12.   Fama & French (2004).
13.   Equivalent to president in an American firm.
14.   Black & Scholes (1973).
15.   Myers & Turnbull (1977).
16.   Dixit & Pindyck (1994)
17.   Kahneman (2011: pp. 278–88).
18.   Keen (2011: p. 386), Legge (2012: pp. 21–22).
19.   Stage-Gate is a registered trade mask of Stage-Gate International.
20.   Volatility is usually defined as the square root of the variance of the closing values of a price per year.
21.   Dixit (1992).
22.   Page 174 ff.
23.   Dixit & Pindyck (1994).
24.   Email to author, June 15, 2013.
25.   Kolstad (1996).

11

Externalities and
Public Goods

We worry about our schools. We worry about our public recreational facilities. We worry about our law enforcement and our public housing. All of the things that bear upon our standard of living are in the public sector. We don't worry about the supply of automobiles. We don't even worry about the supply of foods. Things that come from the private sector are in abundant supply; things that depend on the public sector are widely a problem. We're a world, as I said in The Affluent Society, of filthy streets and clean houses, poor schools and expensive television.
—John Kenneth Galbraith

The concept of perfect markets lies at the heart of neoliberal theory. In such a market, should it exist, every transaction is between a willing seller and a willing buyer, and no third party is affected, for good or ill. Neoliberal theorists also hold that every human need will be satisfied if markets are left to perform their perfect work.

Less ideological economists have observed that many transactions do inflict costs, or sometimes benefits, on third parties. Such costs or benefits are referred to as externalities. Neoliberal theorists argue that either there are no significant negative externalities, or if there are significant externalities, the costs inflicted by government action to rectify them would exceed the harm that they cause.

Economists going back to Adam Smith[1] have observed that there are some necessary services that cannot be provided by a market, or at best cannot be provided satisfactorily. Such services and institutions are referred to as public goods, since without them the majority of the population, and the aggregate population, would be worse off.

Examining the real world shows that there are, in fact, many externalities arising in the normal course of the operation of a capitalist system, and there are many public goods that an unregulated market would not provide.

Public Goods

A public good is one that is available to all the people in a community or to none of them; the classic example is "freedom from foreign invasion." If one's country is invaded and occupied, this affects all the residents: it is impossible for one household to be invaded and occupied by foreign enemies while its neighbors remain free of such problems. For this reason even the most ardent libertarians support the existence of national defense forces financed from general taxation.

Mortality from disease was far higher in the nineteenth century than it is today, and life in the great cities was particularly unhealthy, with typhoid and cholera carrying off as much as 3 percent of the population in some years. While the poor suffered more than the rich, no one was immune: Queen Victoria's consort, Prince Albert, died relatively young, probably of typhoid fever. Doctors had various explanations for illness and contagion, but it wasn't until the work of Louis Pasteur in the 1860s that the germ theory of disease became established. Pasteur and those convinced by his arguments and demonstrations had to overcome the protests of the more conservative doctors who were unwilling to see their learning discredited and who resented the implication that their poor hygiene had killed many of their patients.

In 1854 Dr. John Snow demonstrated that cholera was a waterborne disease and that it was particularly prevalent where sewage contaminated the water supply.[2] When Snow's work was combined with that of Pasteur, it became clear to those who were prepared to learn that cholera and typhoid could not be eliminated without providing a clean water supply and effective sewage disposal. Everyone in a community had to be provided with clean drinking water and effective sewage disposal before anyone was safe from cholera and typhoid.

The wealthy could afford to buy pure water and have their sewage carted out of their neighborhood; but they still had to eat food that others had handled and admit servants into their houses. Only when their servants and food purveyors also enjoyed the benefits of clean water and effective sewage disposal could the wealthy feel safe from typhoid and cholera. For these reasons the great cities of the developed world built publicly funded water supply and sewage removal systems during the last quarter of the nineteenth century, generally paid for out of property taxes: the rich subsidized the poor.

Externalities

The existence of public goods creates the possibility of "free riding": a wealthy household that refused to pay its share of the cost of a metropolitan water supply and sewage system would, if such a system was constructed anyway, enjoy the benefits of disease-free servants and food suppliers without paying for them. This hypothetical household would, in most developed countries, make its allotted contribution voluntarily or it would be coerced into making it; but it would be made. There is a broad consensus among economists supporting compulsory taxation to pay for the provision of essential public goods, although less of an agreement as to which goods are intrinsically public ones.

The firm that discharges pollutants into the common sewerage system is profiting from an externality in a no less heinous way than a wealthy family that evaded its contribution to the sewerage system's construction.

Free riding is not limited to accepting the advantages of public-good provision without contributing to the creation or the maintenance of these goods. A person or firm that successfully privatizes a public good makes an easy profit. The enclosure movements of the sixteenth through the eighteenth centuries in Britain involved wealthy individuals sponsoring parliamentary legislation that granted them clear title to the common lands previously used by the villagers in their vicinity for cropping and grazing. By creating the legal fiction that the villagers were trespassers on some local notable's land, the new owners avoided the need to compensate the evicted villagers for their lost use of the commons.[3]

It can be convincingly argued that the creation of a pool of landless laborers and replacing strip agriculture by relatively large farms greatly increased productivity and the general wealth of England during the late sixteenth through the eighteenth centuries. The enclosures of the eighteenth century created the migratory labor force that worked in the mines, shipyards, and factories of the Industrial Revolution. The general increase in prosperity and living standards came at a heavy cost in disruption, destitution, and death among the English yeomanry while the greater part of the benefits was concentrated in very few hands.

Externalities are not all bad: Romer's theory of endogenous growth[4] relies on the assumption of positive externalities to innovation. Many innovations have generated large positive externalities: Walter Oi pointed out that Willis Haviland Carrier's invention of air conditioning generated vast economic benefits;[5] and while the Carrier Company prospered, it captured a small fraction of the total value created.

Tropical and subtropical cities like Singapore and Houston could not have attained their present eminence without air conditioning; the US Congress could not legislate in the summer months before air conditioning; and the British textile industry would not have evaporated in the second half of the twentieth century without air conditioning in the developing-country factories that replaced it.

Economic debates over national industry policies and national innovation policies generally boil down to an argument about whether the value created by such positive externalities outweighs the generalized economic costs implicit in establishing and maintaining such policies. Neoliberals tend to fall back on anecdotal evidence, and there are plenty of well-verified accounts of governments supporting fatally flawed ventures to add color to their arguments. On the other hand, there are well-verified accounts of industries that were brought into existence with extensive government assistance.

The Boeing 747 "jumbo" revolutionized air travel. The initial design was completed and prototypes flown under a development contract paid for by the US Department of Defense. The Internet began life as the Arpanet, also a US Department of Defense project, as did the Global Positioning System (GPS), without which many popular apps could not work. Neoliberals, when confronted with the East Asian miracles of Japan, South Korea, and Taiwan, fall back on an unverifiable and implausible claim that the population of these countries would be even better off today had the post–World War II governments pursued laissez-faire policies.

Industrial pollution and infectious disease are generally considered undesirable externalities, and government policies that eliminate one and control the other generally command popular, but not neoliberal, support. The standard neoliberal position is that externalities inflict a minor cost on the public compared to the vast costs of burdensome regulation and any benefits will be offset by increased costs. There is very little evidence to support the neoliberal position.

Greenhouse Gases

There is an active economic debate about the control of negative externalities; the *topic de jour* is the emission of carbon dioxide and other greenhouse gases as a by-product of electricity generation and other industrial activities. Once we set aside the efforts of an alliance of sociopathic billionaires paying a pseudoscientific claque to deny that any externality exists and to assert that the release of CO_2 does not affect the climate, there are three main proposals circulating to stabilize and then reduce anthropogenic greenhouse-gas emissions.

Proposal 1, with very little support from economists but with some ardent "green" advocates, requires a world government to allocate a ration of CO_2 emissions to every living person on the planet and to monitor their usage with a large computer system. Once someone's annual allocation was exhausted they would either be physically prevented from indulging in any greenhouse-gas-emitting activities until their ration was renewed or be allowed to buy someone else's greenhouse gas allocation in a global market.

Proposal 2, with support from economists such as Stern, is to tax the emission of CO_2 at a rate that will make alternative technologies commercially attractive; part of the proceeds of such a tax could be used to reduce the impact of higher energy prices on the economically vulnerable.

Proposal 3 is the one that seems to have attracted most support from neoliberal realists and other economists. This is "cap and trade." Every major emitter of CO_2 would be allocated a CO_2 quota based on their past emissions; if their future emissions were below their quota, they would be permitted to sell the difference, while if their operations were emitting more CO_2 than their license permitted, they would have to buy permits from a more frugal license holder.

The amount of CO_2 that could be emitted under a permit, once issued and to whomsoever traded, would be progressively reduced in line with a predetermined greenhouse gas reduction policy. Proposal 3 is a classic privatization of a public good: instead of treating pure air and a stable environment as a public good, firms, based upon their past abuse of the same public good, are proposed to be granted tradable rights over it. Whereas proposal 2 recognizes the environment as a public good and taxes those who damage it in the course of their business operations, proposal 3 grants current polluters the right to continue polluting and to privatize any benefit from reductions in the harm that their activities do to that public good.

Public Safety

The Police and Military Forces

The deterrence of foreign enemies and the suppression of domestic criminals are archetypal public goods. The expectations of their rights to these goods that various classes of society hold can differ widely. In slave-owning societies, the slaves may see foreign conquest as simply the replacement of one master with another, possibly a gentler one: when the Carthaginian general Hannibal invaded Italy in the second century BCE, one of the great fears agitating the Romans was that he might promise to liberate their slaves if they joined his cause. The Romans anticipated Hannibal by raising two legions of conditionally freed slaves. Hannibal apparently saw slaves as part of the property that he hoped to seize for himself and made no move to promise a general liberation.

Part of the animus of the Putney Debates (see Chapter 14) was the belief that landless men had no stake in the country and could not be relied upon to defend it. Paradoxically, in England during the eighteenth and nineteenth centuries, both the police and the army drew their recruits from the lower classes; with the police this continued well into the twentieth century. Wellington famously described the British soldier of the late eighteenth and early nineteenth centuries as "the scum of the Earth."

Part of the liberal argument against standing armies in eighteenth-century Britain was precisely the assertion that a force drawn from the dregs of society would have no loyalty to the established order and would desert to the cause of any adventurer who offered them higher pay and a free drink. Eighteenth-century liberals may have had a guilty conscience in this matter, remembering the ease with which the then-penniless adventurer John Churchill swayed the English army from its notional loyalty to James II into supporting the Glorious Revolution and the installation of William III and Mary II. This event set Churchill on track to becoming the enormously rich Duke of Marlborough.

Prisons

The use of prisons as a form of punishment is a relatively recent one: until the nineteenth century, prisons might be used to hold suspects awaiting trial or condemned prisoners awaiting execution, but the prison itself was incidental to the punishment. Prisons could also be used as a means of coercion: creditors could have a person sent to debtor's prison until their debts were settled and monarchs could throw unruly citizens into prison until they conformed to the royal will.

Some prisons, such as the Tower of London or the Bastille in Paris were royal fortresses and armories, with the jail as a sideline. Many prisons were private enterprises, with entrepreneurs paid a statutory sum for each prisoner they held, making a profit from the difference between the cost of food and security and the payments. Jailers had a clear financial incentive not to starve prisoners to death or let them escape, as in either case they would lose their payment; but beyond these matters they had no interest in their prisoners' welfare.

In Britain the typical punishment for those crimes that did not attract the death penalty had been transportation, initially to North America and later to Australia; but the American Revolution and political unrest in Australia closed off these routes. Thousands of convicts were held more or less permanently in prisons where the average stay had previously been a matter of days or weeks. The conditions were appalling and mortality among both prisoners and guards was high, and Victorian-era reformers demanded change.

The nineteenth-century reforms made prisons a place of punishment and correction, built and owned by the state and managed by salaried officials. Some of these were motivated by the fear of losing their jobs and their pensions; but many prison officers were motivated by a sincere belief that in performing their duties they were making society safer and more virtuous by discouraging crime, by deterring repeat offenders, and by bringing the straying souls of their charges back to the paths of virtue.

The late twentieth century and the rise of neoliberalism saw a loss of confidence in the ability of public servants to perform their duties diligently out of a sense of duty and social obligation, and a corresponding increase in the confidence with which neoliberally-minded economists promoted market-oriented solutions to public problems, substituting cash incentives for moral ones. Some existing prisons were privatized and others closed to be replaced by new prisons built as "public-private partnerships" or similar. The incentive structure was a return to the eighteenth century: the private operators lost money if prisoners died or escaped, and apart from that the only thing between them and enhanced profits were a few easily circumvented rules and regulations.

One of the problems with the eighteenth-century prison system was that the private operators were free to make money by supplying creature comforts to their charges, and a sufficiently affluent prisoner, or one with sufficiently powerful friends, might find the doors unlocked and the guards asleep at an opportune time. Privatization has led to similar results in the twenty-first century: although technology and the threat of contractual penalties has limited the rate of escape, the privatized prisons have been dismally ineffective at controlling criminal syndicates within their jails or limiting the inflow of drugs and the spread of blood-borne viruses such as Hepatitis C and AIDS.

Public Health

Deadly contagious diseases such as typhoid and cholera are obviously a proper matter of public concern; communicable diseases such as AIDS and gonorrhea are generally considered matters of public interest, although there are certainly those who would argue that those who acquire such diseases do so through voluntarily undertaking risky behavior.

AIDS and Hepatitis C can both be acquired through unprotected sexual contact but also through blood transfusions and other involuntary exposure to contaminated bodily fluids. There has been some attempt by those who equate sexual contact with immorality to distinguish between deserving AIDS and Hepatitis C sufferers and undeserving ones; but such distinctions are easier to make in a political debate than as a clinician dealing with a patient.

There are also many conditions with no obvious external cause, including most autoimmune and degenerative conditions and most cancers. Lung and bronchial cancers are clearly associated with cigarette smoking; but the correlation, though very high, is not 100 percent. Some nonsmokers get lung cancer, and some smokers die at a ripe old age without any sign of the disease. Most cancers appear to arise without any overt contribution from the patient; there are only a few where the causal link is as clear as it is with cigarette smoking and respiratory cancer.

People may also be affected or incapacitated by psychiatric illnesses, some of which are not well understood while others may be clearly traced to metabolic imbalances, seldom self-inflicted. In addition to disease, many people suffer from injuries of one sort or another, very few of them deliberately self-inflicted and many quite unavoidable from the victim's perspective. Diseases and injuries, however acquired, have social costs: this is most obvious when the disease is fatal or incapacitating. The victim will require care, which will distract others from more productive pursuits; and many victims have dependents, whose care, however provided, also requires a diversion of resources from other activities.

In practice these costs will be divided between the victims and their families, insurance schemes, and public provision that provides free or subsidized care at the point of delivery. The people delivering the care will be a mixture of self-employed professionals, employees of profit-seeking firms, employees of *pro bono* enterprises, and employees of government or statutory authorities.

Individual Health Care

The boundary between publicly provided care and private arrangements is politically contentious, as is the way public provision should be delivered. There is a long historical tradition of public care for the insane and those suffering from incurable, debilitating, or infectious diseases, such as leprosy or tuberculosis. Free or heavily subsidized health care is available for those too old or infirm to earn an income in most developed countries and some developing ones.

From the laws penalizing "sturdy beggars" in sixteenth century Elizabethan England to Reagan's demonization of "welfare queens" in the late-twentieth-century United States—and probably before, and certainly since—there are those who argue that the public should only help those who have exhausted their personal resources. The alternative view is that disease and accidents affect everyone and some form of universal insurance is the most equitable and efficient way of defraying the associated expenses.

Those neoliberals arguing for strictly private health-care provision (including for-profit insurance for those who can afford and wish to pay for it) must contend with the fact that the lifetime health-care costs for individuals are not distributed along a normal (or "bell") curve, but heavily skewed. Everybody will die eventually—many in accidents or after a short illness; but some will survive for many years as the beneficiaries of expensive medical and paramedical treatment and care. Private individuals and organizations cannot accept unlimited commitments, and so there will always be individuals whose insurance and other provisions, no matter how generous, will run out while costs continue. In the United States, medical expense incurred by the uninsured and those whose insurance had been exhausted was the largest single cause of personal bankruptcy prior to the implementation of the Affordable Care Act, or "Obamacare." In most of Europe, the government stands as insurer of last resort for those with private health insurance as well as insurer of first resort for those without it.

Payment for health care is a point of acute conflict between neoliberal orthodoxy and common morality. To the committed neoliberal, a health-care professional is just another service deliverer, and the more such professionals hope to gain from providing treatment, the more diligently they will provide it. Any form of restriction on their incomes or the way that they choose to practice will, according to neoliberal orthodoxy, lead to a poorer quality of service and worse overall outcomes.

The interaction between a health-care professional and a patient is not, however, as simple as the relationship between a customer and a stall holder at a food market. Not only is there a large information asymmetry; there will be times in the relationship between doctor and patient when the patient physically cannot discuss the proposed treatment. Given the complexity of human metabolism, it is simply impossible to set out a closed contract completely defining a doctor's actions in advance.

Every patient ultimately falls back on trust: trust in their doctor's honesty and good intentions, and trust in their doctor's professional competence. Trust is an alien concept to a neoliberal theorist. Neoliberalism postulates a universe in which everyone is pursuing his own self-interest. Even a self-interested doctor might not want a reputation for killing patients and so takes care not to do so (or at least, not to be caught doing so): but every doctor has opportunities to gain personally from the doctor-patient relationship by overservicing in one form or another. To the convinced neoliberal, patients who suffer physically or financially from overservicing have only themselves to blame: they should have monitored their doctor's actions more carefully.

Health Insurance

The US health system is structured on neoliberal lines and is the world's most expensive in terms of the fraction of the country's GDP it absorbs and one of the least effective in terms of outcomes per dollar spent. The bogy of "socialized medicine" has delayed and weakened all attempts at reform of the US system, while many of the attempts to address its inequity and extraordinary cost have generally made things worse, adding layers of bureaucracy and expense without improving outcomes.

The Affordable Care Act of 2010, instituting some modest reforms of the US health insurance system, was the subject of bitter political dispute, and in the 2012 US elections, the Republican Party and its presidential candidate promised to repeal the act, including its modest financial savings. Fortunately for many millions of American families, including many who voted Republican, the Republicans lost.

One powerful reason why the US medical profession fights "socialized medicine" so forcefully is that most students pursuing medical education in the US pay enormous tuition fees, and only by charging what the market will bear can they get a return on this investment. American doctors fear that fees and stipends set under a national health system would not include an adequate return.

There are two public health-insurance schemes in the US: Medicare, which provides coverage for the disabled and the elderly; and Medicaid, which offers some support to the indigent and those of very low incomes without private health insurance. Both operate fee schedules well below the "market rate," and Medicaid is frequently subject to more or less arbitrary cuts intended to reduce the federal budget deficit. These incidents contribute to the fear among US doctors that a single-payer, government health-insurance scheme would significantly reduce their incomes.

As explained in Chapter 10, economists who believe that the assumption of perfect foresight is a reasonable approximation to reality will set the administered return on any investment too low; and American doctors have every reason to fear that such economists would take charge of their incomes if a system of universal health care was initiated.

When the British National Health System was implemented, Aneurin Bevan, then the health secretary, explained how he had secured the doctors' consent to the scheme: "I stuffed their mouths with gold." Parallel reforms in Britain introduced free university education, so doctors entering the system after the inauguration of the NHS expected incomes at a level that rewarded them for their skill and their investment of their time studying but did not have to provide a return on exorbitant tuition fees as well.

Viewed from Britain, Canada, or Western Europe, the United States' Affordable Care Act seems extraordinarily tentative: there is no government provider or insurer and the act merely places some constraints on the private health-insurance industry and mildly penalizes those who are not covered by their employer's health insurance and choose not to insure themselves if they have the financial capacity to do so.

In public systems where services are free or heavily subsidized at the point of delivery, no one is refused treatment outright; but those whose condition is not life threatening may be required to wait a considerable period of time for treatment.

As soon as a nation moves from purely private health-care provision, there will be an apparent, and possibly a real, need to set some limits on what the public provider will provide or the public insurer will pay for.

Already fringe medical practices such as homeopathy, chiropractic, and acupuncture are at least partly covered under some public or publicly underwritten schemes: if someone wants to form a witches' coven and summon the devil in search of a cure, should the public provider pay for the cloaks and broomsticks? Public providers generally pay for restorative plastic surgery after an accident, but should someone be able to enhance their appearance at public expense? German and French experience suggests that operating an open-ended public provider does not lead to an unlimited demand on public funds and saves the costs of an intrusive bureaucracy splitting hairs over distinctions between necessary and unnecessary treatments.

Education

By far the greatest proportion of education from kindergarten to first undergraduate degree is provided to children and young people without the personal means to pay for it: "user pays" may be a slogan often used by neoliberal advocates, but it does not reflect reality in any society where the majority of the population is expected to be literate and numerate. In every developed country and many developing ones, the provision of basic education is seen as a public obligation, and so the costs are wholly or partly defrayed by the proceeds of general taxation. The public purse may be supplemented by parental contributions and charitable (generally tax-exempt) foundations.

Higher Education

Postsecondary education in public institutions is still free to the recipient in many countries, but those under neoliberal influence have instituted substantial copayments by students—in the United States in the form of government-guaranteed loans and in England (but not Scotland) in the form of income-contingent loans from the government.

The arguments in favor of such copayments fall into two groups: some argue for the economic efficiency assumed to be generated by making costs visible; while others argue that higher education delivers a substantial private benefit, and copayments are a just way of preventing the privatizing of a public good. The first of these arguments has been challenged above: there are substantial information asymmetries between students and education providers, and the perfect foresight needed to establish market efficiency is based entirely on faith since it has no basis in reality.

The claim that higher education creates a private good rests almost entirely on studies of the salaries of graduates and nongraduates, and even then there are two significant issues unresolved. One is the question of the positive externalities associated with the work of many professionals. A surgeon may earn a high income while carrying out life-saving procedures. If this enables people who might have died or become invalids to return to a productive life, are there no public benefits arising from the surgeon's education?

In a hypothetical perfectly efficient market, the cost of a procedure (including the surgeon's share) will exactly equal the private benefit conferred on the most marginal patient, and this will include sufficient profit to provide a sufficient incentive to train an adequate number of doctors, surgeons, and paramedical staff; but this is not the case in reality.

The most cursory contact with a fee-paying medical system will reveal that the fee for every procedure far exceeds its short-run marginal cost; and in a pure market system this implies that many people who could gain a net benefit from treatment at its marginal cost will not be able to afford the fees and so will not realize the relevant benefit.

If higher tuition fees and copayments reduce the number of medical professionals and paraprofessionals, a certain number of people who might have lived will die or become incurable invalids, and their residual lifetime economic contribution will be lost. When fully worked through, the justice of charging fees based on the earnings potential of graduates may prove to be seriously overstated, with much of the benefit of advanced education accruing to the community rather than the individual practitioner.

A second flaw in many of the arguments justifying fees and copayments is the assumption of perfect foresight, a necessary precondition for perfect competition. Students generally forgo a substantial income during their studies, and in the case of many professionals, including surgeons, these studies may continue for many years after the completion of their first degree.

Many would-be upper-tier professionals drop out for one reason or another before obtaining a well-paid senior post, and many qualified professionals have their period of high earnings cut short by illness or accident. When these uncertainties are properly taken into account in determining an appropriate discount rate (see Chapter 10) for evaluating the decision as to whether someone with the capacity to obtain advanced professional qualifications should do so, the relative private benefits of advanced education will be seen to be greatly reduced if not eliminated.

School Education

The dogma of choice suggests that users should be able to choose providers; but who is the user when an education provider is selected for a minor? Policy seems to have developed on the assumption that children are the property of their parents, rather like a pet dog; and much as a dog owner is free to teach it tricks or not, parents are assumed to have the right to subject their children to an arbitrary form of indoctrination. Avoiding the teaching of evolution is often the overt issue driving the establishment of sect-based schools, while exposure to sex education is often the undercurrent. There is a general consensus against allowing parents to abuse their children's bodies for their own amusement or profit; abuse of their minds seems to be acceptable to many.

As with medical service providers, the integrity and competence of an education provider is always going to be a matter of trust. There are good reasons for offering all children a tax-funded education system; but the benefits of such a system may be wasted if the teachers and administrators should place their own interests above those of their students, as neoliberal theory asserts that they will. The information asymmetries implicit in a teacher-student relationship and the absence of even nearly perfect foresight mean that markets cannot be trusted to eliminate incompetent or abusive teachers before they have caused incalculable harm to many children. An effective public education system must include measures to detect and correct inadequate teaching and to detect and eliminate abuse.

One of the drivers of independent education is the existence of problem children. Most people whose psychological profile leads them to become teachers will respond to student needs rather than to their own ambitions, and they may devote much of their time to helping the most troubled and difficult of their students. In a mixed class, this will often lead to a feeling among the brightest students and their parents that the teachers are neglecting them.

Performance-based incentives, much favored by neoliberals, will mean that schools with a high proportion of problem students will suffer funding cuts, while parental choice will mean that the normal and brighter students will flee schools with significant numbers of problem students, making things worse.

Public Transport

Humans are gregarious, and there are many economic, cultural, and social activities that require large numbers of people to assemble in a relatively small area. At the same time, people value the private spaces in which they pursue solitary or small-group activities. Even if people permit themselves to be crammed into miserably small apartments in multistory tower blocks, there will be necessary journeys that cannot easily be undertaken on foot.

Prior to the achievement of modest general affluence during the nineteenth century, the very rich traveled in private carriages or on horseback, the well-off traveled in hired carts or mail coaches, and the rest walked. Affluence brought on two effects: people of even modest means moved into larger apartments or even single dwellings; and there were many more occasions to travel for both business and pleasure.

The suburban railway and the electric streetcar were invented in the nineteenth century to address these needs. With the streetcar system supplemented or replaced by diesel buses, they do so today in many European (including British) and Asian cities. In the United States, New York and to a somewhat lesser extent San Francisco, Boston, and some other US cities retain extensive public-transport systems.

The introduction of the mass-produced motor car in the first quarter of the twentieth century and the explosive growth of car production and ownership through the second half of that century meant that many journeys that might have involved public transport were completed in private cars. The reduced patronage, particularly by full-fare passengers, led to many US cities abandoning their fixed-rail public-transport systems and replacing them with a skeletal bus service for schoolchildren and those few adults who were incapable of driving.

The private motor car is ineffective for many journeys in cities with a total population of much over 350,000 because the requirements for roads and parking become obstacles to accessing their objective. The car is unchallengeable for journeys from one suburban or rural household to another, but as more journeys converge on a common destination, the use of private motor cars becomes increasingly self-defeating. Standard parking system designs require 36 square meters per vehicle, so to service an activities district (such as downtown San Francisco) with 400,000 people entering it daily would require 15 square kilometers of parking space; to move all these people in or out over a two-hour period would require roads that are in aggregate 1.2 kilometers wide.

A standard office layout requires twelve square meters per person, so in an all-car city, there has to be three times as much space devoted to car parks as to people. If cars in such a city are parked in multistory buildings, three out of every four buildings must be a car park. With only ground-level car parks, as little as 3 percent of each site may be used for buildings, with the rest used for car parking. Either way the economic cost is considerable.

A public-transport system that attracts even a small number of commuters from their cars enables space otherwise devoted to low-value car parking to be reallocated to high-value office and retail use, to the considerable benefit of property owners: US studies suggest that simply replacing buses with a more passenger-friendly fixed-rail system raises the value of commercial and residential property served by the enhanced systems by between 15 and 20 percent. Although in the US outside New York, private motor cars remain the dominant transport mode, even small increases in public transport commuting have a significant economic effect.

The Dallas Area Rapid Transit (DART) authority began light-rail operations in 1996 in what had been one of the most car-dominated cities in the United States, and one in which the downtown area had more bombsite car parks than buildings. Light-rail vehicles are expensive compared to buses, and while the rail track is no more expensive to build than an equivalent road, buses do not, in general, require exclusive use of the road. These factors lead to fierce arguments and claims that light rail is an expensive indulgence in Dallas and elsewhere.

The DART authority has commissioned several studies into the relative impact of light rail and other forms of public transport. A recent one concluded the following:

> Properties located within 0.25 miles of DART Rail stations appear to be valued at higher rates than those located within the same distance of our control group intersections. The assessed values of multi-family residential, office, and retail properties, in particular, greatly exceed the values of similar properties not associated with a DART Rail station. Large projects at Bush Turnpike and Irving Convention Center stations will create mixed-use, urban districts that drastically alter the current landscapes associated with those two stations. The rapid expansion of multi-family homes near DART Rail stations highlights a strong demand for higher-density urban living in the region, following trends observed at the national level. The benefits of development near light rail stations is not only felt

by the individuals who have increasingly used the service, but also by developers who continue to see business opportunities near rail stations, and by local governments that receive increased property tax revenues associated with development.[6]

The DART report highlights a significant externality: the apparent users of a public-transport system are the people riding in public-transport vehicles, but much of the economic benefit of their choices goes to building owners, who aren't apparently users of the system at all. Not entirely surprisingly, it is impossible in most cities to recover the fully allocated cost of a public-transport system from fares. Since traveling to work is generally regarded as a private expense, it is reasonable to ask commuters to pay something, but it is definitely not reasonable to ask commuters to pay the full cost.

A further externality flows from public-transport users to commuters in private cars. Where car commuting is mainly on freeways, each person who chooses to use the public transport service reduces the travel time for other users in the lane that they would have used by about two seconds; a single car removed from traffic in a suburban street saves those who continue to use it about five seconds per lane.

The individual effects are small; but the aggregates are quite significant, considering that a single busy suburban railway can carry twenty thousand or more passengers an hour while a three lane freeway starts becoming congested at around five thousand vehicles per hour. A car commute that normally takes thirty minutes would blow out to over four hours if all twenty thousand train passengers on a parallel train line decided to take their private cars to work on the same route.

It is also necessary to recognize that the street-based part of the public-transport network performs multiple roles: it provides local transport to those who do not, for any reason, use a private car for a particular journey; it also carries a (generally minor) part of the commuter load; and it provides the first and last leg of many multimode commuter journeys where the main mode is light or heavy rail. When the local service is provided by streetcars or light rail, there is a "halo effect," raising property values within four hundred meters of the service. As with the owners of central business district property, suburban property owners can benefit from the existence of light rail services in their vicinity even if no one in their household actually uses it.

Natural Monopoly

When faced with the fact of positive returns to scale and the high and increasing concentration of many industries, economist defenders of the *status quo* invented the term "contestability." Even if a business had no competitors, they argued, the fear that competitors might enter their market forced them to behave "as if" they were operating in a state of near-perfect competition.

As I showed in Chapter 3, even firms in a highly competitive market set their prices as if they were individual monopolists; but when the products of an industry are easily substituted or forgone, a rapidly rising elasticity of demand deters excessive price gouging. A single operator or an oligopoly of operators supplying a product that is not readily substituted may set very high prices without customer resistance cutting into their profits.

Air services between cities without a rapid surface transport alternative provide a good example of such pricing patterns, at least for business travelers. Business travelers require frequent services, ready substitution of bookings on short notice, and modest traveling comfort. These markets are barely even contestable because an entrant would have to match the incumbent's service frequencies long before they had the passenger numbers needed to fill the aircraft used for this purpose. Airlines also offer services to tourists and family travelers; and these passengers are relatively flexible in their timetable requirements and usually plan their journeys well in advance. This segment of the air-services market is clearly contestable as shown by the development of low-cost carriers such as Ryanair,[7] which offer no flexibility, awkward schedules, uncomfortable seats—and very low fares.

There remain industries that are not even remotely contestable. These include the fixed-line telephone system and the electricity, water, and gas distribution systems. These all require enormous fixed investments prior to providing a service, and for an entrant any attempt to duplicate this would be an act of financial suicide. In a market system, even a potential first mover would hesitate to start building such a system for fear that a second entrant would "cherry pick" the most profitable parts of the market and deprive the first entrant of critical revenue and early profit.

For these reasons practically all utility systems were originally built as public monopolies or closely regulated private monopolies. The Bell System, the national telephone system once operated in the United

States and Canada by AT&T, is the most globally famous example of a regulated private monopoly.

Two models emerged during the nineteenth century, both tending to be based on municipalities rather than regions or nations. Under one the relevant level of government granted a franchise to a private enterprise that would build and operate a utility system; under the other, the government would establish a board of commissioners who would build and subsequently manage the utility. In some instances the commissioners would let contracts for the necessary construction; in others they directly employed the necessary workforce.

Both models were susceptible to corruption: aspiring franchisees might find it necessary to pay substantial bribes before securing their contracts; while publicly operated utilities might favor private interests in the award of construction contracts or even the layout of their systems. Tammany Hall in New York became famous, or infamous, for the shameless way it extorted money from the city's franchisees in the interests of the Democratic Party and its politicians.

As Melbourne, Australia, was growing in the nineteenth century, a publicly owned suburban railway suddenly appeared amid the empty paddocks beside Port Phillip Bay a few miles south east of the city. To nobody's great surprise, the admirably named Tommy Bent owned most of the land now made accessible, and the attractive and very affluent suburb of Brighton was born. A statue of Sir Thomas Bent stands on the boundary.

There are many examples of commissions completing their work diligently and honestly. Joseph Chamberlain initiated a program of civic reform in Birmingham, England, in 1873, leading to the construction of a pure water supply, sewerage, gas supply, tramways, and public housing. By and large these projects were not marred by corruption and made a significant contribution to the quality of life and economic prosperity of the city. Joseph Bazalgette, chief engineer of London's Board of Works in the late nineteenth century, is honored to this day for the foresight and energy that he brought to the task of building a sewerage system and in the process slashing the death rate from cholera and typhoid.

When these great service enterprises were publicly owned, their managers earned substantial salaries and could retire on substantial pensions, and in many cases their public service was recognized with honors and awards. In return they were expected to be diligent and honest, and most of them were. Their incentive and reward was their self-respect and the respect of the public, as confirmed by various honors such as knighthoods.

Privately owned service monopolies once put significant effort into convincing the public that they were benign and could be trusted not to exploit their market dominance. The American telephone monopoly AT&T funded Bell Laboratories, where distinguished scientists and engineers were allowed a largely free hand: Shockley's invention of the transistor was one of the many contributions by Bell Laboratories to advances in science and technology.

Privatization and Deregulation

Calls for "reform" of the way utilities were delivered probably go back well into the nineteenth century; but they became strident in the 1970s as neoliberalism came to dominate the political and economic debate. There were a number of strands to these calls, many logically flawed and others disproved by events.

Among them were the following:

- The doctrine of "regulatory capture"—the assertion that those entrusted with the regulation of natural or other monopolies would identify with the interests of the industry that they regulated, to the detriment of the public at large.
- Public Choice theory, whose advocates argued that anyone in a position of authority, whether a politician or public servant, would place their own self-interest above the interests of the public on whose behalf they were supposed to act.
- An assertion that competition could replace regulation in ensuring that suppliers of essential services did not abuse their monopoly power, and where it was impossible to introduce competition, economists could set prices using simple rules that would eliminate the possibility of regulatory capture.

In the background there was the possibility of enormous profits, including spectacular capital gains. The first of these came because standard accounting rules value assets at their historic cost, and when an enterprise has been operating for fifty or more years, its balance sheet valuations can be a long way short of their market value. This meant that governments could make an apparent profit on the sale of assets while the buyer acquired a bargain. One extreme example was the privatization of Britain's Royal Ordnance Factories, the main suppliers of small arms, artillery, and ammunition to the British armed forces, in 1987. The buyer, British Aerospace plc, sold surplus land that it had acquired with the factories for more than the entire purchase price of the factories and their ongoing contracts.

The second quick source of profit came from the shedding of social obligations such as the training of apprentice tradespeople (Chapter 8) or, in the case of the benevolent American telephone monopoly AT&T, the generous support of the Bell Laboratories. Following privatization and deregulation, these schemes were eliminated or drastically cut back; the resulting public losses became private profits.

Even when the ghost of former benevolence remained, as with Bell Laboratories, the former freedom to undertake curiosity-based research was greatly restricted; Bell Laboratories is now one of many contract research businesses, addressing specific problems for specific clients.

Notes

1. See page 32 above.
2. http://www.ph.ucla.edu/epi/snow/removal.html.
3. We hang the man and flog the woman/Who steals the goose from off the common/But let the greater villain loose/Who steals the common from the goose (Trad.).
4. Romer (1986).
5. Oi (1996).
6. Clower, Bomba, Wilson-Chavez & Gray (2014).
7. Ryanair operates primarily in Europe. The United States' best-known low-cost carrier is Southwest Airlines, which is much more passenger-friendly.

12

Intervention and Laissez-Faire

Our progress as a nation can be no swifter than our progress in education. The human mind is our fundamental resource.
—John F. Kennedy

The committed neoliberal economist assumes that the economy works best when individuals are allowed to pursue their own self-interest, and any intervention that restricts individual freedom causes more economic damage than it can possibly prevent. When Mrs. Thatcher asserted that there was no such thing as society,[1] she treated this assumption not simply as a postulated way to achieve certain desirable outcomes, but as an incontestable fact.

I explore some implications and responses below.

Justice

The term "justice" implies that there is such a thing as injustice—behavior that in some way abuses some general concept of "right" behavior. If one person's pursuit of her self-interest leads to another person's harm, even when no law is clearly broken, many people will hold that such an outcome is unjust and it is proper for governments, acting in society's interest, to take balancing actions.

Neoliberals generally oppose such redistributive actions, arguing that primitive concepts such as fair dealing and succoring the weak are historical anomalies. If there is no such thing as society, then there can be no actions that draw social disapproval and hence no valid arguments in favor of any form of compulsory redistribution. Some neoliberals go further and argue that unequal rewards for equal effort are a necessary price to pay for social progress.

Neoliberal economists recognize that human weakness might lead to individuals taking the pursuit of self-interest too literally, stealing

233

rather than trading, or psychopaths might interpret their self-interest in ways that conflict with the self-interest of others. Institutions, such as a police force and a criminal justice system will be needed to limit the activities of thieves and psychopaths; but as far as possible, these institutions should be allowed to emerge spontaneously and should operate on market principles.

London in the mid-eighteenth century had an "emergent" system for controlling crime, and it reflected neoliberal principles quite well. The pursuit of criminals was a private matter. Lower-middle-class victims of crime relied on the "hue and cry"—chasing down offenders and dragging them before the magistrates.

In the lowest classes, crimes led to arguments settled with fists, clubs, and knives; the magistrates were not usually involved. The upper-middle and upper classes could engage thief takers who, for a fee, would identify and arrest a criminal. The Bow Street "runners" who operated between 1749 and 1839 were a more professional body of thief takers, but even they did not initiate the pursuit of criminals. A victim of crime had to persuade the magistrates to issue a warrant before the runners would act.

Because neoliberals assert that freedom is incompatible with social obligations, they conclude that there should be no such thing as social justice, since this would require the reconciliation of differing individual opinions. In this they are building on one aspect of the Protestant Reformation of the sixteenth century, and its rejection of Papal authority.

From the time of the Roman emperor Constantine (b. 272 CE; emperor 306–337) to the Reformation in the sixteenth century CE, the official ideology in Europe was based around the concept of divine order. At the top was God and His son, ruling from heaven; but the Regent of Christ on Earth was the pope, who had the ultimate responsibility for interpreting God's law to humans. Everyone below the pope to the most humble serf had a place in the divinely ordered hierarchy. Disputes between two people at the same level in the hierarchy were settled by appealing to the first person above them in their common hierarchy; and the magistrate judging every case was expected to act "justly" and to apply divine law. Peasants took their disputes to the lord of their manor; squires and knights appealed to a baron; barons appealed to the monarch; and monarchs appealed to the pope. Courts, at this point in history, were simply the places where lords, kings, and the pope lived and where they could be approached for justice. Judges were originally royal delegates, appointed to free the monarch's time for other activities.

The Protestant Reformation rejected the structure of divine order and asserted the primacy of the individual conscience. This did not seriously affect community attitudes to murder and theft, but it left the handling of many other disputes in limbo: not merely the facts of a case had to be determined, but also the intentions of the parties.

During the eighteenth century, this dilemma was resolved on proto-neoliberal lines in England. The traditional Court of Chancery dispensed justice on traditional lines; but over the century the Court of the King's Bench progressively replaced Chancery as the primary place of dispute resolution, and in the Kings Bench intentions and circumstances ceased to matter: the court determined what the contractual relationship between the contending parties was, and then enforced it.[2] A contract could be overturned if one of the parties had been induced to enter it by force or fraud or if the contract outraged public policy; but otherwise it could be enforced, no matter what hardship to one of the parties resulted.

Society

Attempts to put the neoliberal idea of total freedom into practice have generally had poor outcomes. Where there are no regulations control-ling pollution, or regulations without effective enforcement, entrepre-neurs have polluted the environment to the point that human lives are severely affected. Failure to institute and enforce transnational regula-tions to limit overfishing has seen the stocks of species after species reduced to the point that their habitat is invaded by less commercially interesting species, and commercial fishing, or even subsistence fishing, ceases to be possible. Failure to regulate conditions of employment has led to grotesque exploitation and a reckless indifference to the life and health of employees. Before food standards were rigorously enforced, adulteration, including the use of poisonous additives, was rampant. (In the early twentieth-century novel *Peter Pan*, the children are warned against a cake with green icing. Not long before, an arsenic salt was frequently used as a green food color.)

Markets are a social construct, and without some form of civil soci-ety they cannot exist: the strong will seize what they will and the weak will survive, or not, on what is left. Social relationships are an essential precursor to market relationships.

My relationship with my butcher is one of mutual benefit and clearly has market characteristics: he provides meat and related products, and I pay him for them; but at the same time, I know his name and the names of his longer-serving staff and he knows mine; and I do not attempt to drive his prices down, and he does not try to sell me unsuitable or poor-quality products. Our relationship is social as well as commercial, as it is with my baker, greengrocer, doctor, dentist, pharmacist, optician, and even my publisher.

Two distinguished philosophers, John Rawls[3] and Amartya Sen, have examined the question of whether society exists, and if it does, whether its existence constitutes a benefit to all or most of the people comprising it. Evolutionary sociologists such as Richard Dawkins and Robert Putnam[4] have demonstrated that innovation and social development depends on the existence of a web of mutual cooperation—a society. We could not have obtained our present level of technologically-supported affluence without a society, and Rawls and Sen provide convincing arguments to the effect that it is the existence of a society that permits us to enjoy our technology and our affluence.

Rawls asked us to carry out a thought experiment in which we had to consider a conflict between two parties, one of whom was ourselves; but we would not know which until after we had made our decision. We would be under considerable pressure to propose a solution that was fair to both parties. Sen provides a very perceptive short summary of the argument:

> Early Indian legal theorists talked disparagingly of what they called *matsyanyaya*, "justice in the world of fish," where a big fish can freely devour a small fish. We are warned that avoiding *matsyanyaya* is an essential part of justice and it is crucial to ensure that the "justice of fish" is not allowed to invade the world of human beings.[5]

Scarcity

The environment is very large compared to any single human being, but large is not infinite. There are various desirable resources within the environment, and several of them are not present in particularly large quantities compared to the demands modern industrial society makes upon them.

When confronted with a shortage of anything desirable, neoliberal (and many neoclassical) economists have a very simple answer: such goods should be sold to the highest bidder because this will ensure that they are put to their "best and highest use." Tracing the logic backward leads to the prior assumption that all the money that may be offered to buy such rare and precious goods was honestly earned in a perfect labor market where everyone was paid the true marginal product of their work.

The possibility that someone's wealth may have been accumulated by successful acts of peculation, bribery, piracy, banditry, or terrorism, or by laundering the proceeds of such acts, is eliminated by assumption. To fully committed neoliberals following the advice of Friedman, it is equally impossible for anyone to have acquired wealth by monopolizing a market in one or more desirable commodities. The fact of possession of wealth becomes proof that the possessor has an unlimited right to spend it or hoard it as he or she chooses.

Allowing wealth to determine who gets to consume or use a scarce commodity has no particular moral implications when there are functional alternatives. Most people cannot afford to dine regularly at expensive restaurants, but this does not mean that they must starve. Some choices are harder.

Renal failure can be ameliorated by regular dialysis and reversed by a transplant; but there is only a limited supply of donor kidneys. Should a wealthy roué receive a transplant ahead of the hard-working parent of a young family? To a neoliberal economist, the answer is an obvious affirmative; but to a normal human being, the issues are less clear cut.

The Role of Government

There have always been two main streams of opinion about human nature: one considers that people are naturally evil, and governments are necessary to limit the damage that they will cause if not controlled; and the other is that people are naturally good, and governments are instituted to exploit the general population on behalf of vested interests. Advocates of either position have little trouble pointing out examples: on the one hand, the "nasty, brutish and short" lives of people in places where law and order has collapsed; on the other hand, the awful oppression of the general population under governments such as that of North Korea under the Kim dynasty, who claimed that their policies would free the people from exploitation.

For those who see people as naturally evil, governments should be strong and their powers unlimited, since the forces of the state should be directed to suppress evil wherever it appears and to promote good whenever opportunities arise. For those who see people as naturally good, the state should have strictly limited powers to be used only in cases where abuses can clearly be proven, and not necessarily even then: sometimes the cure can be worse than the disease. "Good" and "evil" are usually interpreted in an interpersonal context, but it is not a major leap to use the terms to describe the behavior of people and firms operating in a market and to constrain their behavior by laws and regulations.

Neoliberal theorists manage to combine both traditional views of government: they argue that government should be limited and individual freedom maximized; but they also argue that human motivation is dominated by greed. Allowing the free exercise of greed will, they claim, maximize welfare.

Greed and the undeviating pursuit of self-interest drive the neoliberal vision. In this vision, when every transaction takes place in a market where the seller seeks the highest price and the buyer the lowest, their common greed will lead to a perfect balance. At the prices so determined, everyone enjoys the maximum utility that their talents (and that of their ancestors) deserve. Since, in this theory, governments cannot improve this allocation of benefits from economic participation without treating someone unfairly, governments should avoid any actions that might alter market outcomes.

Neoliberalism derives such coherence as it has from neoclassical economics and its "calculus of pleasure and pain"[6] adopted from the work of Bentham. By ignoring the many flaws in the theory of perfect competition,[7] they argue that markets will naturally come to a welfare equilibrium and the proper role of government is to "hold the ring"— ensure that the contestants obey the rules but otherwise leave them to it. Since real markets do not come to a welfare equilibrium but rather create a few winners and many losers, it should not be altogether surprising that the political parties and think tanks that most ardently support laissez-faire draw most of their support from billionaires whose wealth comes because they—or their ancestors—made fortunes from the ownership or control of successful market enterprises.

Markets and Society

The very existence of a government modifies the behavior of both businesses and consumers, although it is unlikely that a market economy, and therefore a distinction between businesses and consumers, could come into existence or survive without the presence of a government of some kind. A market brings buyers and sellers together to exchange valuable things; but in the absence of a government, the most powerful will take what they want and offer nothing in return.

Markets did not emerge spontaneously: they are a deliberate social construct. Feudal societies were explicitly based on the right of those higher in the hierarchy to seize the goods of those below them and on the duty of those lower in the hierarchy to surrender their goods peacefully and without complaint to their superiors. Pragmatic noblemen left their peasantry enough of their property to allow them to survive and reproduce, and local and specific customs emerged that morphed these concessions into continuing rights. But there were few sanctions against nobles who repudiated their forebears' concessions and increased their exactions or even evicted the peasants entirely to turn their land into parks or game preserves.

Markets were one form of concession: in return for an agreed-upon fee, a nobleman might permit a market to operate at a designated place and for designated times and there permit exchanges to take place without the threat of sudden seizure. Some of the more significant markets obtained their license from the king, and so were freed from the caprices of the local nobles; some entire towns obtained royal charters that exempted them from all feudal dues and obligations apart from royal taxation, and in such towns markets and trades flourished. The charters typically set out governance arrangements to keep the peace and continue the flow of taxation.

Under the overall town, government guilds established the rules for the conduct of each of the individual trades. The bourgeois in the towns had escaped (most of the time) the depredations of the local landed nobility, but only by placing their trust in the monarchy; and they were far from immune from arbitrary royal exactions.

It took two rebellions against the Stuarts before the English bourgeoisie secured their Bill of Rights in 1689 from William and Mary, and although the English continued to be (and still are) described as subjects of the monarch, the monarchy accepted these limits on its authority. Property owners were now generally free from the threat of confiscation on the basis of a royal whim. Property in land in England had been relatively secure for most landholders with a clear title since Magna Carta was proclaimed in 1215: the Glorious Revolution extended this to moveable property and so offered the emerging bourgeoisie a similar level of security for their growing fortunes.

During the "long eighteenth century" from the Glorious Revolution of 1688 to the First Reform Act of 1830, most of the economic constraints carried forward from the feudal period were abolished in Britain and entrepreneurial capitalism began to emerge, led by

Wedgwood and the early cotton masters. These were closely followed by Boulton and Watt's pioneering steam engines and Wilkinson's iron-making and the beginnings of a machine tool industry. George and Robert Stephenson and other entrepreneurs developed the railways that by 1845 had turned Britain into a single economic unit.

England's economic dominance became apparent during the Napoleonic Wars: Wellington was well rewarded for his skillful command of the British, and on occasion, allied armies; but it was the bottomless vaults of the Bank of England that kept Napoleon's enemies in the field and the economic importance of British manufactures that forced Russia to leave Napoleon's Continental System. Napoleon's fury at this Russian "betrayal" inspired him to lead the *Grande Armée* to Moscow, and the successful Russian defense forced his army into a disastrous winter retreat, losing over 80 percent of its strength.

By the end of the Napoleonic Wars in 1815, Britain in general and England in particular had risen to a position of economic dominance in Europe and had begun to extend that dominance to Asia by conquering India.

The Napoleonic Wars encouraged rather than disrupted the Industrial Revolution in Britain, and as the wars ended, the Industrial Revolution spread to agriculture with the introduction of threshing machines. Initially the mechanization of agriculture increased the number of destitute laborers and kept industrial wages low even as middle-class incomes rose. The benefits of the Industrial Revolution were very unevenly distributed in Britain, and it wasn't until the 1850s that living standards for the working classes began to improve in line with the growing national income.

The historic record demonstrates quite conclusively that the extension of freedom of contract and free trade in England during the eighteenth and nineteenth centuries did not reflect the spontaneous emergence of the relevant institutions but was rather the result of a series of deliberately planned political, legal, and social initiatives.

Free Trade

Ricardo published his theory of comparative advantage, setting out the arguments for free trade, early in the nineteenth century, but it took decades before his arguments became the basis for public policy. Smith used the term "invisible hand" only once in his *Wealth of Nations*, which was that the supply of a domestic market with imported goods would encourage the development of national manufacturing industries to replace the imports. This is not Ricardo's recommendation.

In modern terms Ricardo's argument was based on differences in "total factor productivity." Even if another country had potentially higher productivity in manufacturing than Britain, it should stick to the production of agricultural commodities if its relative productivity in agricultural pursuits compared to that of Britain was higher still.

In 1846, well over a hundred years after the start of the Industrial Revolution in England and over thirty since the publication of Ricardo's Theory of Comparative Advantage, Sir Robert Peel persuaded the British parliament to repeal the Corn Laws, which had previously put a floor under the price of wheat in England, Scotland, and Wales.

The move was prompted partly by the ten-year campaign by the Anti-Corn Law League, but made urgent in Peel's eyes by the Irish famine. In direct terms it must have been one of the most perverse responses to a crisis in history: as a million Irish starved to death, Peel encouraged the export of Irish-grown wheat to England, Ireland having previously been deemed a foreign country for Corn Law purposes.

In more general terms, Corn Law repeal was an economic success for Britain: Britain's manufacturing industries had saturated their home markets and needed exports to survive and grow; and by allowing predominantly agricultural economies access to British markets, a degree of trade balance was restored, for a few years. The continued growth of British industry soon saw exports rising ahead of imports again, and British investment, primarily in North and South America, filled the gap.

British economists were naturally impressed by these events, and soon came to believe that the British example was one that everyone else should follow, with deregulated markets, freedom of contract, and free trade. These rules certainly worked for Britain in the nineteenth century, especially when potential rivals were persuaded to adopt them: some of Britain's trading partners failed to develop any competitive manufacturing industries; while in others such industries were financed by British capital and operated with at least as much attention to British interests as to those of the host nation. The current Washington Consensus, the most public affirmation of neoliberalism, is a direct descendant of this school of thought, with the startling exception that the United States and the EU subsidize and protect their agricultural industries to the point that developing countries can only pay for manufactured imports and technology licenses by allowing the free entry of foreign capital.

The United States adopted free trade as a policy, if not always a practice, in 1933 after over a century developing industries behind protective tariffs. The US had little to lose: it dominated the global motor car industry, the machine tool industry, the electronics industries, photography, and many others, and the likely American sufferers from free trade in that period would have been Southern smallholders, mostly black and voteless. As high-value exports grew, these people would become factory fodder in the Northeast and Midwest. The United States' only potential rivals appeared to be in Western Europe, where wages were relatively high.

World War II appeared to confirm American superiority. When the German submarine campaign threatened to strangle Britain and prevent the Americans building up an invasion force, the US response was the liberty ship: cargo ships built faster than German submarines could sink them. When the American women recruited to build the invasion fleets found welding above their eye level difficult, US shipyards starting building landing ships keel up, flipping them just before their launch. On top of building two invasion fleets and hundreds of thousands of airplanes, and lavishly equipping a multimillion-man army, the United States could afford the Manhattan Project[8]; and Hiroshima and Nagasaki felt the full weight of American vengeance for Pearl Harbor.

America exited World War II as the global superpower, untouchable in manufacturing capacity, the sole holder of nuclear weapons, and thanks to Keynesian economic management during the war, about to enter an unprecedented period of general prosperity. The myth of American exceptionalism began to take hold well outside America's borders.

During the postwar period, a "technology train" developed: a plant that had become technologically obsolescent in the United States would be moved to Latin America or to some other less technologically advanced country. Its lower-economic-quality output could not be sold in the United States, and the earned margins could only cover somewhat lower wages. When the next generation of US plant was put into service, and the newly obsolescent plant moved to Latin America, the Latin American plant now made redundant would move to India, leaving that country two quality steps behind the United States and Western Europe and paying correspondingly low wages. The benefits of free trade became less obvious to the majority of Americans from 1980 onwards with the coincidence of an event and an intellectual transition.

The event was Deng Xiaoping's opening of China, attracting US firms with a docile, low-cost workforce. China refused to permit the import of second-hand machinery except as steelmaking scrap, and so the economic quality of its factories' output was comparable to that of contemporaneous US factories. The intellectual transition was the adoption of neoliberal dogma in the United States, particularly Friedman's assertion that the social responsibility of business was to make as much profit as possible.

US corporations discovered that they could pay Chinese wages, deliver competitive economic quality, and collect US prices. Friedman having relieved them of any moral responsibility toward their workforce, they moved their manufacturing operations to China as fast as the Chinese could build supporting infrastructure. Median US incomes stagnated, and the United States, for the first time since the start of the twentieth century, began running substantial trade deficits; but many US corporations enjoyed record and growing profits while their senior executives collected huge bonuses on top of rapidly rising salary packages.

The rise of manufacturing in China and its decline in most of the developed countries is a graphic illustration of the flaws in Ricardo's reasoning. China's advantages as a base for manufacturing are not the result of natural endowments but rather the result of deliberate and sustained policy. Following the communist victory in the Chinese civil wars in 1948, Mao Zedong initiated a mass literacy campaign; when Deng Xiaoping declared that Mao had been "70 percent right," this was probably one of the policies that he was referring to.

When Deng set China on the path to global manufacturing supremacy, he and his colleagues left little to chance. Even while China struggled past the barriers that separate less developed from developing countries, the Chinese invested in a developed-country infrastructure: the ports, railways, and roads that made efficient manufacturing possible. Having made China an attractive place for manufacturing investment, its government, as mentioned above, insisted that only first-rate, modern equipment could be imported and that production should be by best practice, not simply exploitation of a low-wage labor force.

Whether China's economy should be described as capitalist, communist, or "socialism with Chinese characteristics" is a moot point; but the institutions behind its success owe nothing to spontaneous emergence and everything to deliberate, formalized, and centralized planning.

The Free Trade argument, in spite of its weaknesses[9] has achieved the status of sacred dogma for much of the economics profession, and politicians under their influence have spent much of the late twentieth and early twenty-first centuries executing free-trade treaties, many of which represent egregious interference with traditional sovereignty, none of which are popular, and none of which have produced the results that their advocates promised.

Industry Policy

To believers in free trade and in Hayekian economics, government-determined industry policy is an abomination, distorting the perfect operation of the market and leading to suboptimal if not outright disastrous outcomes. China's experience since 1980 is not the only example of countries adopting policies that worked in practice, if not in theory.

The nineteenth-century German economist Friederich List (1789–1846) was well aware of the basis of British industrial success, but considered that Britain's continued dominance under free trade was based on what are now referred to in the management literature as first-mover advantages. British firms had the advantage of experience[10] in the manufacture of export products, keeping their variable costs low; and their capital costs could be recovered from sales to an extensive market, allowing them to crush emerging industries in other countries by exports priced at the British variable-cost level.

List's initial work was in the United States, where he was influenced by Alexander Hamilton's arguments for protection; and there he formalized his concept of a "National System." He returned to Germany in 1833, where he continued to advocate a national system and argue for extensions to the Zollverein, a free-trade area comprising most of the German-speaking states and levying a common external tariff against manufactured imports.

List's ideas continued to influence policy in the United States and Germany after his death, and by the end of the nineteenth century, the total value of industrial production in the United States exceeded that of Britain, and per capita incomes in both the United States and Germany had overtaken those in Britain. There was more to the German system than a simple tariff barrier against British manufactures. Nineteenth-century Germany offered an extensive system of technical education and training to provide a skilled workforce and universal health insurance to ensure that the workers stayed productive.

The Cambridge economist Ha-Joon Chang continues to work in List's tradition and based the title of one of his books[11] on a quotation from List:

> It is a very common clever device that when anyone has attained the summit of greatness, he kicks away the ladder by which he has climbed up, in order to deprive others of the means of climbing up after him. In this lies the secret of the cosmopolitical doctrine of Adam Smith, and of the cosmopolitical tendencies of his great contemporary William Pitt, and of all his successors in the British Government administrations.
>
> Any nation which by means of protective duties and restrictions on navigation has raised her manufacturing power and her navigation to such a degree of development that no other nation can sustain free competition with her, can do nothing wiser than to throw away these ladders of her greatness, to preach to other nations the benefits of free trade, and to declare in penitent tones that she has hitherto wandered in the paths of error, and has now for the first time succeeded in discovering the truth.[12]

The pattern of development of Germany through the nineteenth century showed a further, more subtle development: while at the start of the twentieth century Britain remained dominant in the first-generation industries of the Industrial Revolution—pottery, textiles, iron, and steam power—German firms dominated the second-generation industries of steel, chemicals, and electricity. Much of English manufacturing industry remained essentially artisanal while Germany had moved to a scientific approach. The English scientist and entrepreneur W. H. Perkin (1838–1907) invented aniline dyes, but German firms such as I. G. Farben soon dominated their manufacture. Manufacturers in the United States enjoyed tariff protection comparable to the Zollverein, and from the late 1870s began to emulate Germany's technical high schools with the foundation of "agricultural and mechanical" colleges, of which Texas A&M University is one of the most famous surviving examples.

Michael Porter is an IO economist and an ornament of Harvard University. In 1990 he published a massive survey volume *The Competitive Advantage of Nations*.[13] In this he distinguished competitive advantage, which is the result of deliberate investment in skills, innovation, and infrastructure, from Ricardo's comparative advantage, which is a consequence of natural endowment.

Porter emphasized the importance of industrial clusters with many competing firms in an industry building plants close to each other. In nineteenth-century Britain, this became so pronounced that certain cities gave their name to entire branches of production, as with Manchester for cotton goods and Sheffield for cutlery. Clusters form because the advantages of colocation, including access to skilled workers and common infrastructure, exceed the higher costs for land and labor, with many firms competing for both.

Economic growth is almost entirely a matter of working smarter, not harder (Chapter 9), and creating a regulatory climate that rewards innovators and encourages innovation may involve inconveniencing businesses that do not innovate or even keep abreast of modern practice. Businesses that neither innovate nor follow the innovations of others may survive for a time by increasing the intensity with which they exploit their workers; but they are dead men walking, and their continued existence is a detriment to the generality of the population and the economy.

There are two roads to economic development: the high road of innovation and international competitiveness based on product excellence; and the low road of international competitiveness based on cost.[14] The high road leads to rising median incomes, falling inequality, and given appropriate laws and regulations, a reduced environmental footprint; countries on the high road seek competitive advantage (in Porter's sense). The low road leads to falling median incomes (although average incomes may still rise because the rich may get richer faster than the rest of the population get poorer), increased inequality, and increased environmental damage; countries on the low road seek comparative advantage (in Ricardo's sense).

One of the decisive events in modern economic history came in Japan as it emerged from US tutelage after the end of World War II. The unanimous economic advice given to the Japanese government was to exploit its country's comparative advantage by encouraging low-wage, low-capital industries such as clothing; at a considerable short-term cost the Japanese Government forced the development of high-wage, high-capital industries such as optical and automobile manufacturing. Modern Japanese society is not without its problems, but Japan is home to the world's largest and most successful automobile manufacturer, and its companies grew to domination of the precision optical and electronics industries.

Other East Asian countries—Taiwan, South Korea, and then the People's Republic of China—followed the Japanese path. From the desperately poor members of the third world that all three countries were in 1950, South Korea and Taiwan now enjoy developed-country living standards while China is now a middle-income country rapidly approaching developed-country status. The South Korean conglomerates LG and Samsung have seized domination of the global consumer electronics industry from Japan.

Globalization

Ricardo's theory of free trade was discussed on pages 95 and 240, and I noted that several of his assumptions, possibly justified in the conditions of the early nineteenth century, do not apply today. A majority of economists, not simply neoliberal ones, still hold that free trade is always an unconditional improvement over any system of tariffs, quotas, or restrictions. The known weaknesses in Ricardo's argument are not sufficient to alter these opinions.

Many economists argued that the Great Depression was prolonged and deepened by the adoption of domestic protection by many developed countries: some go so far as to argue that the Smoot-Hawley Act of the US Congress, passed in 1930 and raising tariffs on imports to the United States, was the prime cause of the Great Depression (which started in 1929). These arguments persuaded twenty-three countries to sign the General Agreement on Tariffs and Trade treaty (GATT) in 1947.

The original treaty called for mutually advantageous and balanced reductions in tariffs and other preferential arrangements: had the trade economists been taken seriously there would have been no need for a treaty, as these economists argued that even the unilateral abandonment of tariffs and other forms of protection would make the countries that did so better off whatever their trading partners did. This relatively extreme argument failed to gain traction until the 1990s, and then in only a few countries.

In the years following 1947, there was a succession of extensions to the GATT, and more countries acceded to the treaty, until in 1986 an extension to the GATT created the World Trade Organization. This set up a quasijudicial review process under which countries could complain that another country's practices constituted a banned form of protection. Countries that were found to have breached the revised GATT were obliged by the treaty to abandon the practices complained of, and if necessary to change their laws, under threat of sanctions.

There have been continuing attempts to broaden the GATT further, but these have been frustrated by popular opposition and the reluctance of the developing countries to make further concessions without access to the markets of Europe and the United States for their agricultural products.

If trade were the only issue, it would be hard to see much room for further liberalization; but trade is no longer the major focus of trade talks. There has been a continuing drive to use the trade talks to establish a Hayekian paradise: a world in which there are no citizens, only consumers. While these ambitions have been frustrated so far, at the global level they have been reflected in a number of regional "free trade" agreements, the most important of which are the North American Free Trade Association (NAFTA) uniting the US, Canadian, and Mexican markets, and the European Single Market Act. NAFTA made extensive provision for "investor protection," not merely mandating compensation for any assets expropriated, but allowing companies to sue governments if regulations prevent those companies from making profits, even if these regulations reflect current law. The complaints are not tried by the relevant national law courts, but rather by a panel of arbitrators selected in a manner that favors corporate appellants. Most notoriously, NAFTA's Chapter 11 has been used repeatedly to overturn environmental regulation and force all three member countries to modify democratically enacted laws in order to favor corporate interests.

The European Single Market Act had no provisions directly comparable to NAFTA's Chapter 11, but it still establishes panels of economists with the power to order changes to the national laws in the member countries of the European Union. The EU provides a minimal level of democratic oversight, in that some of its decisions are subject to ratification by the Council of Ministers and/or the European Parliament.

The proposed Services Directive, which among other things would have required every EU member to have accepted any EU member's trade and professional qualifications, was frustrated when the ministerial council responded to popular concern. Alert citizens realized that the directive set the stage for a race to the bottom: if any EU member chose to certify as brain surgeons anyone who presented three coupons from a popular brand of breakfast cereal, every other country would have had to offer such "surgeons" appointments in their hospitals. The minimum level of qualifications and experience to be found in any trade or profession in any country in the EU would have become the general level.

No doubt the economists who proposed this policy sincerely believed that every consumer's perfect foresight would protect them from the harm an incompetent surgeon might cause; but the rest of the population were less sanguine.

One of the preconditions for perfect competition—or for any sustained market competition in the absence of procompetition laws and regulations—is that there are no, or limited, economies of scale. By assumption, once companies reach a certain size, further growth will place them at a competitive disadvantage, and smaller companies will be able to thrive in competition with them. Globalization, as distinct from free trade, only makes sense if there *are* economies of scale: larger markets will allow companies to become larger and more profitable. For an orthodox economist to support globalization means rejecting one of the foundation stones of orthodox economics.

The fact that many economists are enthusiastic supporters of globalization is not so much evidence of hypocrisy as a cultivated immunity to the effect of contradictions. Good orthodox economists do not revise their opinions if presented with contrary facts; rather such challenges make their belief stronger. In this and other ways, orthodox economics resembles a religious rather than a scientific system of viewing the world. Globalization along the lines of NAFTA and the Single European Market is seen by such economists as a good thing because it forces more people to submit to rules written by economists, even if no other justification can be established.

Consumer Protection: Warranties and Product Liability

Most developed countries have quite strict consumer-protection laws; in the EU the laws are so strict that contracts that purport to evade them may be voided. These laws are a direct contradiction of the neoliberal argument for freedom of contract and deregulation. The failure of the neoliberal argument to lead to legislative and administrative action lies deep in history.

Markets are always at risk of a "race to the bottom"; if a dishonest trader can get away with offering short weight, he will gain a competitive advantage that previously honest traders must match or leave the market with their goods unsold. In the nineteenth century as food production moved from local artisans to larger factories, tales, many confirmed, of gross adulteration and the use of poisonous additives such as alum to whiten bread led to demands for strong regulation and the creation of food inspectorates in many developed countries.

Every market in recorded history has been subject to regulations guaranteeing fair weight and honest lineal measures, with heavy sanctions for defaulters. The warranties of merchantable (now defined as "generally acceptable") quality, truth to specification, conformance to supplied sample, and fitness for specified purpose have a long history and make it possible for markets to function.

The first three basic warranties appeared when most markets dealt with raw materials or simply transformed manufactures, and buyers could be reasonably expected to assess the quality and suitability of the products on offer after examining them. The warranty of fitness for specified purpose is relevant to more complex products and allows buyers to rely on a seller's assurances about the application of a product. It is conditional: buyers who do not ask a seller whether a product is suited to a given purpose cannot invoke the warranty if the product proves unsatisfactory.

Since the Industrial Revolution, products have been getting steadily more complex to the point where very few consumers have the knowledge, equipment, and skills to determine the quality and effectiveness of the various products they may be offered. As a matter of practical necessity, consumers will normally rely on their previous experience and the recommendations of their friends and colleagues when choosing a product (see Chapter 9 above). Entrants to a market must provide incentives simply to secure a trial of their product, in the hope that the trial experience will be sufficiently satisfactory to encourage repurchase and recommendation.

At the extremes, some products will deliver value to practically all their users and harm to none of them, while others will fail instantly and obviously without harming more than their users' pride. Markets work quite well in such circumstances: the first product will succeed unless the company selling it is unusually incompetent; while the second will almost certainly fail to make a profit or even cover its launch costs and will be withdrawn. Even if the second product causes physical harm to its users, it does so promptly and directly, and aggrieved users (or their surviving relatives) can pursue pecuniary remedies through the courts.

Problems, as always, occur in the messy middle. Some products (like cigarettes) do serious harm to their users, but the harm does not become apparent until after many years of use. Some products work perfectly well in the hands of sufficiently competent users, but may cause serious injury to their users and third parties when misused, even when the misuse is only slightly different from safe and proper use (like motor cars, particularly before the appearance of Ralph Nader).

It is clearly not possible for ordinary consumers to completely understand all the short- and long-term consequences of becoming the users of a novel product, and neither is it possible for a typical consumer to secure a private remedy for any adverse consequences of such use. Litigation is expensive beyond the average citizen's means, and if the adverse consequences appear over the longer term, the responsible party may no longer be in business or may not have the means to provide compensation.

An excessive reluctance by consumers to try new products would have a negative impact on economic growth (Chapter 9), and a variety of statutory and legislative remedies have been developed to provide consumers with basic reassurance that the products that they buy are likely to be safe. The supply of unsafe products has been criminalized in many countries, and in the United States the class action and the award of punitive damages both emerged to make it possible for aggrieved consumers to litigate.

In the purely commercial sphere, the emergence of large companies with strong brands offers a second line of reassurance: brands have a measurable value and internationally recognized brands are extremely valuable. The appearance of an unsafe product under a widely recognized brand is likely to have a sharply negative impact on that brand's value, outweighing any short-term profit from the sale of the unsafe product. For these reasons even if a brand owner was free from any moral scruples, it would still attempt to avoid introducing unsafe products or permitting the quality of established products to fall to the point that they might cause harm.

One of the major neoliberal causes of the period since 1980 has been to roll back these consumer protections under the aegis of tort law reform and deregulation. To the extent that these campaigns have not been purely venal exercises, they have been justified by turning the assumption of perfect foresight required by neoclassical marginal economic analysis into an assumed fact about consumer behavior. If someone suffers from the use of a product, the immediate assumption made by neoliberal polemicists is that they knowingly accepted the risks implicit in becoming a user of it, and so any damage is self-inflicted.

From the macroeconomic perspective, this particular twist of neoliberal thinking has all the common sense of a man sawing off the branch of a tree upon which he is sitting.

Conditions of Employment

Master-and-servant relationships lie at the very heart of the argument for freedom of contract. While the terms "master" and "servant" have largely been replaced by the less condescending terms "employer" and "employee," neoliberals, and many other orthodox economists, argue that every form of regulation of employer-employee relationships, whether to set a minimum wage, maximum hours of work, or the concession of legal rights to trade unions is a distortion of the labor market that must inflict unseen but damaging costs to all participants in the economy.

The unconditional right of masters to set employment conditions and dictate duties to their servants has historic antecedents going back to long before neoliberals, or even classical liberals, existed. The word "servant" has roots going back to the Latin word for slave; and while Roman jurists debated the question of whether the killing of a slave by a master was murder, or any crime at all, none disputed the right of masters to treat slaves any way they liked short of killing them. By the start of the nineteenth century, British jurists had come to the view that servants were not slaves and that slavery itself was incompatible with the laws and traditions of England; but an aggrieved servant's rights went no further than the right to leave an abusive employer.

Slavery presents a challenge to the neoliberal exaltation of freedom of contract. Roman jurists argued that any man who surrendered on the battlefield rather than fighting to the death had consented to enslavement. Women and children had already been, in Roman law, the property of their husbands or fathers, so their capture represented a change of master, not of status. No neoliberal theorist that I am aware of explicitly endorses slavery, but endorsing an unrestricted freedom for employers and employees to agree to a contract, including any terms short of murder or suicide, is at least an implicit endorsement of contracts indistinguishable from slavery.

A neoliberal advocate might argue that no one could ever be in the position of choosing between slavery and a somewhat less onerous employment contract, but only by asserting the prevalence of perfect labor markets. As I showed in Chapter 8, labor markets aren't and can't be perfect.

Britain managed to complete the nineteenth century without any legislation that addressed the working conditions of adult males employed on shore, although the repeal of the Combination Acts allowed unions to oppose the most egregious forms of exploitation and mistreatment. Sailors were an early exception to the principle of laissez-faire in employment in Britain, partly because of a degree of sentimental goodwill for the heroes of Trafalgar but also because the objective conditions of employment on a ship at sea were so obviously different to those on a farm or in a factory.

Victorian sentimentality, vigorously inflamed by Lord Shaftesbury, saw a series of Factory Acts address the hours and conditions of employment of women and children before the midpoint of the nineteenth century. From the early twentieth century, the British Parliament addressed the working conditions of adult males, partly as a response to the appearance of the Labour Party but also as a way of preempting the actions of the increasingly powerful union movement.

Practically all developed countries now have some statutory regulations of wages and employment conditions, generally including a minimum wage and maximum hours of work. Most countries also have some form of employment protection: sacking someone because they have been called up for jury duty is illegal in many countries.

According to the economics of the elementary textbooks, such interference with the freedom with which employers may engage, direct, or dismiss employees is unequivocally bad for both employment and productivity. The actual situation is much more nuanced; the evidence suggests that while employment protection has a slight depressing effect on employment in low-skill, low-value-added jobs, it has a positive effect on employment in more-skilled, higher-value-adding work. The effects seem related to the employer's investment in education and training: labor turnover is lower in the presence of job protection, investment in education and training higher; so productivity and therefore firm growth is higher and the net effect is an increase in employment.

Some economic commentators continue to claim that the minimum wage depresses employment in spite of conclusive evidence to the contrary. They usually base their arguments on the "law" of supply and demand, some comparing this economists' assumption to Newton's law of universal gravitation and as impossible to avoid. In reality employers hire more workers when they expect to sell the increased output profitably, and if they have no expectation of increased sales, they will not hire more workers, whatever the going wage.

Workplace Health and Safety

For the first three quarters of the nineteenth century in Britain, and for the whole of it in the United States, workplace injury came under the common law, and the common law position at that time was that workers accepted the risks when they accepted a job: injured workers only had a claim against their employer if they could prove that their injury followed a deliberate act by their employer with the specific intention of causing them harm. Neoliberals who argue for freedom of contract in employment are restating the traditional legal view.

The Triangle Shirtwaist disaster in 1911, where 142 workers, mainly women, were burned to death or died after jumping from windows to avoid the flames, was the worst loss of life in a single incident in New York until the attack on the World Trade Center in 2001. The owners and managers of the Triangle Shirtwaist Factory were acquitted of charges of manslaughter. They had locked some of the fire-escape doors and permitted finished goods and raw materials to be stacked against others, but it couldn't be proved that they knew that these acts put their workers' lives at risk. The employer's insurer paid a small sum to each of the victims' families after a long delay.

Britain introduced occupational health and safety laws in 1878, and the rest of the developed world slowly followed suit; but the principle that an employer was responsible for keeping the workplace safe, as distinct from not deliberately creating hazards, was not generally accepted in the developed world until the 1950s. Developing countries have generally adopted appropriate laws, but enforcement is another matter.

Even in the developed world, there are jurisdictions where the compensation payable to injured workers and their dependents may be reduced if it can be shown that their actions contributed to the accident in which they were hurt. Very few neoliberal polemicists argue for the repeal of laws mandating a safe workplace, but they maintain a drumbeat of demands for fewer inspectors and less detailed regulation. Acceding to these demands must eventually have the same effect as repeal.

Provision of Public Goods

I set out the need for public goods and the impossibility of expecting a private organization to arise spontaneously in order to deliver them in chapter 11 above. Nevertheless, since the mid-1970s there has been a relentless push to delegate the provision of public goods to private enterprises, on the ungrounded assumption that prospective profit is a more powerful motivator than the respect due to a public servant discharging his or her duties conscientiously and effectively.

The principal motives of most private enterprises are, first, survival, and then, making a profit. If the public is better off as result of any given private enterprise's activities, it is, to paraphrase Smith, no part of the owners' and managers' intention. Even a private enterprise specifically chartered to deliver public benefits must cease doing so should these activities became unprofitable or a threat to the enterprise's survival. A public enterprise, backed by the sovereign power to tax, is a more direct way to deliver specific public benefits than waiting for an invisible hand to force private enterprises to do so.

A compromise, with historic roots at least as far back as the sixteenth century, is the chartered monopoly: a private company protected from competition by laws. The railways in Britain and the United States were generally built by such companies, special laws giving each of them the legal right to survey and then acquire land for the right-of-way.

The first public organization formed to deliver a public good in England was the Royal Navy, and Henry VIII (b. 1491, king 1509–1547) is generally credited with its founding. Before that time national defense was treated as a private good to be paid for by the king (including calling up feudal rents in kind). Well after the founding of the Royal Navy, privateers continued to flourish: these legalized pirates preyed on the king's enemies and remunerated themselves from the loot. Loot was also an incentive for the king's commissioned officers in the Royal Navy: captured enemy warships were sold to the crown and the proceeds divided among the officers and crew of the capturing vessel, with the lion's share going to the officers.

Nelson's comprehensive victory over the combined French and Spanish fleets at the Battle of Trafalgar in 1805 was soured for many of the British officers by the sight of French and Spanish warships exploding or sinking before they could be captured; fortunately for these officers, a grateful British parliament voted the Trafalgar survivors a special bonus, making up for the lost prize money.

Henry VIII also introduced the first royal mail service, initially for the carriage of government business—orders out, reports in—but the public were eventually able to use it at considerable expense, with charges based on both the number of sheets posted and the distance. The Post Office was reformed in 1840 to become a universal service with a common low postage rate for letters delivered anywhere in Britain.

The British Army did not become a public responsibility until the reign of George III (1760–1830), who assigned most of the royal revenues to the parliamentary government in return for a guaranteed privy purse. The police force only became a national responsibility in 1829, and then partially, when the Metropolitan Police were set up under the then home secretary, Sir Robert Peel (hence "Bobbies").

In the United States and Britain, the railways were built and operated by private companies, although in Britain in 1844 Gladstone's Railway Act forced them to offer regular low-cost services to every station and introduced other regulations. In Germany the railways were built and operated by the relevant governments almost from the start of their construction: the public good aspects of an efficient railway system led to the creation of very large state enterprises in these and many other countries.

As the nineteenth century progressed, municipally owned enterprises were created to provide tramways, gas, and electricity for Britain's largest towns; the London Underground was brought into public ownership in 1933, and the British railway system was nationalized in 1948. Universal primary education came to Britain with the 1870 Education Act, and universal health care arrived in 1948 with the founding of the National Health Service. By the mid-1970s the British government had assumed direct responsibility for providing higher education, rail transport, the telephone system, electricity supply, gas supply, steelmaking, coal mining, and even a few public houses as well as national defense. Central and local government jointly controlled school education, the police, and street-based public transport, while the London County Council operated the London Underground.

The New York subway remains the world's largest and one of the world's busiest transit systems. While it is now owned by the City of New York, various parts of it were initially built by franchised private companies or built by the city and then leased to private operators. Most of the US electricity supply industry is owned by regulated monopolies, but there are some federally owned systems and some municipally owned ones, notably that of Los Angeles.

While many of these activities are natural monopolies, the argument for state or municipal ownership was generally based on equity rather than economic efficiency, and different industries had traced different paths into public ownership. Those who equated public ownership with socialism and the interests of the workers were generally disappointed: governments used capital rationing and price restraint to force the managers of publically owned industries to behave much as did the managers of private enterprises in similar circumstances; and while egregious mistreatment of workers is rare in publically owned industries, it is also rare in large private corporations.

The Thatcher government in Britain made a devastatingly effective strike against the British Labour Party when her government privatized British Telecom in 1984 at a significant discount to its commercial value. She ensured that vast numbers of middle-class households were allotted a tranche of shares the value of which rapidly rose well beyond their purchase price. Labour entered the British 1987 election ahead of Mrs. Thatcher's conservatives in the opinion polls, but Labour's promise to renationalize British Telecom saw middle-class voters desert it in droves, and Mrs. Thatcher's majority was barely dented.

The reelection of Margaret Thatcher as Prime Minister of Britain in 1987 led to the progressive privatization of the rest of Britain's state-owned trading enterprises. By 2012 the only major enterprises still in government hands in Britain were the National Health Service, the railway tracks (but not the trains) and the Royal Mail. Gas, water, electricity, telecommunications, rail transport, coalmining and steel making (what is left of them), the Royal Dockyards, and the Royal Ordnance factories were all privatized, with the profit motive replacing the spirit of public service as managerial motivation. At the time of writing, the Conservative British government (elected in 2010 and reelected in 2015) had privatized the Post Office and was planning to privatize the National Health Service.

We now have over twenty-five years' experience with the effects of privatization and deregulation of public utilities and state enterprises. There is no unequivocal evidence that privatization and deregulation have improved the lot of the typical consumer, while in several cases they have made things much worse. British experience strongly suggests that privatizing water supply and public transport has been a disaster for both users and the Treasury, with dramatically increased subsidies, much higher charges, and generally worse service.[15]

Electricity privatization in Britain conspicuously failed to deliver the promises its advocates had made, but apart from a more brutal approach to slow payers, there is little evidence from Britain to suggest that costs have risen or service standards declined. The attempt to force "almost-perfect" competition on the generating companies by a half-hour market was a conspicuous failure in Britain. In California a similar scheme created an opportunity for the criminal manipulation

257

of the electricity market by Enron, which it exploited vigorously. While most of California endured blackouts, brownouts, and soaring prices, the inhabitants of Los Angeles enjoyed the reliable, low-cost supply provided by the municipally owned Los Angeles Water and Power.

Gas privatization has not, apart from the more ruthless pursuit of those with accounts in arrears, demonstrated any great benefits or losses to the British public. Privatization and deregulation of the telecommunications infrastructure has accelerated the provision of new types of service, which is a benefit of sorts. Incredible sums of money have been wasted in ill-judged investments, but that is just capitalism.

Regulation of Natural Monopolies

The undergraduate economics textbooks suggest that perfect competition forces prices down to marginal cost;[16] but the conditions for perfect competition are not compatible with the observed world or the laws of mathematics. Real competition (Chapter 3) leads to monopolistic pricing.[17]

In many markets the products on offer are readily substituted, either by technically equivalent alternatives or by simply going without. While the monopolistic price is higher than the price under the purely theoretical conditions of perfect competition, the difference is relatively modest. Price regulation of such markets is unlikely to deliver much consumer benefit; neither is social ownership of any of the enterprises serving them.

There remain markets where there are no realistic alternatives as far as the average consumer is concerned. Patented medicines and copyrighted software are well-established examples; but so are utilities such as electricity supply and water supply and sewage disposal. In a totally deregulated environment, prices in such markets could be expected to rise to the point that a substantial fraction of the population was denied access entirely or at best restricted to a fraction of the supply considered necessary for a decent standard of living.

Water supply and sewage disposal deliver important public goods (Chapter 11); in this industry a profit-maximizing monopolist freed from the public health consequences of its actions would set pricing and supply terms that favored large users and penalized small ones. Low-income households are vulnerable to infectious diseases, which can then infect their more affluent neighbors and employers. It is for this reason that the Victorian-era reformers treated water supply and sewage disposal as a public good primarily supported out of taxation with only a minor role for usage charging. Until very recently almost no British households had water meters. Privatization involves a blind belief in market forces and an automatic rejection of the possible existence of externalities. Privatization of the water supply in some less developed countries is already recreating the public-health problems of the mid-nineteenth century.

Electricity, even when sold at its fully allocated cost, including a "normal" profit, faces an inelastic market in most countries, and a profit-maximizing monopolist would raise the basic tariff to between two and three times the fully allocated cost of supply. Large and medium businesses and affluent households would be able to negotiate substantial discounts by threatening to establish private generating plants, while the least affluent would be hardest hit. In the United Kingdom, the privatized electricity supply companies install pay-as-you-go meters in households with a record of slow bill payment, with the meter rate set at a multiple of their standard tariff. The public good aspects of a household electricity supply are less obvious than is the case with water supply, but such an overpriced supply creates an additional disadvantage for those who are already disadvantaged.

The electricity supply industry faces certain intractable technical issues that are likely to affect the reliability of the supply offered irrespective of the price; one is the sharp limit on the output of generating plants and the relatively short permissible duration of overloads. Boilers (in steam plants) and turbine blades (in both steam plants and gas turbines) are operated at a temperature close to their metallurgical limit in the interests of technical efficiency, but this means that even a slight overload if allowed to persist for more than a few minutes, or in some cases seconds, can lead to catastrophic failure. An efficient generating plant is expensive, and unless a proposed plant has an assured load at an attractive price, it will not be built as a private-sector venture.

Transmission of electric power over medium distances requires expensive power factor correction equipment and over long distances requires even more expensive AC/DC inverters at each end of a DC link. In addition, linking many geographically dispersed generators into a single grid creates a system liable to instability. For these reasons most generating plants are located relatively close to their principal loads, and a single new unit represents a nontrivial addition to the total capacity within a local market.

Without a regulator to guarantee a minimum revenue level, or a public owner prepared to accept short-term operating losses, there will be no investment in new base load generating plants until the system as a whole is clearly overloaded and subject to long periods of dependency on expensive power from a peaking plant, or subject to frequent blackouts, or both.

Regulation and public ownership provide the only known ways to maintain an assured electricity supply at a stable and moderate price. Public ownership has the additional advantage that the cost of capital is lower (Chapter 10). With a publicly owned supply, there is no division between the financial and political accountability for supplying the vulnerable and the involuntarily indigent with sufficient power to maintain life and minimal dignity.

The use of patents to maintain the prices of life-saving pharmaceuticals can also lead to the infliction of pain and worse on the most vulnerable. The best practice, as established in most civilized countries, is to establish a centralized buying agency that can use its monopsony to negotiate prices with the monopoly suppliers of various patented medicines.

Other Regulation of Monopolies

Among those who have convinced themselves both that the economy may be analyzed as if it were perfectly competitive and that the general interest is best served by guiding it into such a state, collusive price fixing is regarded as one of the worst of crimes. In the United States, executives convicted of collusive price fixing may be sentenced to jail while in Europe and several other countries such convictions can lead to multimillion-dollar fines.

Since competition in the real economy is not even nearly perfectly competitive and real competition leads to prices close to the pure monopoly level, the prompt economic damage from price fixing to the customers of colluding firms will in most cases be negligible.[18] If the only thing the collusive firms did was to settle on a common price list, there might be no economic damage at all—and no benefit to the colluding parties.

Collusion is more likely to lead to a market-sharing agreement, because such agreements can deliver major economic benefits to the colluding firms and do significant long-term damage to society as a whole. With a market-sharing agreement in place, the colluding firms can make deep cuts in their sales and marketing expenses without triggering any loss of revenue; they can allow product quality and customer service levels to fall; and they can also abandon or restrict their efforts to develop competitive innovations. It is this latter practice, with its adverse impact on economic growth, that is the most objectionable.

Notes

1. Margaret Thatcher quoted in Keay (1987).
2. Atiyah (1979).
3. Rawls (1999).
4. See page 8 above.
5. Sen (2009).
6. See page 26.
7. Chapter 3, Keen (2001, 2010).
8. The Manhattan Project ran from 1942 to 1945 under the command of Major General Leslie Groves with Dr. Robert Oppenheimer as chief scientist. The project designed and built the first atomic bombs.
9. Schumaker (2013).
10. See page 53.
11. Chang (2002a).
12. List (1885: pp. 295–96) quoted in Chang (2002b).
13. Porter (1990).
14. Marcea, Sicklen & Manley (1997).
15. Whitfield (2006).
16. $P = MC$
17. $MR = MC$, see Chapter 3.
18. Harberger (1954) caused a furor in economic circles by an econometric demonstration that oligopoly and implicit collusion on prices had a negligible economic effect: "Less than one steak dinner per year per American household."

13

Corporations

Corporation: An ingenious device for obtaining profit
without individual responsibility.
—Ambrose Bierce

Incorporation

We have become so accustomed to incorporated persons—companies—
as a normal way of doing business that most of us are not aware of the
anomalies implicit in the corporate form. Adam Smith was scathing
about companies. He was convinced that the directors would place their
own interests ahead of those of the shareholders and the company's
creditors. To Smith the only legitimate business structures were the sole
trader and the partnership; in either case there was no barrier between
the owner-manager's personal assets and claimants against the firm.
Smith and many of his contemporaries saw these arrangements as the
only way to guarantee prudent management.[1]

The collapse of the South Seas Company bubble in the early eighteenth century and the scandals surrounding Warren Hastings's management of the East India Company reinforced the view that companies
were a shield for reckless or worse management behavior. (Not that
Hastings did anything particularly scandalous; as imperial proconsuls
went, he was relatively enlightened. He was impeached on his return
to Britain but acquitted after a seven-year trial.) The Bubble Act of
1720 greatly restricted the creation of new joint stock companies until
its repeal in 1825. (The Bubble Act was initially passed to protect the
South Seas Company from having to compete for investors' money,
but after the collapse of the South Sea bubble, it acquired the *post facto*
justification of protecting investors from the predations of any future
"projectors," as company promoters were then called.)

The repeal of the Bubble Act was followed by the incorporation of
many new companies, and the directors of some of the new companies

exhibited every form of malfeasance that Smith had warned against as well as many that he had not imagined. Limited liability protected shareholders from anything worse than the loss of their subscriptions, while the free hand given to the founding entrepreneurs in drawing up Articles of Association (also known as Charters or Constitutions, depending on the jurisdiction and the date) ensured that shareholders had little or no opportunity to interfere with management, even to prevent the founding entrepreneurs or their successors squandering their investment.

Rather than reinstate the Bubble Act, the British and other governments passed progressively more prescriptive Companies Acts and established regulators with the authority to prosecute companies and directors who breached any of these laws and regulations. The coming of the railway demanded a corporate form, since it was physically impossible for a single owner-manager to oversee all of a railway's operations, and the capital required was often too great for any individual to provide. Toward the end of the nineteenth century, initially in the United States, large corporations began to emerge in other industries as former rivals merged or were taken over.

These early American corporations were marked by ruthlessness or corruption, and sometimes both. Unionization of their workforces was violently contested; the environment was treated like a bottomless sewer and critics were treated with contempt or worse. When a conflict between two railroad magnates brought on the Northern Securities crisis in 1907 and threatened a major collapse of credit and a consequent depression, the banker J. P. Morgan returned from England to force the contending parties to a solution. At one stage a journalist asked Morgan whether he owed the public an explanation for his role in the crisis: "I owe the public *nothing*," he replied.[2]

Ruthless corporate behavior continued well into the twentieth century. Ford's thuggish security staff beat up workers and their wives if they showed any interest in forming or joining unions. In 1932 many unemployed former Ford workers rallied outside Ford's Dearborn plant: the security guards opened up on the crowd with machine guns, killing four and wounding many. The Dearborn massacre was one of the factors leading to Roosevelt's landslide win in the 1932 presidential election.

The Wagner Act, passed during the Roosevelt administration, guaranteed workers the right to join a union, while the onset of full employment in the United States with the start of World War II and persisting after its end greatly reduced the relative power of corporate employers. The post–World War II US corporation was a far more pleasant place to work, both for blue-collar and professional staff, than its prewar predecessor. Union bargaining led to relatively generous wages and other conditions, while the destruction of much of European industry during the war and its rebuilding under the Marshall Plan after it ensured US corporations could access ample global markets. Professional staff benefited from extensive training programs after their initial hiring, a promise of lifetime employment and frequent opportunities for promotion.

X-inefficiency

In the period between 1945 and 1980, senior executives in most companies were normally promoted from within the corporation. In the largest firms they enjoyed extensive perquisites, including private dining rooms supported by fully staffed private kitchens, golf and country club memberships, salaries that were considered generous at the time and generous superannuation and stock purchase schemes. Such generosity to senior executives was most pronounced in the United States, but it was not uncommon elsewhere.

The economist Harvey Leibenstein[3] observed the way that corporations in the postwar period appeared to pamper their workers, staff, and senior executives when economic theory asserted that they should be trying to minimize their costs. Leibenstein and those with similar views appeared to think that the lack of machine guns and massacres outside Ford's factories in the 1960s showed a lack of determination to manage properly.

Leibenstein's concept of X-inefficiency was at least partly an attempt to explain the prevalence of monopolistic pricing and the dearth of perfectly competitive pricing in the real world; but since there is no valid reason to believe that any competently managed firm in the real world would deliberately adopt strategies leading to perfectly competitive pricing, no additional explanation is strictly necessary. As mentioned above (Chapter 3) the whole idea of a competitive equilibrium where prices are forced to equal marginal cost is based on a set of utterly unreal assumptions combined with an elementary mathematical error.

The evidence for X-inefficiency was inferred from the way very senior corporate executives were pampered, with perquisites that even the most eminent of economists have few chances to enjoy. What may have been missed is the dual incentive effect of these provisions: they made diligent striving to further the corporation's interests in the hope of promotion a reasonable personal strategy for less senior employees, since most companies that seemed X-inefficient tended to promote from within; and to the extent that the pampered senior executives enjoyed their perquisites, it became an incentive for them to perform such tasks as came their way diligently in order to keep enjoying them.

Conventionally trained economists saw a number of problems apart from X-inefficiency with the emergence of the large, professionally managed firm. One was that the assumption underlying the theory of perfect competition, that firms had no market power and that they were price takers in the markets that they served, was a patently false description of the behavior of the major corporations.

The first of these problems was claimed to be solved by Friedman's "F-twist": since the assumption of perfect competition produced answers pleasing to Friedman, his sponsors, and his followers, the objective evidence of the prevalence of not-even-nearly perfect competition should be ignored. As mentioned above (page 51), the F-twist is a rhetorical device without any logically valid basis.

The proposed solutions to the X-inefficiency "problem" were developed by applying principal-agent theory to the management of large corporations. Doing this required studied ignorance of both history and common observation. Many economists made the assumption or asserted that the principals in the company-shareholder relationship were the shareholders. This required the extralegal assumption that the shareholders were the owners of a corporation and the directors their agents; X-inefficiency was to be eliminated by aligning management incentives with shareholders' wishes.

This was to be achieved by aligning their remuneration with the stock price, a logical conclusion only if one believes in the Efficient Market Hypothesis (EMH) in its strongest form. (The strong form of the EMH asserts that the stock price is always an accurate reflection of the value of a company, and there is no action that the directors can take that will cause the stock price to diverge from the company's underlying value.)

The solutions to X-inefficiency are built on a series of false assumptions, which is to be expected, given that X-inefficiency is a myth in any case.

The myth of shareholder ownership has been dispelled by John Kay, Aubrey Silberston, and Lynn Stout.[4] The historic pattern of the development of corporations does not reflect the principal-agent model.

Companies are formed by entrepreneurs who raise cash for expansion by selling shares in the prospective profits to investors. The company, as an incorporated person, is not really owned by anybody; but it is called into existence to further the entrepreneur's ambitions, not those of the shareholders. The attempt to solve the X-inefficiency problem by the application of principal-agent theory has led to an explosion in the salaries and other benefits enjoyed by senior corporate managers and an even more cautious approach to productive investment by the corporations that they manage.

In the rush to eliminate X-inefficiency by the provision of what economists describe as appropriate incentives, the cost to the economy as a whole of supporting the lifestyles of top management has grown by at least one and possibly two orders of magnitude: by some estimates senior management remuneration is now consuming 10 percent of corporate profits in the United States. Similar effects are probably occurring in the rest of the English-speaking world; but only in the United States is transparency taken to the point that the necessary data to form a conclusion is readily and freely available.

The Nature of a Corporation

At the time that early corporations such as the Dutch East Indies Company, the British East India Company, and the Bank of England were formed, they were seen as something extraordinary. When Smith condemned the separation of ownership and management implicit in incorporation, he was reflecting the informed opinion of his day. Those who supported incorporation considered that it could only be justified by particular circumstances, and corporate charters were (by modern standards) highly specific.

The repeal of the Bubble Act and the failure of the new American states to pass equivalent restrictive legislation paved the way for an explosion in the number of incorporated bodies on both sides of the Atlantic.

The "projectors" who offered shares in their companies for sale were generally determined to allow themselves maximum freedom of action and to work under the least possible scrutiny, and so proposed articles of association that supported these objectives. The chartered companies created by acts of the British parliament granted shareholders limited liability, promising subscribers that the worst that could happen was the loss of their subscriptions, and company projectors generally offered their subscribers the same benefit. By 1840 limited liability had become a more or less general condition of stock ownership, meaning that when companies failed, society at large took on their liabilities, with the principal impact falling on the failed company's creditors.

Over the years since 1840, the idea that companies are formed for a special purpose has been abandoned; in typical Articles of Association (also known as Charters or Constitutions), every commercial activity that experienced corporate lawyers can think of is set out as the purpose of incorporation. Limited liability is taken for granted.

The Efficient Market Hypothesis

In 1970 the finance economist Eugene Fama (b.1939) proposed the Efficient Market Hypothesis or EMH.[5] While the EMH comes in three flavors, the basic assertion embedded in all but the weak form is that the stock price is an accurate reflection of the future prospects of every company listed on a properly run stock exchange. Boards of directors who accept the EMH principle now have a way to decide whether a given course of action is right or wrong: if it leads to the stock price increasing, it was right, and otherwise it was wrong.

Many corporate boards in the English-speaking countries have enthusiastically endorsed this conclusion, and reinforced it by tying the remuneration of the CEO and some other senior executives to the stock price: if the stock price goes up, the management team are assumed to have been performing well. Much of the remuneration has been in the form of stock options that vest if a few undemanding targets are achieved: in this way 10 percent of the shares in all listed companies in the United States measured by value have passed into the hands of a few thousand current and former CEOs.

In thirty years the EMH has never attained even the equivocal status of an economic law, and the many attempts to establish it empirically have all failed. Fama, who first formulated it, has published papers suggesting that the EMH may not be even approximately true.[6] Work on the artificial stock market maintained by the Santa Fe Institute suggests that real stock markets are far too active to even reflect well-known information: for the EMH to hold, investors would need perfect foresight of a company's future performance and would not be affected by what other investors are doing.

As Keynes pointed out, most active stock-market investors attempt to profit from buying and selling shares: but they know it isn't their opinion that drives the stock price; it isn't even the average opinion of a company's prospects that drives the stock price; it is what the average investor thinks that the average investor thinks about short-term movements in the stock price. This is an indefinite recursion: ideal for the generation of chaos, and devastating to any suggestion that rational factors drive stock prices.

Since, in fact, corporations operate in not-even-nearly perfect markets, executives have a number of ways of manipulating the stock price. Explicit stock price manipulation is illegal in most jurisdictions, but putting a favorable spin on the accounts is generally regarded as innocent, especially when analysts with the patience to wade through a hundred pages of boring tables can generally uncover the facts—if they want to. Since market analysts tend to get excited about reported profits, senior corporate executives on incentive contracts will strive to achieve growth in their firm's reported and projected profit. Many do not appear to be concerned if the search for profits leads to the exploitation of employees, despoliation of the environment, and gouging of customers; when all else fails, there are plenty of examples of large companies taking on "off balance sheet" debt and using the cash so raised to declare a trading profit.

The modern X-efficient corporation produces strong short-term results for its shareholders, but these come at the expense of its relationships with its customers and employees, and often at the expense of society at large when devotion to shareholder interests is seen to justify tax evasion and environmental destruction. One particular concern is the degree to which the promotion of shareholder interests is seen to justify the corruption of the political process with lobbying and targeted donations to friendly politicians and their parties.

The world's most profitable company, ExxonMobil, has become notorious for its attempts to disrupt and delay action to prevent anthropogenic climate change. ExxonMobil has used front organizations and made barely disguised attempts to corrupt scientists. One of the company's predecessors, Exxon, was exposed after the *Exxon Valdez* disaster (when the ship of that name ran aground in Prince William Sound, Alaska, in 1989 and triggered an ecological crisis in the region) as having made a solemn promise to the US Congress to use double-hulled tankers on the environmentally sensitive route between Alaska and the Lower Forty-Eight and then having shamelessly broken that promise. Proximal causes of the disaster included drastic reductions in crewing and a failure to maintain the ship's collision-avoidance radar, both measures intended to reduce operating costs.

In the short term, a focus on quarterly profits and the stock price tends to increase both; but in the medium and long term, companies that place short-term shareholder returns above all other considerations do not do so well. This does not affect senior executive behavior. Most CEOs have a relatively short tenure and a golden parachute to soften the blow when their failures can no longer be concealed. Shares that have vested and bonuses that have been paid are not reclaimed. Companies that invest for the medium and longer term are often seen as the proper prey of hedge funds and other short-term investors.

Corporate Governance

Corporations are legal fictions: a corporation is an artificial person. Nevertheless, a corporation is capable of entering into contracts and capable of suing and being sued in courts of law. This raises the question of corporate action: what acts are corporate acts, and what are purely those of individuals with some relationship to the corporation? Who decides what actions a corporation should take, given that circumstances arise requiring a decision? And what are the legal obligations placed on those who make these decisions? Some of these questions can be answered uncontentiously. A corporation has a board of directors that is responsible for the corporation's actions, either in response to the board's own resolutions or to the instructions of some person to whom the board has delegated its authority.

In practice a corporation will have a chief executive officer (CEO) who may be the chairperson of the board or a person appointed by the board. In normal English practice, a CEO who is not the chairperson will be referred to as the managing director; in US practice such a CEO may be titled president.

While the CEO carries the full delegated authority of the board, every action that he or she orders that does not directly contravene a board instruction will be an action of the corporation. When the CEO delegates, he or she can place further restrictions on the scope of that delegation. Actions that any employee of a corporation, from the CEO down, takes within his or her delegated authority are actions of the corporation as far as the law is concerned. Certain matters are "strict liability" (including certain forms of pollution), and if relevant offences are committed, the corporation cannot use as a defense the argument that the offender was acting outside his or her delegated authority.

There is some contention about the issue of corporate manslaughter. If a natural person behaves in a reckless or negligent manner and this leads directly to the death of another person, the reckless one may be found guilty of the serious crime of manslaughter, with a penalty of up to twenty years imprisonment or more in some jurisdictions. If, however, the reckless or negligent behavior is by an employee of a corporation acting in accordance with his or her instructions, the corporation, not the individual, has committed the manslaughter.

One of the most notorious instances of directors avoiding responsibility for proven corporate manslaughter came in the aftermath of the *Herald of Free Enterprise* tragedy, when a vehicular ferry operated by P&O plc capsized while leaving Zeebrugge harbor in 1987, causing 143 fatalities. The directors whose instructions for staff reductions and faster turnarounds made this tragedy inevitable avoided a conviction for manslaughter by demonstrating that their instructions, while they may have made a fatal accident inevitable, did not directly cause this *particular* accident.

There have been discussions, in England and other countries, about removing or at least restricting the use of this "get out of jail free" card, particularly in the case of workplace accidents, but company directors have lobbied powerfully and so far successfully to retain it.

Directors' Duties

The question of what obligations directors have when making corporate decisions is generally uncontentious. Friedman stated the common position concisely: "A corporate executive is an employee of the owners of the business. He has direct responsibility to his employers. That responsibility is to conduct the business in accordance with their desires, which generally will be to make as much money as possible."[7] When economists are asked to justify Friedman's position, it is common to quote the Michigan Supreme Court's decision in Dodge Brothers v. Ford in 1919. The consensus view is that shareholders own companies, and the directors have a fiduciary duty to act in the shareholders' interests.

Unfortunately the consensus is wholly wrong. As John Kay and Aubrey Silberston pointed out, Friedman is certainly not summarizing the law as it exists in Great Britain.[8] Kay and Silberston quote the English Law Lords: "Shareholders are not, in the eye of the law, part owners of the undertaking. The undertaking is something different from the totality of the share holdings."[9] Lynn Stout cogently argues that the law in the United States is equally dismissive of the idea of shareholder ownership.[10]

Stout notes that the remarks made by the Michigan Supreme Court that appeared to make directors fiduciaries of the shareholders were *obiter dicta*, not part of or relevant to the main judgment. The real basis of the argument between the Dodge brothers and Henry Ford was about Ford's attempts to prevent Dodge emerging as an effective competitor and to force the Dodge brothers to sell their minority shareholding in the Ford Motor Company to him at a discount to its real value. Establishing the principle that directors must not discriminate between shareholders by no means implies that directors should place their shareholders' interests above all other considerations.

Stephen Bainbridge picks up on Stout and concludes that "we can throw Friedman's concept of ownership out the window, along with its associated economic and ethical baggage."[11] Shareholders own a share of the profits, and of anything left after all other creditors are satisfied in the event of liquidation; but that is far from owning a share of the business itself. Bainbridge argues that in law, as well as in practice, companies are run by their boards of directors, and these boards act in the interests of their various companies, not as delegates or fiduciaries of any shareholder or all of them.

Kicking the economic and ethical baggage associated with shareholder ownership out of bounds leaves open the question of how directors should interpret their duty to "act in the interests of the company."

They certainly can't be expected to ignore the need to make a profit and to deliver a fair return to their shareholders. The way that this return is delivered often interacts with the taxation system: if capital gains are favored over dividends, directors will be tempted to favor share buybacks instead of increasing dividends as a way of distributing profits in excess of the investment needs of the business. Thanks to the work of Dixit and Pindyck (Chapter 10) it is possible to calculate the quantum of a fair return given a firm's profit history and the available returns on fixed-interest investments. Well-managed firms should aim to match or modestly exceed these benchmarks but should be required to justify excess returns by demonstrating the successful introduction of innovations. In the absence of such innovations, returns substantially in excess of the benchmarks are a sign of bad, not excellent, management.

Takeovers

Directors are not acting in the interests of their company when they arrange for it to be taken over and asset-stripped: even if this generates a substantial capital gain for the shareholders, it is clearly damaging to the company and generally harmful to the economy as a whole.

US and British law favor hostile takeovers while Japanese and German law and practice make them extremely rare. This works very much in the interests of the median citizen in Japan and Germany but has prevented the rise of a class of immensely rich merchant bankers.

Economists and others in favor of liberal takeover laws like to cite averages and ignore international trade imbalances, demonstrating that the *average* American is better off than the average German. When the executives of companies involved in zero-value-added activities in the finance, insurance, and real estate (FIRE) industries are stripped out of the figures, and national income is adjusted to remove the effect of trade imbalances, Germany and Japan are seen to be more prosperous countries than the United States. This is obvious to the most casual tourist: it is only the figures that lie.

The threat of takeover has been lauded by English-speaking economists as a way of forcing directors to maximize shareholder returns or be replaced by a new set of directors that will. However, since there is no sound legal, moral, or economic argument that justifies making the maximization of shareholder returns the primary duty of directors, there is no justification for the existence of laws and practices that facilitate hostile takeovers.

The one thing most at risk from directors whose sole objective is to maximize the stock price is any sense of socially responsible management. Society is the ultimate guarantor of every limited liability company's debts and so has a legitimate interest in the way corporations are managed.

Corporate Social Responsibility

Friedman's definition of corporate responsibility (above) sounds outrageous; but since he claimed to believe that corporations operated in "as-if" perfect markets in which "excess" profits were impossible, these remarks are not quite as outrageous as they sound. His statement is without legal foundation: shareholders are not the owners of a corporation in US or British law, and directors are not the shareholders' employees.

Friedman deliberately ignored, and those who quote his opinion with approval are deliberately ignoring, the difference between a limited liability corporation and a partnership. Partners in an enterprise are, indeed, joint and several owners of that enterprise, responsible for its debts to the limit of their personal wealth, and the managers that they employ are indeed their servants. Shareholders, safe behind limited liability, are not liable for the debts or other obligations of the company in which they have invested and are not partners and are not owners.

Economists challenged to account for the unrequited benefit of limited liability tend to fall back on the assumption of perfect foresight: corporations cannot, under this assumption, go broke unless their managers are incompetent or worse; and creditors who are left holding unpaid debts recklessly failed to use their perfect foresight before extending credit.

Real markets are not even nearly perfect and neither real corporate managers nor a corporation's real creditors have perfect foresight. For these reasons limited liability has a significant financial value: the community, by sharing commercial risks with the shareholders of corporations, has a clear interest in corporate behavior.

Corporations pay taxes, and it might be argued that honest accounting and the prompt settlement of liabilities to the tax authorities completes a corporation's social responsibilities; but this approach has several problems. One is that sole traders and partnerships also pay taxes but do not enjoy the benefits of limited liability. Another discrepancy springs from the existence of externalities (Chapter 11). The normal operations of a business inevitably consume resources; but only some corporations actively replenish them. A single corporate taxation regime does not discriminate between corporations whose overall operations are sustainable and those whose operations are not.

The two critical social responsibilities of corporations are to the natural environment and to the general population; and no corporation can be considered to be acting responsibility if as a result of its operations either is, individually or in aggregate, worse off.

Environmental Sustainability

Corporations consume resources in the act of delivering services and supplying goods for sale; they will inevitably, in the course of their operations, affect the environment by the release of waste. In a perfectly sustainable world, corporations would replace the resources they consumed and absorb or neutralize any environmentally problematic by-products.

Many corporations have realized that their public image requires them to be believed to be operating sustainably and have engaged public relations companies to create the impression that their operations are, in fact, sustainable. Unfortunately not all of the companies that claim to be operating sustainably are, in fact, doing so. To the extent that a company's operations are not sustainable, its reported profits include unrequited externalities (Chapter 11). Allowing a company to profit from externalities means tolerating the moral equivalent of theft from the broader community, and much as individual thieves have their loot confiscated, such profits should also be confiscated.

Some jurisdictions have moved in the reverse direction: in the United States, oil companies are allowed to claim a tax deduction in respect to the oil that they extract on the basis that the supply from which they drew it was depleted. The fact that the subsequent combustion of that oil is a major contribution to urban pollution and to global climate change is an additional externality that the oil majors have generally avoided paying for. It should not be surprising that the most profitable company in the world today is the US oil giant ExxonMobil, or that it spends tens if not hundreds of millions of dollars in lobbying for the preservation and extension of the tax concessions that it enjoys.

Certain resources are so abundant that a modest royalty is a reasonable offset for any depletion of them: among these are iron and aluminum ores. The capture of solar energy does not in any real sense deplete a limited resource: there is plenty of space on the planet for all the solar collectors mankind could need for the foreseeable future without disrupting other activities, whether profit-seeking or recreational.

The capacity of the biosphere to absorb CO_2 is certainly finite, and while there are no technical problems with converting developed societies to operate within these limits, there will be some expense and some plant made prematurely obsolete. Rather than get unduly excited about such issues, it should be remembered that the normal operation of a capitalist system involves various expenses and the premature obsolescence of various items of plant.

Skill Replenishment

Two of the resources eagerly consumed by corporations are professional staff and skilled workers. An individual's skill set can be considered as having three major components: generic skills as taught in schools and enhanced in post-secondary education; industry-specific skills that may be partly acquired through professional and trade education, but can only be fully developed by appropriate experience supplemented by on-the-job training (formal or otherwise); and firm-specific skills that can only be learned on the job or in firm-based education and training programs.

Skills, whether trade or professional, decay if not refreshed, and they are embodied in a human being who will eventually die or retire. The combination of economic growth and advancing technology means that the proportion of skilled and professional workers in the labor force must steadily rise, and the demands on those who have joined the labor force also rise.

Historically a great deal of trade training took place in public enterprises and regulated monopolies, and when these were corporatized, privatized, or deregulated, the various apprenticeship schemes were cut back or eliminated entirely. These schemes lasted long enough to breed a sense of entitlement among major corporate employers, at least in the English-speaking countries: they now believe that the state has an obligation to provide skilled, experienced workers. Since the major corporations were generally in favor of privatization, corporatization, and deregulation, and lobbied for such policies through their industry associations, their current position lacks logical consistency.

A corporation with a need for a number of skilled or professional workers has a number of options. They can recruit recent high school and first-degree university graduates and provide them with appropriate experience and training; or they can recruit appropriately trained and skilled staff from other corporations in their industry; or they can lobby the government to make up the shortfall. Governments who respond to such demands can bend their school and undergraduate education systems to produce graduates more suited to industry's requirements, but they can't, once their various semicommercial operations have been privatized and corporatized, provide the experience needed to turn theoretical education into practical skills. Governments can also liberalize their immigration laws to permit companies to recruit skilled and professional staff from other countries, as for example the US H1B visa.

These skilled migrants had been educated and trained at the expense of governments and firms in countries much poorer, in most cases, than the destination country. The fact that these costs were not borne by the host government or by the employing firms does not stop their recruitment being an externality; and draining the resources of relatively poor countries to boost the profits of firms in rich ones is neither fair nor moral.

The lack of expenditure on education and training by British and American firms is not solely an issue of morality. As long as any major firms choose to recruit trained staff rather than bear the fair costs of that training, those firms that do provide staff training will see many of their expensively trained staff recruited by other firms. Myopic investors and stock-market analysts may even criticize the firms that conduct training for their excessive cost structure and praise those that rely on piracy and immigration to meet their need for skilled staff.

Companies that profit from the work of skilled and professional staff but do not contribute to their training are profiting from externalities as effectively and immorally as firms that profit from polluting the environment. Applying a special levy to eliminate any profits created by a firm's failure to make an equitable contribution to education and training would not be in any sense excessive.

By some estimates there are up to eleven million "undocumented" immigrants in the United States, including skilled workers holding vital jobs across the US economy. The threat of exposure to the immigration authorities keeps their wage demands modest, possibly even below the statutory minimum rate. It is hard to believe that a country that could put a man on the moon couldn't enforce its own immigration laws—if it really wanted to.

Britain's membership in the EU allows it unlimited access to skilled workers from former Soviet bloc countries, and these fill many jobs, particularly in building and construction, where defective local training schemes have led to a shortage of local workers.

A Safe Workplace

A socially responsible corporation should take steps to maintain a safe and healthy workplace whether or not there are laws and regulations requiring it to. Unfortunately a constant theme of neoliberal propaganda is that the nineteenth-century common law was correct. Neoliberals argue that if an employee is hurt, it should not be the employer's fault unless a criminal act can be proved. OHS regulation is, they claim, an unwarranted interference in the right of shareholders to earn the maximum possible profits on their investments.

A civilized society does not return evil for evil, and the idea of locking a number of neoliberal advocates in a room on the eighth floor of a building and setting the building on fire must remain a pipe dream; but every time we read of a call for "less regulation," we know that this is exactly what they plan for others. The managers of a socially responsible corporation want its employees to live safe and healthy lives, and they extend the same attitude to its customers and the community at large.

Appropriate Incentives

Attempts to legislate moral attitudes have generally failed in the past, and there is no reason to believe that they would succeed in the future. Neoliberals may seek to justify the behavior of psychopaths in management positions, but it is in the nature of psychopaths to seek positions where they can dominate and abuse people, and if this means evading regulations or acting immorally, they do not hesitate to do so.

What is required is some form of incentive that will encourage ordinary managers to oppose the promotion of psychopaths and encourage psychopaths to control their urges. The taxation system may be a convenient way to create appropriate incentives. Rather than punishing antisocial and irresponsible behavior, the incentives should be structured to encourage socially responsible behavior. This could be done by raising the general rate of company income tax and then offering a deduction, or scale of deductions, to corporations meeting various objective standards.

Among the requirements placed on firms claiming the tax deduction to be earned by socially responsible corporations could be the following:

- Environmental responsibility, perhaps demonstrated by a significant reduction in or total elimination of pollution per unit of output.
- Human responsibility, perhaps demonstrated by zero significant workplace trauma or a significant reduction in the annual incidence of such trauma.
- Education and training responsibility, perhaps demonstrated by spending a minimum fraction of the total payroll on providing education and training to staff or making an equivalent contribution to a social education and training provider.
- Commitment to equity, perhaps demonstrated by limiting inequality in total remuneration for employees, including executive directors, to a multiple of twenty times the average remuneration in their company.

The tax deduction for social responsibility could not totally eliminate psychopathic management, but even a modest surcharge on badly behaved corporations would have a major signaling effect: a significant number of people would neither wish to work for nor invest in a company that chose to be socially irresponsible. Corporate bad behavior would not be eliminated but it would be marginalized.

Notes

1. See pages 123 ff.
2. Josephson (1934 [1961]).

3. Leibenstein (1966).
4. Kay and Silberston (1995), Stout (2008).
5. Fama (1970).
6. Fama & French (2004).
7. Friedman (1970).
8. Kay & Silberston (1995).
9. Evershed, L. J. in Short v. Treasury Commissioners, 1948, A.C. 534 H.L. quoted in Kay & Silberston (1995).
10. Stout (2008).
11. Bainbridge (2003).

14

After Neoliberalism

So I returned, and considered all the oppressions that are done under
the sun: and beheld the tears of such as were oppressed, and they had
no comforter; and on the side of their oppressors there was power.
—Ecclesiastes 4:1

Neoliberalism is a term that refers both to a body of economic theory and to a political ideology. The theory is essentially orthodox neoclassical economics with a superstructure built around the work of von Mises, Hayek, Friedman, and their followers. The ideology is widely described as Thatcherism, after the late British prime minister; in the United States it may be described as libertarianism or possibly Reaganism after the late president; it may also be referred to as "economic rationalism."

Neoliberalism is a body of theory and practice based on the following points:

- "There is no such thing as society. There are individual men and women, and there are families."[1]
- "The agent of economic theory is rational, selfish and his tastes do not change."[2]
- Theories need not be based on reality as long as they produce the right answers.
- Economies are at or close to an equilibrium state where changes will generally be for the worse.
- All firms are price-takers: none of them can affect the market price by their actions.
- Banks are mere intermediaries, accepting deposits and then repackaging them into loans.
- Inflation only appears when greedy workers are appeased by weak monetary authorities.
- Keynes and all his works may safely be ignored. Schumpeter and all his works may also be ignored, except for his phrase "creative destruction," which may only be used out of context.
- Trade deficits are self-correcting, and their magnitude does not matter.

- Wages reflect each worker's marginal contribution, and prescribing minimum wages or any other regulation of the labor market damages the economy.
- There are no significant externalities: every firm's impact on the environment is fully reflected in its costs and prices.
- Welfare is maximized in countries that adopt free trade and freedom of contract.
- Corporations are owned by their shareholders and the directors are their agents.

The body of neoliberal theory includes assumptions, logical arguments, predictions, and conclusions. To the extent that a theory claims to describe reality, it must be subject to testing: its assumptions must reflect reality, its arguments must be logically complete, and its predictions must be borne out. Neoliberal theory fails all four tests.

Neoliberal ideology is a set of beliefs that, while they may have been originally inspired by neoliberal theory, are quite separate from it. Unlike theories, belief systems cannot be subjected to logical testing and possible disproof. To the extent that neoliberals claim that their policies and recommendations have theoretical support, they are mistaken, but pointing this out may not change their beliefs. Neoliberals may make predictions that prove to be erroneous, but they can always find extraneous factors to blame.

Even if events and arguments raise doubts in a neoliberal's mind, some at least will prefer to persist rather than admit their previous mistakes:

> All causes shall give way: I am in blood
> Stepp'd in so far that, should I wade no more,
> Returning were as tedious as go o'er.[3]

The late Baroness Thatcher described herself as a "conviction politician," a lady who was "not for turning." No doubt self-confidence approaching arrogance is an essential quality in someone taking on the job of prime minister, but her refusal to change her mind, even in the face of overwhelming evidence, eventually caused her colleagues to remove her from office.

This book will probably not appeal to conviction politicians, whether neoliberal, socialist, or any other cult. When Keynes was accused of being inconsistent, he is supposed to have responded, "When I learn new facts I adjust my opinions. What, sir, do you do?" Cromwell wrote to the Scottish covenanters, "I beseech ye, in the bowels of Christ, believe it possible that you might be mistaken." (Cromwell was trying to avert an armed clash, but the covenanters insisted on a battle. It took place at Dunbar, and the covenanters lost bloodily and comprehensively.) In our complicated world, new facts will emerge all the time, and only those societies where these facts are taken into account and policies adjusted appropriately can prosper in the medium and longer term.

Neoliberalism and conviction politics have dominated governments in the English-speaking world for over thirty years, and the result has been a Great Recession in the United States, a renewed Great Depression in the countries of Southern Europe, unsustainable international trade imbalances, the return of contagious diseases once thought eliminated, and many other unintended and unwanted consequences. Its time is up.

Change Is Needed

Neoliberalism is the current ideology used to maintain the social order and ensure that those at the top of the economic pyramid are secure in their possessions and their income. By asserting the sanctity of property, it gives ideological support to campaigns to eliminate estate duties and so permit the perpetuation of privilege based on inherited wealth. By identifying shareholders as the owners of a company and the managers as their agents, it justifies the unlimited growth in executive salaries. By pretending that competition is perfect or that society can be analyzed as if competition was perfect, its followers are able to blame the poor and the sick for their own predicament and so justify reductions in social provision.

The fundamental basis of neoliberalism is the assertion that property rights are superior to all other rights; and since ownership of property is unevenly distributed, those with greater property have greater rights than those with less, and those with no property have no rights at all.

There is a long historical tail to this argument: the Putney Debates of 1647 between members of Cromwell's army pitted the Levellers, who asserted that landless men had rights—in particular, the right to vote and be elected to Parliament—against the rest.[4]

The argument ended with a number of the Levellers hanged. Manhood suffrage did not arrive in England until 1918, and adult suffrage was delayed a further ten years. The Levellers' program was finally completed in Britain in 1948 when the university seats and the property vote were abolished. (Before 1948 graduates of Oxford, Cambridge, and the Scottish universities had a second vote in parliamentary elections to elect a member representing their institution.)

Neoliberal governance is fundamentally unstable. Because there are increasing returns to wealth—"To those that have, more shall be given"—a neoliberally governed society becomes progressively more unequal, eventually degenerating into a tiny and fabulously wealthy elite ruling a mass of impoverished servants. Hayek wrote *The Road to Serfdom*[5] to explain his belief that government intervention in an economy would lead to a new form of feudalism; but experience since 1979 shows that it is precisely the withdrawal of government from the economy that sets a society on that road.

Thomas Piketty[6] has documented the path inequality has followed over two centuries, and predicts, rather gloomily, that western civilization is headed back to the eighteenth century, with government of, by, and for the inheritors of vast wealth.

For most of human history, civilization has involved hierarchical relationships, with orders passing down and taxes and rents flowing up; those high in the hierarchy were rich in property and income; those at the bottom had little of either. The situation is intrinsically unstable; inequality in a hierarchical society steadily increases, and no matter what justification those at the top of the hierarchy offer for the *status quo*, eventually those at the bottom will find a leader who will enforce a more even distribution of the available wealth. The leader may arise from the downtrodden masses, but often, from long before Caesar to Lenin and after, the leader arises from the upper levels of society. Such a person will harness popular discontent in order to achieve power; once in power, history suggests, not all such leaders actually resolve popular grievances.

Democracy has made popular revolutions less bloody than many of their historical antecedents. Franklin D. Roosevelt's election halted the United States' slide into fascism, and his New Deal set in train an unprecedented period of general prosperity during which, in John F. Kennedy's words, a rising tide did in fact lift all boats. The conservative counterrevolution under Reagan and the two Bushes removed the constraints on growing inequality set in place by Roosevelt and his immediate successors. With the constraints relaxed, both inequality and economic instability were allowed to return to pre-Roosevelt levels.

Roosevelt's enlightened response to the economic crisis of the 1920s and 1930s was not the only one. The same period saw the rise of Mussolini and Hitler and a flock of their imitators across Europe promoting corporation-friendly dictatorships. Fascism and the appointment of a dictator who will redress all wrongs can be sold to a suffering population at least as easily as Roosevelt's moderate reformism.

Those at the top of an established hierarchy will generally attempt to protect their position from real or imaginary revolutionaries, and they will seldom hesitate to use force to do so if they see no alternative. Since there are few at the top and many at the bottom, the use of force is problematical. As Caesar's successors learned, a praetorian guard can be very effective in a revolutionary situation—on either side.

Revolution

The combination of extraordinary wealth alongside extraordinary deprivation creates fertile ground for demagogues, usually of the Right. Communism in one form or another has been present for a long period; but the capture of power brings opportunities for self-aggrandizement to the point that notionally left-wing dictatorships, such as those of Stalin or Pol Pot, have been even more oppressive and as ineffective at remedying the problems of the middle and working classes as the fascist dictatorships of Mussolini or Franco.

One could construct a terrifying counterfactual history by assuming that Father Charles Edward Coughlin's[7] clerical Fascist movement had been able to insert a more pliant president than Roosevelt into the White House in 1937 and initiate a clerical/fascist regime in the United States. The forces behind Father Coughlin were subdued but not eliminated. In the 2010 US midterm elections, the Tea Party, a quasi-fascist front group manipulated by a number of extremely unpleasant billionaires, seized control of the Republican Party. Their program calls for a return to the 1920s economically, politically, and socially.

Right or left, revolutions are not conducive to economic progress.

Neoliberals are not, in general, fascists; but neoliberalism leads inexorably in that direction. To the sort of pure economist who feels that ethical issues have no place in their discipline—or in government, for that matter—Fascism might be seen as having a "bad rap." Mussolini did make the trains run on time, and at least until the start of World War II, there were few massacres (at least of Italians; Libyans and Abyssinians were not so fortunate). It is not entirely sure that Mussolini would have lost an election or that in winning it he would have used more fraud and violence than that which is acceptable in many notionally democratic countries. If Mussolini had shown as much sense as Spain's General Franco and not joined Hitler's war, he too might have died in his bed, still Il Duce, long after World War II was over.

In 1994 and again in 2001 and 2008, Italians elected a direct heir to Mussolini to take charge of the Italian state: Silvio Berlusconi exploited lower-class resentment to win political office and included acknowledged Fascists in his governing coalition. Berlusconi certainly used his office to further his own interests—in particular his wish to avoid prosecution for many alleged criminal acts. He did not need thugs toting castor oil bottles to win over the public: monopoly control over Italian commercial TV and a near monopoly over the press sufficed. (Mussolini continued to conduct elections after his coup in 1923, but anyone who showed signs of opposition was at risk of being seized by a gang of Fascist youth and forced to swallow a large quantity of castor oil.) Campaigns against Roma and various refugee groups proved a successful distraction from the Berlusconi government's failures to actually do anything to improve the Italian economy.

Ultimately, rejecting Fascism is a personal and ethical choice. Men motivated by pure self-interest did well under Franco and Pinochet and under Mussolini as well until his overwhelming vanity led him into making a fatal alliance with Hitler. Since unchecked neoliberalism must cause indefinitely rising inequality, and such rising inequality can lead to Fascism or worse, endorsing neoliberalism is to accept Fascism as a possible ultimate destination.

Although there is no reason to suppose that Fascism leads to a Benthamite "greatest good for the greatest number," it has generally been kind to those who took a leadership role in installing it. Caesar's murder by a group of aristocratic plotters led by two of his close associates is unusual in this sense; but his nephew Octavian, later the Emperor Augustus, completed Caesar's work and utterly crushed the aristocratic opposition to the imperial power. As in modern Russia, the oligarchs were allowed to enjoy and increase their wealth but not to use state power to pursue their personal interests, whether venal or altruistic.

There is no logical reason to believe that placing additional obligations on the wealthy and those enjoying very high incomes would have adverse economic consequences for those with lesser wealth and earning lower incomes. There is reason to believe that such populist measures will postpone or avert the crisis of legitimacy that must arrive should a clear majority of the population refuse to participate in the democratic process, or should only participate to support antidemocratic groups. Such measures should also postpone or ameliorate financial crises that might otherwise be triggered by a large-scale diversion of investment from productive purposes to speculation.

The detachment of the people at large from the political process provides the space for demagogues to flourish.

British history in the nineteenth century makes a remarkable contrast with that of the rest of Europe: on the Continent, 1830 was a year of revolution; in Britain, the passage of the first Reform Act. On the Continent there were even more violent revolutions in 1848; in Britain, the Chartists submitted a huge petition to the parliament, most of which was acted on a mere nineteen years later. The relatively peaceful transitions in Britain owned much to a split in the aristocracy between the pragmatists led by the Duke of Wellington and the "ultras" who lacked such a distinguished leader. The Iron Duke knew when and how to organize a strategic retreat.

The result of the duke's moderation and the general respect for public opinion by all British governments after 1830 was not anarchy but rising general prosperity—a prosperity that the aristocracy certainly shared in. By and large British politics worked by consensus: Liberal, and later Labour, governments would introduce reforms over Conservative opposition; yet subsequent conservative governments might have modified the resulting institutions but made no effort to reverse the reforms.

The arrival of the neoliberal crusaders led by Thatcher ended the consensus and replaced it with conviction. The results have not been pretty.

Where to Begin?

Neoliberal policies were voluntarily adopted by elected governments in the English-speaking countries, but they have been forced on developing countries by the IMF and on many Latin American countries by military dictatorships. Following the Eurozone crisis[8] in 2012, Greece, Italy, Spain, and Portugal were forced to follow the neoliberal path irrespective of popular wishes: democratic institutions still operated but as theater only; executive power was in the hands of a committee of bankers.

During the early years of postcommunist Russia, some neoliberal economists openly talked about the desirability of a Pinochet-style dictatorship in which opponents of neoliberal policies could be "disappeared" and the secret police would persuade the common people to accept the loss of their previous rights to education and health care. The privatization of Russian state enterprises was deliberately rigged to create an oligarchy of billionaires. They could be counted upon to use their wealth and influence to resist any backsliding from neoliberal orthodoxy by the Russian government, however it might be formed in the future.

Neoliberal policies have never been popular, and as explained by Naomi Klein,[9] elected governments have been unable to implement them without claiming that a crisis, real or synthetic, makes drastic and unpopular action necessary. Now that neoliberalism itself has led to a crisis, the claim that the solution is still more neoliberal measures is being greeted with widespread skepticism. While most developed countries still have elected governments with sovereign powers, they can use them to escape from the neoliberal morass, even if this involves some reduction in the rights of property owners.

A democratically elected sovereign parliament, such as the British House of Commons, clearly has the power to pass laws diminishing property rights and has frequently done so; the process started even before the First Reform Bill and gathered strength through the nineteenth century.

The culmination of the process in Britain was probably the election of the Atlee government in 1945. World War II had been "the good war" as far as the mass of the British public was concerned, with the people from the king down united in the defense of their country and the defeat of the unspeakably evil Nazi regime in Germany. Attlee's unexpected and overwhelming victory was built around his promise to address Britain's social problems with the same determination as the war had brought to the military ones.

The welfare and other reforms inspired by Keynes and Beveridge relied on redistributive taxation and the creation of the National Health Service, one of the world's largest employers. Taxation in Britain in the years following World War II was highly progressive, with a very high top rate and the heirs of the wealthy paying substantial inheritance taxes. Atlee proved that it could be done—that society could be made fairer and more equal without reducing economic growth or frustrating an accompanying rise in living standards. I argue that it should be done.

What Are Property Rights?

Proudhon may have come to regret his invention of the phrase "property is theft"[10] (La propriété, c'est le vol!), not least because it is self-contradictory: theft is the act of taking someone's property, so if theft exists so must rights in property. Proudhon may have meant that conceding to property owners an unrestricted right to do what they pleased with it is a violation of the natural rights of others.

History tells us that real property really is the result of violent theft. William the First of England ("The Conqueror") declared that his success at the Battle of Hastings in 1066 meant that the whole of England was his personal property and he could grant the use of any part of it to whomsoever he pleased. To drive the point home, William dated his reign from the day before the Battle of Hastings, making those who fought on the former king Harold's side traitors who had to beg for pardon and the use of what fraction of their former property the king would permit them to retain.

In the process of white settlement of North America, the land was seized by the British crown without any attempt to secure the consent of the native inhabitants: unalienated parts of Australia are still referred to as "crown land." In Britain those who arrange the sale or rental of land and property are referred to as Real Estate agents; in the United States they are called Realtors; but in both cases "Real" is an alternative spelling of "Royal": title in land is granted by the monarch whose original claim is based on simple conquest.

However based, individual ownership of real property is well established in the developed Western countries and no significant group appears to advocate a radical revocation of property rights. Remembering the morally tainted basis of real property rights should, however, serve as a reminder that such rights are provisional, and claims that they are unconditional cannot be sustained on moral grounds.

To the extent that property rights are going to be limited, the experience of England before and after the Glorious Revolution of 1688 suggests that while arbitrary interference with property rights is likely to be economically damaging, the general application of a legislative set of rules to all property owners, or to a well-defined class of property owners, need not have negative economic effects.

During the nineteenth century, two entire classes of property rights were abolished in Britain: the ownership of seats in parliament ("rotten boroughs") and the ownership of slaves. Defenders of property rights vigorously opposed both reforms and predicted economic ruin in consequence; but all that actually happened was that prosperity continued to increase.

Populism

Neoliberalism does not lead to popular policies: it is not simply that neoliberals use the term "populist" as a form of criticism of proposals with which they disagree, but also that public-opinion polls and referendums regularly demonstrate that neoliberal policies lack popular support. When the proposed European constitution was put to referendums in France and Holland, it was decisively defeated; and when the same proposals were dressed up as the Lisbon Treaty and put to a referendum in Ireland, they were defeated again.

Public opinion polls in Britain and France showed that the Lisbon Treaty would have been decisively rejected in those countries too; much political maneuvering was required to prevent the issue being put to a popular vote. When, in 2011, the prime minister of Greece proposed a referendum to seek popular approval for the crippling austerity measures demanded by France and Germany, he was forced to withdraw the proposal and resign in favor of a "technocrat"—an economist approved by the European Commission and the European Central Bank. In 2015 a new Greek prime minister called a referendum to consider further austerity measures demanded by the "Troika" of the European Central Bank, the European Commission, and the International Monetary Fund. The voters overwhelmingly rejected the austerity program: the Troika then imposed an even more severe one.

The liberal-left parties in the developed countries were largely founded to counter social exclusion and economic injustice. These are popular (and populist) ambitions. While today there may be some rhetorical flourishes in favor of "equality of opportunity," the liberal-left has been thoroughly captured by Mrs. Thatcher's slogan TINA—"There Is No Alternative" (to be spoken with every word capitalized), ensuring that no practical steps are taken that might actually equalize opportunity, since such steps must necessarily interfere with inherited privilege and the property rights of those with great wealth.

The refusal by the leaders of all the major political parties in the developed countries to endorse popular policies has, not unnaturally, made these leaders and their parties unpopular. One of the most visible signs of this effect is, in those countries where voting is voluntary, the fall in electoral participation.

The number of those who didn't bother to vote exceeded those who voted for any party in the 2004, 2006, 2008, 2010, and 2012 US federal elections and the 2005 and 2010 British general elections. In the British General Election of 2015 the vote for the victorious Conservative Party just passed the total of nonvoters. In the 2014 US election, barely 20 percent of the population voted at all. In Germany after the 2005 national elections, the Social Democratic leader Gerhard Schroeder surrendered the chancellorship rather than maintain it with the support of the populist Party of Democratic Socialism (der Linke). In the 2013 Italian elections, a party led by a clown won over a quarter of the vote.

On the face of it, it is surprising that politicians such as Schroeder would prefer to lose office rather than adopt popular policies, although for those who ascribe venal motives to all politicians there is an easy explanation: Schroeder, like many other former leaders from both sides of politics in many countries in recent times, earned far more from the company directorships and consultancies offered him after his resignation than he had earned as chancellor of Germany.

Rejection of TINA would mean desanctifying wealth gained from anything other than personal exertion. In particular, executive salaries and personal consultancies paid at more than ten times the average hourly earnings in the employing enterprise cannot be justified on the basis of the performer's economic contribution and so should be subject to significant marginal tax rates.

A New Agenda

Executive Pay

Effective measures must be taken to prevent executives in incorporated companies drawing excessive salaries, including bonuses and incentives: a blanket limit of twenty times the average income in that enterprise (including its subsidiaries) would almost certainly raise productivity and in due course revenue and profits. There is no need to apply such measures to the owners of and partners in unincorporated enterprises: such people are genuine owners and risk-bearers and have a legitimate interest in their rewards. Founding entrepreneurs should be permitted to earn dividends or make gains from selling part or all of their interest exempt from regulated limits: the social benefits from encouraging genuine entrepreneurship outweigh any possible gains from restricting entrepreneurial rewards.

Wealth gained in a person's lifetime may be earned through skill and exertion or acquired by the abuse of trust or power. Even in the hyperegalitarian USSR, successful sportspeople and artistic performers could become relatively wealthy; and those politicians in the Western democracies who wished to reduce the top rate of income tax from the relatively high levels of the 1940s through the early 1970s often cited the injustice of applying such rates to sportspeople and performers, many of whom would only enjoy a few years of high incomes. These arguments gained considerable popular support and are still used by chief executives of public companies to justify their very high emoluments.

Entrepreneurs such as Andrew Carnegie ("No man will make a great leader who wants to do it all himself or get all the credit for doing it") and now Warren Buffet and Bill Gates claim a double legitimacy for their great wealth. They founded enterprises that competed in the market and earned revenue and profits by delivering value to their customers, while protecting the interests of their other stakeholders; and they divested, or intend to divest, themselves of the accumulated wealth so gained by applying it to various charitable and other worthwhile causes during their own lifetimes.

Carnegie, Buffet, and Gates did not become rich by drawing an excessive income from the enterprises that they created; rather, they sold shares in the enterprise itself to investors. Note clearly that Carnegie, Buffet, and Gates were *not* the agents appointed by a group of investors to manage the investors' money: they were the principals, and the investors purchased an interest in the wealth-generating corporations that Carnegie, Buffet, and Gates had created. Gates until his retirement was one of the *lowest*-paid chief executives of a major American corporation.

Few top executives in Britain or the United States match Gates's forbearance. While in pure theory a board of directors is responsible for the success of their company and so should be frugal with the expenditure of shareholders' funds, in practice boards of directors align their shareholders' interests with those of the chief executive by waving through increases in executive remuneration. Whatever the rhetoric, directors appear to have been persuaded, or chosen to pretend, that increasing the remuneration of the chief executive will lead to better outcomes for the shareholders. As a result the spread between the average wages and salaries paid by corporations and that paid to the chief executive has risen from 40:1 to 300:1 in the United States in a little over twenty years, and has risen at a similar rate from a lower base in the United Kingdom.

Many studies have shown that there is no correlation between chief executive rewards and corporate performance; and those not versed in statistics can recall the many cases where hopelessly incompetent executives were sent on their way with generous severance packages.

Excessive executive pay has two malign effects on corporations that indulge in it. One is direct: pay is cash drawn from an enterprise that might otherwise be invested within it or paid as dividends to shareholders. As soon as the pay passes the level needed to draw a maximum performance from the executives who receive it, the cash drain weakens the company and reduces its profits and growth.

The second malign effect of excessive executive pay is indirect and probably even more damaging. Setting aside people traumatized congenitally or by subsequent injuries and assuming an equal opportunity for training and education, a span of ten to one covers practically every measurable aspect of human performance. Pay differentials outside this range for people of similar experience and educational attainment are certain to be perceived as unjust, and the persons who benefit from such excesses will be seen to be claiming the reward for others' effort.

Sportspersons have been mentioned before: but it is noticeable that the salary differentials *within* a successful sporting team are often less than ten to one and seldom much more.

Many sporting leagues, including many American ones, operate under an agreement that limits total player payments. Some leagues allow a specific exemption for "marquee" players; in others every player's salary is counted. In leagues without such an exemption, a star player's payments will appear to be at the expense of the rest of the team members. Even with such an exemption, the remaining players may see the exceptional payment offered to the star as unfair.

Injustice always breeds resentment, and resentment eliminates cooperation. The threat of being sacked or having a career sidelined into a dead end may prevent open rebellion, but employees so affected will see every impending problem as a chance to enjoy *Schadenfreude* rather than something that they should try to avert. This can be visibly true for sporting teams, but is equally significant inside corporations.

Psychological studies suggest that diligently performing an employee's assigned tasks may not be the way to secure promotion to the top levels of a corporation, at least in the English-speaking countries.[11] When plausible rogues make it to the corner office, the interests of the company that they are ostensibly responsible for are completely subordinated to their own. If a subordinate does do an outstanding job or proposes a valuable innovation, the first reaction of such chief executives will be an attempt to claim the credit; if this fails, the subordinate will be seen as a threat, not an asset.

Capping senior executive salaries will divert the interest of such plausible rogues from robbing public companies to some other malfeasance. Borderline psychopaths may be diverted from amassing personal wealth to securing the admiration of their friends, colleagues, and the broader society, making us all better off.

Estate Taxes

Estate taxes are, in theory at least, painless. The person who left the estate has no further interest in it: as the popular saying goes, "you can't take it with you." Outright confiscation of deceased estates would offend most people's sense of justice, but levying substantial taxes on very large inheritances will be an important part of any measures limiting the growth of inequality.

A majority of the populations of developed Western countries appear to recognize a distinction between earned rewards and other sources of wealth. Few would dispute the right of a wealthy person to leave enough for the decent support of a surviving spouse and minor children; but beyond that many would agree with Andrew Carnegie that "I would as soon leave my son a curse as the almighty dollar." Inherited wealth has no more place than inherited status in a democratic society. In particular, inherited wealth based on land is seldom more than violent theft sanctified by time.

Education and Training

The standard used by many economists to assess the effectiveness of solutions to any problem is the omniscient social planner. Such a planner would assess society's future needs for professional and skilled workers in every relevant category and assign every young person to an education and training program that, subject to society's overall requirements, best matched their aptitudes and aspirations while incurring the lowest overall cost. The authorities in the USSR attempted to control their economy, including the education and training function, by a centralized planning system, and although they succeeded in producing a well-educated and highly skilled workforce, the overall economy performed badly and the USSR disintegrated.

Orthodox and Hayekian economists argue that the economic failure of the USSR proves the impossibility of successful centralized planning, and so the provision of education, training, and experience on anything other than commercial terms is an intervention in the market, leading to inefficiencies and suboptimal outcomes. They argue that, in the absence of any centralized planning or control, individuals will use their perfect foresight to devise an education and training program that matches their aptitudes and aspirations, while institutions will spontaneously arise to deliver the required education and training programs at the lowest possible total cost consistent with an adequate level of delivered quality. Such self-serving rubbish should be rejected with the contempt that it deserves.

One of the successes of the conservative network from the 1980s onwards was to reduce the element of public subsidy to education at all levels. This took several forms. One was the introduction of fees for formerly free public higher education. Another was subsidizing fee-paying schools and degrading the public school system to make private schools more attractive to parents. At the same time, by promulgating the doctrine of shareholder sovereignty, the orthodox and the Hayekian economists were able to persuade many employers that their in-house education and training schemes conferred a private benefit on their employees at the cost of the shareholders—a situation that, the economically orthodox claimed, was both inefficient and immoral and so should not be allowed to continue.

In recent years in the United Kingdom and the United States, many employers in attractive white-collar fields have started to offer internships where would-be employees work without pay in order to build their networks and gain work-related experience. Some employers actually charge would-be interns a substantial premium, to the delight of conservative economists but the dismay of any aspirants for work in that field who do not have rich parents.

Governments following neoliberal theory have welcomed private, for-profit institutions into the education and training market, arguing that competition will reduce costs and raise quality. The record of the largest of these private entrants, the University of Phoenix, gives some cause for doubt: some of its students have been awarded nursing degrees without ever having set foot in a hospital; other students paid large sums pursuing a doctorate in psychology, only to discover that the university was not qualified to offer degrees in that field.[12]

The arguments for allowing for-profit institutions to provide education and training are based on clearly false assumptions, including the existence of perfect credit markets and perfectly informed buyers (if someone was perfectly informed about an education and training program, they would have no need to undertake it). Because there are genuine differences between those requiring education and training and the type of training required for various trades and professions, the probability of a spontaneous outcome being optimal are quasi-infinitesimal. It remains possible that such an outcome would be superior to an administered one; but such a conclusion is a matter of faith rather than logic.

We need to return to the basic Bismarckian model, at least as far as operating well-funded public school systems, an effective national health system, and alternative low-cost paths to high quality higher and further education. Such measures will increase social mobility and economic growth rates; and it will be necessary to tax the wealthy for the benefit of the rest of society.

Deprivatization?

The case for privatizing natural monopolies is based on falsified theories and has been exposed as bad for consumers in practice.[13]

Such enterprises should be taken back into public ownership as rapidly as possible, and no further natural monopolies should be privatized.

The European Alternative

The Social Market Model provides a starting point for a discussion of a practical alternative to neoliberalism.

The Social Market Model: Origins

Neoliberalism is sometimes described in continental Europe as "Anglo-Saxon economics," reflecting its origins and its direct descent from the economic policies adopted by Britain after the repeal of the Corn Laws in 1846 and giving laissez-faire and free trade totemic status. Under these policies Britain's entrepreneurs exploited their global preeminence in manufacturing. Its navy dominated the world's oceans while its merchants and soldiers created "an Empire on which the sun never sets."

The German economist Friederich List argued cogently that Britain's dominance of global manufacturing was so complete that no nation that adopted free trade and laissez-faire had any hope of establishing a viable manufacturing base.[14]

The argument in favor of creating a significant manufacturing industry was two pronged. There was the matter of simple nationalism: the American Civil War demonstrated that war was increasingly mechanized, with artillery and machine guns more important than rifles and bayonets; and countries without a strong manufacturing industry would not be able to stand on the battlefield against countries that had one.

A lack of artillery was not the only thing that handicapped the armies of nations without a manufacturing base: Lee's advance into Pennsylvania leading to the South's crushing defeat at Gettysburg in 1863 was in part a hunt for footwear for his army.

296

The second prong of the argument for establishing a manufacturing industry was social: manufacturing wages were far higher than rural ones (and still are) reflecting both the higher value added in manufacturing and the higher capital intensity of manufacturing operations. "We eat butcher's meat, Miss," explains the working-class hero of Gaskell's *North and South*,[15] a novel set in mid-nineteenth-century Manchester, while the rural poor the heroine was familiar with might occasionally share in a poached rabbit but otherwise could go without meat from one year to the next.

As Bismarck organized the unification of Germany, he was directly concerned with the military significance of manufacturing and indirectly concerned with the social implications. Bismarck did not share Kaiser Wilhelm II's imperial obsessions,[16] but he did want Germany to be strong enough to resist an attack by any of its neighbors, including an attack supported by Britain. The Zollverein created a German common market in which manufacturing flourished while protected from the more virulent forms of British competition.

Manufacturing, particularly in the days before computer-assisted automation, required a large workforce; and although the wages paid far exceeded those for rural labor, the workers were well aware that their bosses earned an order of magnitude more. A manufacturing workforce, now as much as then, must achieve a high degree of internal coordination, which implies a high degree of cooperation; this in turn predisposed the workers to demand higher wages and other benefits and to cooperate in collective action seeking to persuade their employers to satisfy these demands. A recurrent theme of nineteenth- and early-twentieth-century polemic was that the workers could not have formed these revolutionary ideas without help, and "socialist agitators" rather than workplace conditions were generally blamed for worker dissatisfaction.

Bismarck was temperamentally suited to ordering the massacre of insubordinate workers, but he chose the alternative path of outbidding the "agitators" with programs of his own. A network of technical high schools raised the competence and therefore the productivity of the workforce, enabling German employers to increase wages without losing profits; a publicly funded health system spared employers the cost of supporting sick or injured employees and workers the fear of destitution following illness; and a pension system relieved manufacturers of the cost of supporting retirees.

297

Bismarck was not entirely successful in his attempt to outbid the Socialists; but he did reduce the contest to a relatively manageable squabble over the division of the economic surplus rather than a revolutionary "expropriation of the expropriators." His ghost was duly rewarded when the Socialists voted unanimously to support Germany's entry into the world war in 1914. Revolutionary socialism briefly emerged in Germany in the wake of Germany's defeat in World War I, but the murder of Karl Liebknecht and Rosa Luxembourg by the Freikorps put an end to that.

The Social Market Model Today

Between 1918 and 1945, Germany's history, both social and military, was tortured to say the least; but when the US occupation forces turned to rebuilding West Germany's economy in 1946, their efforts had a distinctly Bismarckian twist. Under the Adenauer government, ownership of the means of production stayed firmly private; but the state accepted a major role as the primary provider of education, technical training, transport infrastructure, and health care.

Even the private ownership of the means of production was less than absolute: corporations were required to establish supervisory boards on which employees, through their unions, had equal representation with management; and although the supervisory boards had no direct executive power, they served to maintain a high degree of workplace harmony.

The German economy now delivers a very high median wage while supporting a comprehensive welfare state and extensive public amenities, including both a high-speed road network and a fast and moderately priced intercity train service with reasonably frequent and comfortable train services to smaller centers. German firms are competitive in spite of extensive unionization, high wages, and high taxes: this is shown by Germany's strong balance of trade.

The published unemployment rate in Germany was, for most of the years preceding the Global Financial Crisis, higher than that in the United States or Britain; but this was at least partly a matter of definition, since in the United States and Britain, anyone who worked for at least one hour in the week preceding the survey is reported as employed while in Germany anyone not working at least thirty-eight hours a week who expresses a wish for more hours of work is recorded as unemployed. The "core" workforce participation rate (the percentage of people between twenty-five and fifty-four years of age currently employed or seeking work) before the Global Financial Crisis was as high in Germany as it was in Britain or the United States; at the time of writing, it is substantially higher.

While the other countries of continental Western Europe differ in the details of their employment law and the reach of their welfare state, they all resemble Germany much more closely than they resemble the United States. Germany, as the largest economy in continental Europe, is the principal ideological battleground and the principal example of a successful economy not organized on neoliberal principles.

Neoliberalism and the Social Market

The intellectual dominance of a combination of neoliberalism and pure neoclassical economics is such that there are few coherent arguments in favor of the social market model to be found in the orthodox economic literature, and not many outside it. The Ordo-liberals in Germany defended the continued role of the state in public provision, but even some German economists proved unable to resist Friedman's siren songs.

In the think tank universe, there were strident calls for "economic reform" in Germany from the start of the twenty-first century. Their agitation was successful to the point that in 2003 Schroeder's Social Democratic government weakened employment security and allowed the employment of "temporary" staff on low wages with few rights. The resulting dissatisfaction split the Social Democratic Party and led to the formation of the new left-wing party, the Party of Democratic Socialism (Der Linke). These events contributed to the Social Democrats' defeat at the subsequent elections while the effective freezing of real German wages led to enormous trade surpluses and the Eurozone crisis starting in 2010.

The oxymoronic "growth and stability pact" (the Maastricht treaty); the establishment and governance of the European Central Bank; and the terms on which the East European states were admitted to the European Union were all structured in order to create pressure for the reform of the Western European economies along neoliberal lines. The proposed European Constitution was an attempt to incorporate neoliberal doctrine into the governance of Europe.

The main obstacle to such neoliberal "reforms" is the great popularity of the European welfare state. Welfare became a term of abuse in the United States when it was successfully demonized by President Reagan and his followers as providing a way for underserving idlers to live a life of ease paid for by taxes on honest workers. Reagan achieved, and the

Republican Party has maintained, a decisive lead over the Democratic Party among white working-class voters. Since Reagan's presidency the Democratic Party has achieved an even greater lead among African American and Hispanic voters. No such polarization has occurred in Britain or Europe: overtly racist and/or xenophobic parties exist but are not mainstream.

This in turn leads to the main argument in favor of the *status quo* in Western Europe: the pragmatic comparison of the neoliberal United States and Britain with the economies of Western Europe. The statistics need vigorous interpretation to support any general neoliberal claim to superiority.

- Comparisons between nations may be made on a total basis or on a per capita basis. Since Germany has a low birth rate and a low rate of immigration, its growth rates will always appear, on a gross basis, to be lower than those of the United States, which has a higher birth rate and a substantial level of immigration, much of it legal. On a per capita basis, the difference is less and on some measures even reverses.
- The "social wage" is often ignored; in particular, the costs of health care. US citizens must pay (or have their employers pay on their behalf) many thousands of dollars per year for a health system under which Americans suffer greater morbidity and mortality than Germans, for whom health care is free at the point of delivery.
- Comparisons are often made on the basis of average rather than median income and wealth. When Microsoft founder Bill Gates sits down in an intimate cafe, its average patron instantly becomes a billionaire.[17] While average US incomes (at least when measured in US dollars) have been rising faster than German incomes measured in Euros, the median US income adjusted for inflation has hardly moved for thirty years. The entire benefits of economic growth and rising productivity since 1979 have been captured by the top quintile of the US income distribution—nearly all of this in the top 1 percent. The median German earns a higher income than the median US or British citizen.
- National balance sheet effects are often left out; but the United States has, of recent years, been running a major deficit on its current account of the order of 7 percent of its gross national product, while Germany has been running a current account surplus of over 5 percent of its gross national product. On the assumption that international debts will eventually have to be repaid, standard comparisons between Germany and the United States overstate relative US incomes by approximately 12 percent.

A leading economist is supposed to have made a study of the Japanese system of economic management and concluded that their methods "may work in practice, but not in theory." The main basis of the neoliberal attack on the German social market model is clearly theory; and when practice confounds theory, the wise will reexamine the theory, as this book has attempted to do.

Germany is not perfect, and its leadership's deference to the shibboleths of Ordoliberalism is unfortunate, since Ordoliberalism is no more soundly based than the tenets of neoliberalism. In particular, the Ordoliberals have not caught up with the fact that "perfect" competition does not and cannot exist (Chapter 3). Schroeder's neoliberal "reforms" have weakened the consensus behind the social market, coming on top of the heavy cost of rebuilding Eastern Germany after the fall of the Berlin Wall.[18] Germany is, however, the most advanced capitalist system in the world, resuming the place it held before the First World War.

Bismarckian pragmatism seems to live comfortably alongside Ordoliberal myth-making inside Germany, but the combination has led to appalling consequences for the Greeks, Portuguese, and Spanish, who from 2011 on were forced to endure a depression enforced by Germany in the apparent expectation that this would turn their countries into little Germanys. Such expectations could only be held by people with no knowledge of economic history from 1834 to the present.

An American tourist is supposed to have asked a gardener at an Oxford college how he was able to create such a perfect smooth, green lawn. His response commenced, "You take a patch of ground four hundred years ago . . ." There is a great deal that the rest of the world can learn from Germany; but expecting other countries to reproduce the effects of 180 years of policy overnight is neither reasonable nor helpful.

The comprehensive failure of the USSR's economy strongly suggests that an economy without markets, or where the only markets are in peasant and artisanal commodities, will not deliver the social or economic progress that the social market economies of Germany, France, the Benelux countries, and Scandinavia have demonstrably achieved.

The human success of the social market economies is not based on extreme egalitarianism, but on a solid social welfare system, a minimum wage sufficient to support a life of dignity and modest comfort, and extensive physical infrastructure. There are wealthy people in these countries and even people living off inherited wealth; but there is usually a recognizable link between an individual's earned wealth and his or her economic contribution, and the wealthy are subject to inheritance taxes and progressive income taxes.

The fact that there are significant policy differences between the various social market economies suggests that the model is capable of improvement, but a comparison with the United States suggests that for at least 90 percent of the population, a social market economy provides greater security and a better quality of life than a neoliberally managed one.

The social market economy is a good starting point for the building of a fair, secure, and just society.

Notes

1. Margaret Thatcher quoted in Keay (1987).
2. Bruno Frey quoted in Kahneman (2011).
3. Macbeth Act 3, Scene 4.
4. Mortimer (2015) provides an accessible account of the Putney Debates and the principal characters involved.
5. Hayek (1944).
6. Piketty (2014).
7. Father Coughlin was a Catholic priest who made weekly broadcasts to a large audience between 1926 and 1939. He was initially a New Deal supporter but from 1934 on became aggressively anti-Semitic and in favor of Mussolini and Hitler.
8. See page 136 ff.
9. Klein (2007).
10. Proudhon (1840).
11. Ronson (2011).
12. Hotson (2011).
13. Quiggin (2011, 2012).
14. See page 244 ff.
15. Gaskell (1854).
16. Wilhelm II may have been bluffed by the German General Staff into allowing World War I to start: see Mombauer (2014) for an accessible discussion of the July 1914 Crisis.
17. Myers (2007).
18. Ascherson (2013).

Bibliography

Andersen, E. S. (1999), "Railroadization as Schumpeter's Standard Example of Capitalist Evolution: An Evolutionary-Ecological Interpretation," *Paper for the Workshop on Evolutionary Thought in Economics* (26–28 August), Jena: Max Planck Institute.

Arrow, Kenneth J. (2007), "Global Climate Change: A Challenge to Policy," *The Economists' Voice* **4**(3).

Ascherson, Neal (2013), "Hanging on to Mutti," *London Review of Books* **35** (11, June 6), pp. 6–8.

Atiyah, P. S. (1979), *The Rise and Fall of Freedom of Contract*, Oxford: Clarendon Press.

Axelrod, R. & Hamilton, W. (1981). "The Evolution of Cooperation," *Science* **211** (4489), pp. 1390–1396.

Bainbridge, Stephen M. (2003), "Director Primacy: The Means and Ends of Corporate Governance" *Northwestern University Law Review* **97**, pp. 547–606.

Bass, Frank M. (1969), "A New Product Growth Model for Consumer Durables," *Management Science* **15**(5), pp. 215–27.

Baumol, William J. (1968), "Entrepreneurship in Economic Theory," *American Economic Review (Papers and Proceedings)* **58**.

Beeching, Richard (1963), *The Reshaping of British Railways - Part 1: Report*, London: HM Stationery Office.

Black, F. & Scholes, M. (1973), "The Pricing of Options and Corporate Liabilities," *Journal of Political Economy* **81**(3), pp. 637–654.

Blanchard, Olivier & Leigh, Daniel (2013), "Growth Forecast Errors and Fiscal Multipliers," *IMF Working Paper* WP/13/1, International Monetary Fund.

Blas, James (2012), "Wheat Soars after Russian Crop Failure," *Financial Times* (November 8).

Blyth, Mark (2013), *Austerity: The History of a Dangerous Idea*, New York: Oxford University Press.

Card, David & Krueger, Alan B. (1997), *Myth and Measurement: The New Economics of the Minimum Wage*, Princeton: Princeton University Press.

Chang, Ha-Joon (2002a), *Kicking Away the Ladder—Development Strategy in Historical Perspective*, London: Anthem Press.

—— (2002b), "Kicking Away the Ladder: An Unofficial History of Capitalism, Especially in Britain and the United States," *Challenge* **45**(5, September/October), pp. 63–97.

Clark, J. M. (1940), "Toward A Concept of Workable Competition," *American Economic Review* **30**(2), p. 241 ff.

Clower, Terry L; Bomba, Michael; Wilson-Chavez, Owen & Gray, Matthew (2014), "Developmental Impacts of the Dallas Area Rapid Transit Light Rail System," Centre for Economic Development and Research, University of North Texas, https://www.dart.org/about/economicdevelopment/January2014DARTPropertyImpacts.pdf, accessed 24 January 2015.

Cohan, William D. (2012), "Is This Big Fish Worth Catching," *Bloomberg Business Week* (December 3–9).

Cohen, Wesley M. & Klepper, Steven (1996), "A Reprise of Size and R&D," *The Economic Journal* **106** (437, July), pp. 925–951.

Colander, David; Holt, Richard & Rosser, Barkley Jr. (2004), "The Changing Face of Mainstream Economics," *Review of Political Economy* **16**(4), pp. 485–499.

Cottrell, Allin & Cockshott, W. Paul (1993), "Calculation, Complexity and Planning: The Socialist Calculation Debate Once Again," *Review of Political Economy*, **5**(1, July), pp. 73–112.

Cowen, Tyler (1995), "A Review of G. C. Archibald's Information, Incentives and the Economics of Control: A Re-examination of the Socialist Calculation Debate," *Journal of International and Comparative Economics* **4**.

Cusumano, Michael A.; Mylonadis, Yiorgos & Rosenbloom, Richard (1992), "Strategic Maneuvering and Mass-Market Dynamics: The Triumph of VHS Over Beta," MITJP 91–68, Massachusetts Institute of Technology, Boston.

Davidson, Paul (2009), *The Keynes Solution: The Path to Global Economic Prosperity*, New York: Palgrave Macmillan.

Dawkins, Richard (1989), "Nice Guys Finish First," *The Selfish Gene* (new edition), Oxford: Oxford University Press, ch. 12.

Denicolò, Vincenzo & Zanchettin, Piercarlo (2012), "Leadership Cycles in a Quality-Ladder Model of Endogenous Growth," *Economic Journal* **122**(561, June), pp. 618–650.

Dixit, Avinash K. & Pindyck, Robert S. (1994), *Investment under Uncertainty*, Princeton NJ: Princeton University Press.

Dixit, Avinash K. (1992), "Investment and Hysteresis," *Journal of Economic Perspectives* **6**(1, Winter), pp. 107–132.

Drucker, Peter F. (1989), *The New Realities*, London: Butterworth-Heinemann.

Ehrenberg, Andrew & Goodhardt, Gerald (2002), "Double Jeopardy Revisited, Again," *Marketing Research* **14**(1, Spring), pp. 40–42.

Ehrenberg, Andrew S. C.; Goodhardt, Gerald J. & Barwise, T. Patrick (1990), "Double Jeopardy Revisited," *Journal of Marketing* **54**(3, July), pp. 82–91.

European Commission (2013), "Antitrust: Commission Fines Microsoft for Non-Compliance with Browser Choice Commitments," ref IP/13/196 Event Date: 06/03.

Ezekiel, Mordecai (1938), "The Cobweb Theorem," *Quarterly Journal of Economics* (February), pp. 255–80.

Fama, Eugene F. (1970), "Efficient Capital Markets: A Review of Theory and Empirical Work," *Journal of Finance* **25**(2), pp. 383–417.

Fama, Eugene F. & French, Kenneth R. (2004), "The Capital Asset Pricing Model: Theory and Evidence," *Journal of Economic Perspectives* **18**(3, Summer 2004), pp. 25–46.

France, Anatole (1894), *Le Lys Rouge (The Red Lily)*, Paris: Calmann Lévy.

Freeman, Chris & Soete, Luc (1997), *The Economics of Industrial Innovation* (3rd edn.), London: Pinter.

Friedman, Milton (1951), "Neoliberalism and its Prospects," *Farmand* **17**, pp. 89–93.

—— (1970), "The Social Responsibility of Business Is to Increase Profits," *New York Times Sunday Magazine* (September 13).

Galbraith, James K. (1998), *Created Unequal: The Crisis in American Pay*, New York: The Free Press.

Gaskell, Elizabeth (1854 [1986]), *North and South*, Harmondsworth Mx: Penguin Classics.

Geroski, Paul A. (1995), "Do Spillovers Undermine the Incentive to Innovate?" in *Economic Approaches to Innovation*, Edward Elgar.

Gleick, James (1987), *Chaos: Making a New Science*, London: Heinemann.

Gorman, W. F (1953), "Community Preference Fields," *Econometrica* **22**(1), pp. 63–80.

Greenhalgh, Christine (2002), "Does an Employer Training Levy Work? The Incidence of and Returns to Adult Vocational Training in France and Britain," *Fiscal Studies* **23**(2), pp. 223–263.

Grieve, Roy H. (2012), "The Marginal Productivity Theory of the Price of Capital: An Historical Perspective on the Origins of the Codswallop," *Real-world Economics Review* (60, 20 June), pp. 139–149, http://www.paecon.net/PAEReview/issue60/Grieve60.pdf.

Grossman, Gene M. & Helpman, Elhanan (1994), "Endogenous Innovation in the Theory of Growth," *Journal of Economic Perspectives* **8**(1, Winter), pp. 23–44.

Grossman, Gene M. & Helpman, Elhanan (1992), *Innovation and Growth in the Global Economy*, Massachusets: MIT Press.

Guttman, J. M. (2003), "Repeated Interaction and the Evolution of Preferences for Reciprocity," *The Economic Journal* **113**(489, July), pp. 631–56.

Hacker, Jacob S & Pierson, Paul (2010), *Winner Take All Politics: How Washington Made the Rich Richer—and Turned Its Back on the Middle Class*, New York: Simon and Schuster.

Harberger, Arnold C. (1954), "Monopoly and Resource Allocation," *American Economic Review Proceedings*, **44**(May), pp. 77–87.

Hayek, F. A. (1944), *The Road to Serfdom*, London: Routledge.

Herzberg, F. (1968 [2003]), "One More Time: How Do You Motivate Employees?" *Harvard Business Review* **81**(1), pp. 87–96.

Hilzenrath David S. (2010), "Commodity Futures Trading Commission Judge Says Colleague Biased against Complainants," *Washington Post* (October 19). Retrieved May 4, 2011.

Hobbes, Thomas (1651 [2010]), *Leviathan. Revised Edition*, eds. A. P. Martinich and Brian Battiste. Peterborough, ON: Broadview Press.

Hotson, Howard (2011), "Short Cuts," *London Review of Books* **33**(11, 2 June), p. 19.

Hodgson, Geoffrey M. (1998), "Socialism against Markets? A Critique of Two Recent Proposals," *Economy and Society* **27**(4, November).

Hsieh Tsun-Yan and Barton, Dominic (1995), "Young Lions, High Priests, and Old Warriors," *McKinsey Quarterly* (May).

Hunt, Shelby D. (2000), *A General Theory of Competition: Resources, Competences, Productivity, Economic Growth*, Thousand Oaks Ca: Sage.

Iacocca, Lee & Novak, William (1984), *Iacocca: An Autobiography*, New York: Bantam Books.

Jevons, W. S. (1871 [1970]), *The Theory of Political Economy*, Harmondsworth Mx: Penguin Books.

Johnson Chalmers A. (1982), *MITI and the Japanese Miracle*, Palo Alto, Ca: Stanford University Press.

—— (1985), "The Institutional Foundations of Japanese Industrial Policy," *California Management Review* **27**(4, Summer), pp. 59–69.

Josephson, Matthew (1934 [1962]), *The Robber Barons*, New York: Harcourt Brace Jovanovich.

Kahneman, Daniel; Knetch, Jack L. & Thaler, Richard (1986), "Fairness As a Constraint on Profit-Seeking: Entitlements in the Market," *The American Economic Review* **76**(4), pp. 728–741.

Kahneman, Daniel (2011), *Thinking Fast and Slow*, London: Penguin Books.

Kay, John & Silberston, Aubrey (1995), "Corporate Governance," *National Institute Economic Review* (153, August), pp. 84–97.

Keay, Douglas (1987), *Women's Own* (31 October), pp. 8–10.

Keen, Steve (2001), *Debunking Economics: The Naked Emperor of the Social Sciences*, Sydney: Pluto.

—— (2009), "Household Debt—The Final Stage in an Artificially Extended Ponzi Bubble," *Australian Economic Review* **42**(3, September), pp. 347–57.

—— (2011), *Debunking Economics: The Naked Emperor Dethroned?* London: Zed Books.

Keen, Steve & Standish, Russell (2006). "Profit Maximization, Industry Structure, and Competition: A Critique of Neoclassical Theory," *Physica A* (370), pp. 81–85.

—— (2010). "Debunking the Theory of the Firm—A Chronology," *Real-World Economics Review* (53, 26 June 2010), pp. 56–94.

Kennedy, Gavin (2010), *Adam Smith* (2nd ed.), Basingstoke: Palgrave Macmillan.

Keynes, J. M. (1936 [1961]), *The General Theory of Employment, Interest and Money*, London: Macmillan.

Kirzner, Israel M. (1982), "Uncertainty, Discovery and Human Action: A Study of the Entrepreneurial Profile in the Misesian System," in I. M. Kirzner (ed), *Method, Process and Austrian Economics: Essays in Honour of Ludwig van Mises*, Lexington MA: D.C. Heath.

Klein, Naomi (2007), *The Shock Doctrine: The Rise of Disaster Capitalism*, New York: Metropolitan Books.

Klepper, Steven (2002), "Firm Survival and the Evolution of Oligopoly," *RAND Journal of Economics* **33**(1, Spring), pp. 37–61.

Kolstad, Charles D. (1996), "Fundamental Irreversibilities in Stock Externalities," *Journal of Public Economics* **60**(2, May): pp. 221–233.

Krugman, Paul (1996), *The Self-Organizing Economy*, Cambridge MA: Blackwell.

—— (2012), "The Microfoundation Thing (Wonkish)," New York Times on the Web (March 2), http://krugman.blogs.nytimes.com/2012/03/02/

the-microfoundation-thing-wonkish/?nl=opinion&emc=tyb1, viewed March 3 2012.

Kurz, Heinz D. & Salvadori, Neri (2005), "Representing the Production and Circulation of Commodities in Material Terms: On Sraffa's Objectivism," *Review of Political Economy* **17**(3, July), pp. 413–441.

Kurz, Heinz D. (2008), "Innovation and Profits: Schumpeter and the Classical Heritage," *Journal of Economic Behaviour and Organization* **67**(1, July).

Lancaster, Kelvin (1975), "Socially Optimal Product Differentiation," *American Economic Review* **65**(4, Sep), pp. 567–585.

Lattimore, R. (1997), "Research and Development Fiscal Incentives in Australia: Impacts and Policy Lessons," *Paper presented to the OECD Conference on Policy Evaluation in Innovation*, Paris, 26–27 June.

Legge, John M. (2012), *Chaos and the Plan: Why You Should Expect the Unexpected*, Melbourne: Information Strategy Planning.

Leibenstein, Harvey (1966), "Allocative Efficiency and X-Efficiency," *The American Economic Review*, **56**, pp. 392–415.

Lindner Fabian (2015), "Does Saving Increase the Supply of Credit? A Critique of Loanable Funds Theory," *World Economic Review* **4**.

List, F. (1885), *The National System of Political Economy*, trans. Sampson Lloyd from the original German edition published in 1841, London: Longmans, Green.

Lucas, R. E. (1972), "Expectations and the Neutrality of Money," *Journal of Economic Theory* **4**, pp. 103–124.

Mahajan, Vijay; Muller, Eitan & Bass, Frank M. (1990), "New Product Diffusion Models in Marketing: A Review and Directions for Research," *Journal of Marketing* **54**(1, January), pp. 1–26.

Manove, M. (1997), "Job Responsibility, Pay and Promotion," *Economic Journal* **107**(440, January), pp. 85–103.

Marceau, Jane; Sicklen, Derek & Manley, Karen (1997), *The High Road or the Low Road: Alternatives for Australia's Future*, Sydney: Australian Business Foundation.

Martin, Stephen (1993), *Advanced Industrial Economics*, Oxford: Blackwell Publishers.

—— (2006 [2012]), "Market Structure and Market Performance," *Review of Industrial Organization* **25** (3, May).

Marx, Karl & Engels, Frederick (1848), *Manifesto of the Communist Party*.

Mccloskey, Deirdre N. (2008), "Not by P Alone: A Virtuous Economy," *Review of Political Economy* **20**(2), pp. 181–197.

Mombauer, Annika (2014), "The July Crisis," *History Today* **64**(7, July), pp. 21–27.

Mortimer, Sarah (2015), "What Was at Stake in the Putney Debates?" *History Today* **65**(1), pp. 50–55.

Moseley, Fred (2012a), "A Critique of the Marginal Productivity Theory of the Price of Capital," *Real-World Economics Review* (59).

—— (2012b), "Mankiw's Attempted Resurrection of Marginal Productivity Theory," *Real-World Economics Review* (61).

Myers, David G. (2007), *Psychology*, 8th Edition, New York: Worth Publishers.

Myers, Stewart C. & Turnbull, Stuart M. (1977), "Capital Budgeting and the Capital Asset Pricing Model: Good News and Bad News," *Journal of Finance* **32**(2, May), pp. 321–333.

Newkirk, Margaret (2011), "Illegal Workers in Alabama: The Exodus," *Bloomberg Business Week* (June 30), (http://www.businessweek.com/magazine/illegal-workers-in-alabama-the-exodus-07012011.html).

Oi, Walter Y. (1996), "The Welfare Implications of Invention" in *The Economics of New Goods*, Timothy F. Bresnahan & Robert J. Gordon, editors, Cambridge MA: NBER.

Passin, H. (1982), *Society and Education in Japan*, Tokyo: Kodansha, p. 97, quoted in Murata, Shoji & Stern, Sam (1993), "Technology Education in Japan," *Journal of Technology Education* 5(1).

Piketty, Thomas (2014), *Capital in the Twenty-First Century*. Cambridge, MA: Harvard UP.

Podkaminer, Leon (2015), "The Euro Area's Secular Stagnation and What Can Be Done About It: A Post-Keynesian Perspective," *Real-World Economics Review* (70, 20 Feb), pp. 2–16, http://www.paecon.net/PAEReview/issue70/Podkaminer70.pdf.

Porter, Michael E. (1990), *The Competitive Advantage of Nations*, New York: The Free Press.

Proudhon, Pierre Joseph (1840), *What is Property? An Inquiry into the Principle of Right and of Government*, Electronic Text Center, University of Virginia Library.

Prahalad, C. K. & Hamel, Gary (1990), "The Core Competence of the Corporation," *Harvard Business Review* (May–June).

Pratt, J. W. (1964), "Risk Aversion in the Small and in the Large," *Econometrica* **32**: pp. 122–136.

Putnam, Robert D (1994), "What Makes Democracy Work?" *IPA Review* **47**(1).

—— (1993), "The Prosperous Community: Social Capital and Public Life," *The American Prospect* **4**(13, March 21).

Quiggin, J. and Horowitz, J. (2003), "Global Warming: Dynamic and Comparative Static Analyses," *Australian Journal of Agricultural and Resource Economics* **47**(4), pp. 429–46.

Quiggin, J. (2010), *Zombie Economics: How Dead Ideas Still Walk among Us*, Princeton NJ: Princeton University Press.

—— (2011), *Zombie Economics: How Dead Ideas Still Walk among Us* (Australian edition), Melbourne: Black Inc.

Rand, Ayn (1957), *Atlas Shrugged*, New York: Random House.

Rawls, John (1999), *A Theory of Justice* (Revised edition), Boston, Ma: Harvard University Press.

Reich, Robert B. (1991), *The Work of Nations*, London: Simon & Schuster.

Reichheld, Frederic F. (1996), *The Loyalty Effect*, Boston, Ma: Harvard Business School Press.

Robinson, Joan (1962), *Essays in the Theory of Economic Growth*, London: Macmillan.

—— (1969 [2013]), *The Accumulation of Capital* (3rd ed.), Basingstoke: Palgrave Macmillan.

Rochon, Louis-Philippe & Rossi, Sergio (2013), "Endogenous Money: The Evolutionary versus Revolutionary Views," *Review of Keynesian Economics* **1**(2, Summer), pp. 210–229.

Romer, Paul M. (1986), "Increasing Returns and Long Run Growth," *Journal of Political Economy* **94**.

—— (1990), "Endogenous Technological Change," *Journal of Political Economy* **98**(5), pp. S71–S102.

—— (1994), "The Origins of Endogenous Growth," *Journal of Economic Perspectives* **8**(1, Winter), pp. 3–22.

Ronson, Jon (2011), *The Psychopath Test: A Journey through the Madness Industry*, New York: Riverhead Books.

Rose, Charlie (2011), "Charlie Rose Talks to Alan Greenspan," *Bloomberg Business Week* (June 23).

Samuelson, Paul A. & Nordhaus, William D. (1995), *Economics* (12th Edition), New York: McGraw-Hill.

Schumacher, Reinhard (2013), "Deconstructing the Theory of Comparative Advantage," *World Economic Review* **2**: pp. 83–105.

Schumpeter, Joseph A. (1934), *An Inquiry into Profits, Capital, Credit, Interest and the Business Cycle* (trans R. Opie), Cambridge, MA, Harvard University Press.

—— (1935), "Analysis of Economic Change," *Review of Economic Statistics* **19**(4), pp. 2–10.

—— (1942 [1976]), *Capitalism, Socialism and Democracy*, London: George Allen & Unwin Ltd.

Sculley, John & Byrne, John A. (1987), *Odyssey: Pepsi to Apple—A Journey of Adventure, Ideas, and the Future*, New York: Harper and Row.

Sen, Amartya (2009), *The Idea of Justice*, London: Penguin Books.

Shapiro, Nina & Sawyer, Malcolm (2003), "Post Keynesian Price Theory," *Journal of Post Keynesian Economics* **25**(3, Spring), pp. 355–365.

Sharpe, William F. (1964). "Capital Asset Prices: A Theory of Market Equilibrium under Conditions of Risk," *Journal of Finance* **19**(3), pp. 425–442.

Skidelsky, Robert (1983), *John Maynard Keynes: Hopes Betrayed, 1883–1920*, London: Macmillan.

—— (2000), *John Maynard Keynes: Fighting for Britain, 1937–1946*, London: Macmillan.

Smith, Adam (1776 [1983]), *An Inquiry into the Nature and Causes of the Wealth of Nations*, Edinburgh: Thomas Nelson and Peter Brown.

Snell, Bradford C., (1971), "Annual Style Change in the Automobile Industry as an Unfair Method of Competition," *Yale Law Journal* **VIII**, pp. 567–613.

Soskice, David (1991), "Reconciling Markets and Institutions: The German Apprenticeship System," in *Training and the Private Sector* (Lisa M. Lynch, ed.), Chicago: Chicago University Press, pp. 25–60 (http://www.nber.org/chapters/c8776.pdf).

Sosnick, S. H. (1958), "A Critique of Concepts of Workable Competition," *Quarterly Journal of Economics* **72**(3), pp. 380–423.

Sraffa, Peiro (1926), "The Laws of Returns Under Competitive Conditions," *The Economic Journal* **XXXVI**, pp. 535–550.

—— (1960), *Production of Commodities by Means of Commodities*, Cambridge: Cambridge University Press.

Stedman Jones, Daniel (2012), *Masters of the Universe: Hayek, Friedman and the Birth of Neoliberal Politics*, Princeton and Oxford: Princeton University Press.

Stern, Nicholas (2007), *The Economics of Climate Change: The Stern Review*, Cambridge: Cambridge University Press.

Stiglitz, Joseph (2010), *Freefall: Free Markets and the Sinking of the Global Economy*, London: Allen Lane.

Stout, Lynn A. (2008), "Why We Should Stop Teaching Dodge v. Ford" in Macey, Jonathon (ed.), *The Iconic Cases in Corporate Law*, Yale: West Publishing.

Swann, G. M. P. (2014), *Common Innovation: How We Create the Wealth of Nations*, Edward Elgar Publishing.

Tremblay, Diane-Gabrielle & Le Bot, Irène (2003), "The German Dual Apprenticeship System Analysis of Its Evolution and Present Challenges," *Research Note*, Quebec: Chaire de recherche du Canada sur les enjeux socio-organisationnels de l'économie du savoir. (http://www.teluq.uquebec.ca/chaireecosavoir/pdf/NRC03-04A.pdf).

Uslay, Can; Altintig, Z. Ayca & Winsor, Robert D. (2010), "An Empirical Examination of the 'Rule of Three': Strategy Implications for Top Management, Marketers, and Investors," *Journal of Marketing* **74**(2, March).

Van Staveren, Irene (2007), "Beyond Utilitarianism and Deontology: Ethics in Economics," *Review of Political Economy* **19**(1), pp. 21–35.

Waldrop, M. Mitchell (1992), *COMPLEXITY: The Emerging Science at the Edge of Order and Chaos*, New York: Simon and Schuster.

Walras, L (1874 [1977]), *Elements of Pure Economics*, Fairfield: Augustus M Kelley.

Wapshott, Nicholas (2011), *Keynes Hayek: The Clash That Defined Modern Economics*, Melbourne: Scribe Publications.

Whitfield, Dexter (2006), *New Labour's Attack on Public Services*, Nottingham: Spokesman.

Wisman, Jon D. (2014), "The Financial Crisis of 1929 Reexamined: The Role of Soaring Inequality," *Review of Political Economy* **26**(3).

Yamashita, Toshihiko (1989), *The Panasonic Way: From a Chief Executive's Desk* (tr. F. Baldwin), New York: Kodansha International.

Index

neoclassical theory, 62, 90, 94, 165, 177, 189, 196
NPV rule, 196–97
productive, 98, 112
public, 30, 118, 151, 205–08
Real Options, 199–202
and recession, 115, 126
speculative, 98, 100, 113–15, 286
and trade, 99, 241
under uncertainty, 52, 62, 69, 190, 195, 200–01
venture capital, 174–75, 205
and wages, 146

Japan, 65, 80, 163, 273
Asian Monetary Fund, 132
banking system, 176–77
economic miracle, 12, 214
few hostile takeovers, 273
industrial relations, 163–64
industry policy, 246–47, 300
kaizen, 172
labor market, 156, 162–64
Meiji restoration, 162
Pacific War, 163
Jevons, W S, 25–26, 42, 83, 87
Johnson, Chalmers A, 176, 188
Johnson, President L B, 113, 119

Kahneman, Daniel, 8, 15, 16–19, 33, 38, 42, 192–93, 201, 210
Keen, Steve, 44, 49, 65–66, 92, 94, 101, 116, 188, 210
Kennedy, President John F, 284
Keynes, John Maynard, 27–29, 70, 92, 94, 127
on banking, 80, 92
bastard Keynesianism, 15, 152
bursar of Kings College, 103
and Chicago School, 30
euthanasia of the rentier, 118
General Theory, 29, 86, 118, 151
and Hayek, 32
ideas adopted, 70, 110, 118–19, 127–29, 288
ideas criticised, 38
ideas rejected, 39, 71, 82, 100, 118, 129, 281
on inconsistency, 282
on interest rates, 81, 128
on investment, 79, 90, 151, 196, 268
macroeconomics, 30, 79, 86, 90, 201

and Malthus, 23
and Marshall, 27
on money, 30, 69–70, 89, 92, 95, 104
on national accounts, 166
postwar prosperity, 12, 242
prioritises full employment, 118
propensity to consume, 112
on public goods, 32
on recession, 15, 30, 84, 114, 118, 127
on trade balances, 100
on unemployment, 91, 128, 150–51
on value, 69
on wages, 103, 128
Klein, Naomi, 132, 140, 288, 302
Klepper, Steven, 173, 188
Krugman, Paul, 27, 38, 88, 101, 116, 138
confidence fairy, 136
predictions vindicated, 136, 139
Kurz, Heinz D, 167, 187

Lehmann Brothers, 117
Leibenstein, Harvey, 265, 279
Lenin, V I, 166, 284
limited liability, 268
liquidity preference, 90, 92, 201
List, Frederich, 244, 296
London School of Economics (LSE), 127

Maastricht Treaty, 299
macroeconomics, 30, 86–87
DSGE, 88
microfoundations, 86, 88
Mahajan, Vijay, 184, 188
Malaysia
and IMF, 132–33
Malthus, Thomas, 23, 30, 142
Manhattan Project, 242
Manove, Michael, 57, 66, 146–47, 164
marketing, 44, 62, 178, 183, 187
cost, 178, 180–82
and economic theory, 174, 186–87
and firm growth, 65, 105
and innovation, 173–74, 177–79, 187
monopolistic competition, 57
necessary expense, 49, 53
research as real option, 200
Marshall Plan, 12, 265
Marshall, Alfred, 26, 29
on investment, 196–97
Marx, Karl, 9, 14, 23–24, 65, 69, 142, 149, 164–66
Minsky, Hyman, 92, 94

Mises, Ludwig von, 9–10
money, 69–73, 92, 103, 108
  business resource, 43, 48, 104
  creation, 69, 73, 77, 80, 92, 110, 118,
    133, 166, 189
  fiat currency, 72
  Friedman on, 71, 104, 203, 271
  Keynes on, 29, 69–70, 89
  market, 76, 134
  neutrality, 73, 95
  time value, 196
money supply, 39, 70–72, 82, 111, 114,
  118, 128, 152, 189
monopoly, 57–58, 65, 84, 151, 166
  chartered, 255
  Hayek on, 33
  management of, 34
  natural, 34, 206, 228–30, 258, 296
  power, 230
  price, 35, 49–50, 59, 170, 260
  regulated, 130, 158, 256, 260, 276
  rent, 148
Morgan, J P, 264
Mussolini, Benito, 284–86, 302
Myers, Stewart C, 200–201, 210, 302

Napoleonic wars, 119, 126, 240
neoliberalism, 31–33, 37–40, 88, 123, 156,
  217, 238, 281–83, 299–301
  adopted, 37–38, 118, 130–31, 230
  alternative to, 296, 299
  denial, 214, 220, 233–34
  exalts property rights, 283
  failed ideology, 283, 288
  and Friedman, 36
  imposed, 287, 289
  precursor to Fascism, 6, 285–86
  and social progress, 41
  stage two, 38
  Stiglitz on, 132
  Washington consensus, 241
Newton, Isaac, 14, 17
Nixon, President Richard, 113–14,
  129
Non accelerating inflation rate of unemployment (NAIRU), 115, 151–52

Oi, Walter, 213, 231
oligopoly, 55–56, 63–65, 105, 170–71
Ordo-liberalism, 38, 301
Organization of Petroleum Exporting
  Countries (OPEC), 114

P&O plc, 271
Pasteur, Louis, 17, 212
Peel, Sir Robert, 241, 256
Penrose, Edith, 56, 63, 174
Piketty, Thomas, 19, 284, 302
Pindyck, Robert S, 62–63, 189, 200–02,
  205, 208, 210, 272
Pinochet, Augusto, 6–7, 286–87
Plato, 17
Poincaré, Henri, 87–88
Political economy, 2, 26
populism, 41, 286, 289
Porter, Michael E, 27, 245–46
Prahalad, C K, 63, 67
prices, 8, 47, 52, 55, 64, 127, 171, 183
  asset price inflation, 93, 111–13, 134
  branded products, 59–60
  bubbles, 93, 113, 116–17
  central planning, 9, 11
  competitive, 29, 49, 71, 169–70, 258
  Cournot-Nash theorem, 54
  and direct cost, 59–60, 109
  Hayek on, 9, 196
  inflation, 38, 103, 108–11, 113–17
  law of one price, 45
  management, 50, 81, 105–06
  marginal cost, 47–50
  mark-up, 9, 50, 59
  minimum viable, 2, 48
  monopoly, 35, 49–50, 55, 60, 207,
    258–60
  neoclassical theory, 30, 44–48, 238
  on pollution, 215
  option, 200
  and quality innovation, 106, 110
  realistic, 48, 51–52, 55, 59, 63, 105, 148,
    168, 170, 178, 208
  Schumpeter on, 29
  securities, 31, 85, 92, 113, 117, 156, 192,
    197–202, 268
  signals, 154–56, 189
  Smith on, 22
  Sraffa on, 53
  von Mises on, 31
  winner takes all, 155
privatization, 158–59, 207, 217, 231, 257,
  259, 276
  in Britain, 131, 136, 230, 257, 258
  electricity, 45
  Hayek on, 34
  and public choice, 34
  of public good, 215

United Kingdom. *See* Britain
United States, 38, 65, 72, 122, 130–31, 146,
 160, 206, 208, 289
 adopts free trade, 242
 adopts neoliberalism, 37, 40, 243
 Affordable Care Act, 219, 221
 Asian Monetary Fund, 132
 banking regulation, 74, 76, 128
 comparison, 12, 273, 298–300, 302
 competition law, 65, 260
 corporation law, 271
 deficit, 39, 98, 100, 152, 243, 300
 economic growth, 18, 165
 executive salaries, 267–68, 292
 Federal Reserve, 76–77, 81, 116–17, 120
 full employment, 151–52
 Great Recession, 38, 117, 121, 125,
  134–35, 283
 Gulf War, 115
 higher education, 119, 222
 immigration, 159, 277
 internships, 160, 295
 minimum wage, 112, 128
 monetarism, 39, 71, 120, 152
 New Deal, 284
 postwar, 119, 264
 protection, 11, 244–45, 247
 Reaganism, 40, 281
 stagflation, 130
 technology train, 242
 Triangle Shirtwaist disaster, 254
 Vietnam War, 113–14, 119, 129
 welfare, 219, 299
 World War II, 70, 163, 242
Uslay, Can, 55, 66
USSR, 11–12, 15, 32, 291
 failure, 294, 301
 former, 91

venture capital, 174–77, 205
 informal, 80

wages, 1–3, 30, 46, 58, 89, 107, 144, 240
 apprentice, 156, 158, 162

blamed for crises, 84
blamed for inflation, 38, 71, 105, 114
blamed for unemployment, 148, 150,
 253
demand, 39, 90, 105
differentials, 153, 292
Galbraith analysis, 144–46
in Germany, 298
and innovation, 106–107, 161, 167
in Japan, 164
Keynes on, 103, 128, 150
Malthus on, 142
Manove on, 147
manufacturing, 297
marginal product, 142–44, 282
Marx on, 24, 142, 166
in US, 40, 147
minimum, 2, 57, 89, 97, 112, 128,
 144–50, 252–53, 282, 301
and productivity, 297
responsibility premium, 57, 147
Ricardo on, 142
share of added value, 107, 148
Smith on, 122, 141–42
social, 118, 300
subsistence, 96
technology train, 242
winner takes all, 60
Waldrop, M Mitchell, 88, 101
Wal-Mart, 59, 198
Walras, Léon, 9, 25–26, 42, 83, 87
Washington consensus, 6, 40, 241
Watt, James, 24, 62, 92, 240
Wedgwood, Josiah, 179
Wellington, first Duke of, 95, 216, 240, 287
Wisselbank, 73
World Bank, 40, 132
World Trade Organization, 247
Wright, T P, 53, 54

Xerox, 173, 179
X-inefficiency, 265–67

Zollverein, 244–45, 297